Auden

IN LOVE

by DOROTHY J. FARNAN

SIMON AND SCHUSTER
New York

Library of Congress Cataloging in Publication Data

Farnan, Dorothy J. (Dorothy Jeanne)
Auden in love.

Includes bibliographical references and index.
1. Auden, W. H. (Wystan Hugh), 1907–1973—
Relations with men—Chester Kallman.   2. Kallman,
Chester, 1921–   .   3. Poets, English—20th century—
Biography.   1. Title.
PR6001.U4Z685   1984   811'.52 [B]   84-5505
ISBN 0-671-50418-5

The author is grateful to the following publishers for permission to quote poems and passages of text from the following works:

The Estate of W. H. Auden: Quotations from previously unpublished writings by W. H. Auden, copyright © 1984 by the Estate of W. H. Auden.

Harcourt Brace Jovanovich, Inc.: *W. H. Auden: The Life of a Poet* by Charles Osborne, © 1979.

(continued at back of book)

ACKNOWLEDGMENTS

AUDEN IN LOVE was not intended to be a scholarly work or a discussion of Auden's poetry. It was intended, rather, as a collection of memories about a relationship that has often been misunderstood: that between W. H. Auden and Chester Kallman. My husband, Dr. Edward Kallman, Chester's father, believed that the love story—for it was a love story—could best be told by one of Chester's contemporaries, someone who had known both Wystan and Chester over a long period of time. Chester and I were a year and a half apart in age, and we were friends for more than thirty-three years.

There are three people without whom *Auden in Love* could not have been written: my husband; Professor Edward Mendelson, Auden's literary executor; and Mrs. Mary Catherine Valentine, my oldest and dearest friend, who shared with me those early days with Wystan and Chester.

First, I wish to thank my husband not only for the many memories he patiently recounted of Chester and Wystan, particularly those of

5

the early days of 1939 and 1940, but also for his permission to publish poems and letters. I wish to thank him as well for remaining married to someone writing a book, even though it was a book he wanted written. His dinners were often late and his house unswept, but he bore all with patience.

Next comes Professor Mendelson, but I find it difficult to express adequately my indebtedness to him. Chester said to me one afternoon during one of his last visits home: "Wystan says that he has just met a young man who knows more about him than he knows himself." That young man was a doctoral candidate called Edward Mendelson, who visited Auden at 77 St. Mark's Place during the "At Homes" he gave in the 1960s. Wystan was right.

Professor Mendelson spent hours out of a busy teaching schedule at Columbia University reading each chapter, making suggestions, correcting my translations of Auden's cryptic hand, rereading typescripts, and giving me the benefit of his scholarship and vast knowledge of Auden, both as man and as poet.

I am also grateful to Professor Mendelson for his permission to publish Auden's poems and letters, particularly the new letters he himself discovered, and for his help with advice related to writing and publishing. I hope I have not made any serious mistakes in this book, but if I have, they are mine alone.

As for Mary Valentine, if *Auden in Love* is Wystan and Chester's story, it is hers as well. She lived through much of it with me, and relived it during the writing.

I wish to thank my editors, Mr. Michael Korda and Mr. John Herman, for taking a chance on an unknown writer and for finding the manuscript worth the time spent on it. I am grateful, as well, to Miss Michele Wolf for her meticulous and conscientious editing of the final copy, and to Mr. Vincent Virga for his fine picture section.

I am indebted to Mrs. Roslyn Targ of Roslyn Targ Associates, my literary agent, for her faith in me and her wise counsel. I am grateful to Mrs. Norma Ammidown and Mrs. Guida Nixon, without whom this book might still be reposing in a bureau drawer.

I wish also to express my appreciation to the following attorneys: Mr. Jeffrey S. Goldstein; Mr. Joel B. Miller, the attorney for the estate of Chester Kallman; Mr. Robert Simpson; and Mr. Robert Zicklin.

I wish to thank Miss Bertha Case, authors' and artists' representative, for graciously reading my manuscript in its early stages and making suggestions.

Mr. Humphrey Carpenter has been more than generous in permitting me to quote long passages from his excellent book *W. H. Auden: A Biography* (Houghton Mifflin Company, Boston, 1981), and for valuable information gleaned from his research into Auden's early life.

I am grateful for the wealth of material and photographs given me by my former professor of English, Professor Albert K. Stevens, and his wife, Angelyn, and for their permission to quote from their letters and conversations. I am indebted to Professor Carlton Wells as well as to my alma mater, the University of Michigan, for specific data requested concerning Chester Kallman and others in this book.

I would like to thank Brooklyn College for continued help in supplying information and photographs.

I wish to add a personal note of thanks to my former principal, Mrs. Harriet Oxman, for daily urging me to write when I was chairman of English at Erasmus Hall High School in Brooklyn. The force of her encouragement in her letters to me since my retirement acted as a spur.

I wish to express my appreciation to the following publishers: Harcourt Brace Jovanovich, Inc., for permission to quote from Charles Osborne's book *W. H. Auden: The Life of a Poet;* Houghton Mifflin Company, for permission to quote from Humphrey Carpenter's *W. H. Auden: A Biography;* Macmillan Publishing Company, Inc., for permitting me to quote from Robert Craft's excellent essay, "The Poet and the Rake," in Stephen Spender's *W. H. Auden: A Tribute;* and to Random House, Inc., for being so gracious about permitting me to quote many of Auden's poems from *W. H. Auden: Collected Poems* (1976), edited by Edward Mendelson.

For courtesy in permitting me to quote Auden's Christmas letter, 1941, I am indebted to Dr. Decherd Turner, director, the Humanities Research Center, the University of Texas at Austin.

The number of people, particularly Chester Kallman's classmates from elementary school through Brooklyn College and the University of Michigan, who responded to my request for information about him and Auden in the early days was most heartwarming.

I would like to thank especially Mr. Eric Drew, Mr. Samuel Exler, Miss Gale Adams Hanlan, Dr. Nathan Kravetz, Mrs. Charlotte Lew, Mr. William McGuire, Mr. Charles Miller, Professor Walter James Miller, Mr. Jerome Rothlein, and Mr. Joseph Wershba for their willingness to permit me to quote from their letters and conversations and for their generosity in sharing with me their memories of school days and the part Chester and Wystan played in them.

Mrs. Margaret Magoun of Cambridge, Massachusetts, has my gratitude for permitting me to recount an amusing event involving Auden
and her late husband, Alan Ansen's professor at Harvard, Francis
Peabody Magoun, Jr.

I wish to thank Dr. Eric Gordon for his generosity in supplying information regarding Marc Blitzstein; and Mr. Barnett B. Ruder, Mr.
Stavros Kondylis, and Dr. Basil Proimos for information about Chester in Greece.

The friends of the old Auden–Kallman circle have my appreciation
not only for their criticism and generous help with this book by permitting me to quote from their letters and conversations and for supplying me with photographs, but for their cherished friendship as
well. I am indebted to Mr. Alan Ansen, Miss Marie Joyce (Mrs. Edward Ennis), Mr. "Keith Callaghan," Mr. "Peter Komadina," Mr.
"Jack Lansing," and Professor and Mrs. Irving Weiss.

I wish to thank my husband's relatives, all of whom were willing to
share with me their memories of Wystan and Chester in the early days,
as well as in more recent times. I am indebted to Chester's Aunt Sadie
(Mrs. Irving Jacobs) and her son and daughter-in-law, Edward and
Phyllis Jacobs, as well as to Chester's brother, Matt Kallman, Chester's sister-in-law, Joan Hanley Kallman, and his niece, Lisa Kallman
Wolfley. I also wish to thank my husband's cousins, Mr. Jack Kahn
and Mr. and Mrs. Frank Nastasi, as well as Chester's only cousin on
his mother's side, Mrs. Bertha (Birdie) Goldman Santamaria, and her
husband, Carmelo, for their help, their encouragement, and, most of
all, for their love.

Finally, I wish to thank Wystan and Chester for coming into my
life and changing it forever. I hope that Wystan is not more cross with
me than usual as he regards me now from that undiscovered country.

Dorothy J. Farnan
New York
November 30, 1983

For
MARY VALENTINE,
EDWARD KALLMAN,
EDWARD MENDELSON,
and all the days gone by

CONTENTS

CHAPTER 1

That Last Night in Vienna

W. H. AUDEN had just closed his summer home in Kirchstetten on the other side of the Wienerwald and planned to fly alone back to Oxford the next morning, but he was not looking forward to the trip. He had left his friends in New York and his apartment there on St. Mark's Place the year before to return to his native England and the college that had nurtured him and now offered him a retreat from the world. But Auden had not been happy at Oxford that last year. He was lonely at his old school and had found to his regret truth in the saying that you can't go home again.

On the night of September 28, 1973, having given a poetry reading at the Palais Palffy in Vienna for the Austrian Society for Literature, Auden had returned to his room in the old Altenburgerhof Hotel nearby and gone to bed. At some time before nine o'clock the next morning, he died in his sleep.

His friends were stricken with grief. To them the only important fact was that W. H. Auden, the greatest poet of his day, had died sud-

denly in Vienna, during the early hours of a rainy morning in a high
room of an old hotel on Walfischgasse. His death at the age of sixty-
six had shocked them. So sure were they of his immortality that they
could not believe his physical death. Yet within each was the nagging
suspicion that Wystan wanted to die, and they recalled a poem he
had written about himself shortly before: "He still loves life / but
O O O O how he wishes / the good Lord would take him."[1]

His death was discovered by Chester Kallman, his companion for
thirty-four years. Auden had asked Chester to wake him at nine, and
a few minutes before the hour, Chester tried the door to Auden's
room. It was locked. He knocked and called out "Wystan!" But there
was no answer, and he had the sudden feeling that the room behind
the door was empty. He banged heavily on the door and called out
again, but there was still no response. Eventually the management
had to break open the door.

When Chester entered, he saw a room that Wystan's untidiness had
made familiar, as if he had wished to put the impress of his personality upon this impersonal chamber as he did upon everything he
touched. He was lying uncharacteristically on his left side, the covers
of the old double bed in disarray. Many years before in a prophetic
moment he had predicted for himself this kind of death "in a *louche*
hotel." Chester knew immediately that he was dead. Auden was cold
to his touch. That large awkward body, always so quick with life, was
still.

Auden was laid to rest on October 4, 1973, on a sunny Thursday
afternoon in the Roman Catholic churchyard of Kirchstetten, his
adopted home, a small village on the Wienerwald, a few miles from
Vienna. Before the funeral, Chester, Wystan's family, and his friends
and admirers assembled in the cottage on Audenstrasse[2] where Chester
Kallman and W. H. Auden had spent much of their time since the
late 1950s, when Auden purchased the cottage with some prize money.
Wystan lay in the coffin, which was placed in his bedroom. The large,
plump, stubby hands, with their bitten fingernails, were folded on his
breast in the manner of laying out the dead in Catholic Austria. All
that was missing was a Catholic rosary, but Auden was an Anglican,

[1] W. H. Auden, *Thank You, Fog: Last Poems* (New York: Random House, 1974),
p. viii. From a poem discovered posthumously and quoted in the introductory note
by Edward Mendelson.

[2] Auden's street, Hinterholz, was renamed Audenstrasse by the community some
years before his death. His stationery still carried the address 3062 Kirchstetten,
Bez. St. Pölten, Hinterholz 6, however. He avoided using the address Audenstrasse.

and the funeral service was to be performed by a Church of England clergyman from the British Embassy in Vienna in concert with the Roman Catholic prelate in Kirchstetten, whose church Auden had attended every Sunday that he was in residence. The service was to be in English and German; Wystan, who was conservative about such things, would doubtless have preferred a traditional Latin requiem.

The mourners waited in the living room to join the funeral procession to the church a half mile away. Chester Kallman kept the promise he had made to Auden some years before and put a record on the phonograph as the mourners stood in silence. It was Siegfried's funeral music from *Die Götterdämmerung*. Soon, however, the recording was replaced by the local band, all bright in uniforms, performing their blaring civic homage to the great man on his last journey. After the short service, Auden was laid in his grave.

Among the crowd that had assembled for Auden's funeral—relatives, childhood friends, distinguished scholars, writers, artists, civic officials, photographers and TV camera crews, members of the international press—there was one that had mattered supremely to Auden himself; that was Chester Kallman.

Many of Auden's relatives and friends could not understand this selfless, one-sided devotion except as a touch of eccentricity and folly in a nature otherwise serious and profound. Later, biographers and the press tended to concentrate on all other elements in Auden's life except Kallman. They touched upon Chester lightly, if at all, much as if he had been a frivolous, sometimes petulant, object of pleasure. Hence they missed an important key to Auden's mysterious nature and a valuable clue to the understanding of many of his poems. They discounted Kallman's talents and his intellect. They even discounted his gift to Auden of companionship, of happy days, and of joy. They discounted most of all Auden's need to love.

The first encounter with Kallman, in April 1939, changed Auden's life forever. For the plain truth is that Wystan loved Chester and was more interested in loving than in being loved. Auden's love for Kallman enriched his life.

On that October afternoon Chester suddenly knew that he would never again be the most important person in anyone's world. Chester, who had taken for granted Auden's devotion for thirty-four years, was now without it. Despite all his friends and his lovers, he was for the first time in his life really alone. ". . . I broke up after Wystan's death," he wrote to his father in May of 1974. Fifteen months after Wystan's last night in Vienna, he himself would be dead. At the news of his death the more romantic of Chester's friends said that Wystan, not able to endure a heaven without him, had called Chester to him.

Who was this companion of Auden who aroused such controversy and jealousy? What was in the character of Kallman that inspired an almost legendary devotion on the part of a man like Auden? If the answer can be found at all, perhaps it lies in the memories of those who knew Kallman best: his father, his brother, his aunt, his cousins, his early schoolmates, his college friends. These were the people who saw Kallman and Auden together in the beginning of their relationship and who knew firsthand what others can only guess—the years together from 1939 to 1973. So this book will be useful, for its pages tell the Auden–Kallman love story.

I first met W. H. Auden in the autumn of 1941, when he was a guest professor at the University of Michigan. Peter Hansen,[1] a mutual friend, introduced him to me one afternoon in an Ann Arbor drugstore. I did not meet Chester until the summer of 1942, when I returned to my graduate studies at the University of Michigan from a term's teaching out of town. Not particularly interested then in meeting poets, I probably would not have become friends with Chester and Wystan at all had I not moved to New York City with Mary Valentine in October of 1943. Little did I guess that in a few years I would fall in love with Chester's father and live with him for more than thirty-five years. Little did I know that Auden would become for me less a celebrity than a member of my husband's family or that Chester would amuse all our old college chums who came to visit with: "Dorothy is now my mother."

---

[1] Not his real name.

CHAPTER 2

Halcyon Days

IN JANUARY 1939, soon to be thirty-two, Auden arrived in New York City from England with his friend Christopher Isherwood. Three months later he was to fall in love for the first time in his life. He was not prepared for what was to happen. For a long time now he had been seeking the mythical beloved in many love objects, but he had been disappointed. Then, suddenly, during his first months in America, he found what he had been looking for, sitting in the front row of a stuffy lecture hall.

In the last stanza of a poem that Auden had written the year before, he asks himself five questions concerning a love that he had more than once despaired of finding:

> *When it comes, will it come without warning*
> *   Just as I'm picking my nose?*
> *Will it knock at my door in the morning,*
> *   Or tread in the bus on my toes?*

> *Will it come like a change in the weather?*
> *Will its greeting be courteous or rough?*
> *Will it alter my life altogether?*
> *O tell me the truth about love.*[1]

Love came to him without warning, it came in the afternoon, and
its first greeting was courteous. It altered his life altogether.

On the evening of April 6, 1939, the League of American Writers,
one of those left-wing organizations that were popular in the thirties,
had invited Auden, somewhat of a cult figure among young writers
and college students, together with Isherwood, Louis MacNeice, and
Frederic Prokosch, to give a public reading. The league, however,
had not advised the speakers of the correct date, so they were notified
at the last minute and arrived two hours late. The audience, full of
eager, excited college students who filled the first rows, had paid their
fifty cents, which was to include beer, and were waiting restlessly.

At about ten o'clock, when the speakers finally arrived, the evening
began. MacNeice read passages from *Autumn Journal;* Prokosch read
from work in progress on a novel; Isherwood talked about the journey he and Auden had made to China the year before. Auden read his
elegy for W. B. Yeats from manuscript: "I can still see Auden, whose
name we had just learned how to pronounce," said a member of that
audience years later, "tall, fair, extraordinarily handsome, reading at
a tremendous angle into the lectern: 'Earth, receive an honoured
guest: / William Yeats is laid to rest.' "[2]

In the audience that evening was a group of students from Brooklyn
College who were on the college literary magazine, the *Observer*.
They viewed Auden as the poetic voice of the future, and they looked
upon his group in England—Christopher Isherwood, C. Day Lewis,
Louis MacNeice, and Stephen Spender—as the prophets of their own
generation. Among these students were Walter James Miller, on the
literary staff of the *Observer,* and Chester Kallman, a junior, the managing editor of the magazine.

After the lecture, the lively group of students from Brooklyn College, along with more staid members of the audience, rushed back-
stage to meet the speakers. Though it was long past Auden's bedtime—
he preferred to be in bed by ten—he was struck by the earnestness of

[1] W. H. Auden, "Twelve Songs," in *W. H. Auden: Collected Poems,* ed. Edward
Mendelson (New York: Random House, 1976), p. 122.

[2] The author's conversations with Walter James Miller and Samuel Exler, June
23 and 30, 1982. The Auden poem quoted is "In Memory of W. B. Yeats."

these American college students. Auden was at first attracted not by Kallman but by Miller, who was talking to Isherwood about poetic drama. Auden, overhearing the conversation, expressed a desire to read an essay Miller had written about modern poetic drama for the *Observer* called "Aeschylus Returns."

While Walter was talking to Isherwood, Chester Kallman and another boy were concentrating on Auden. They asked for an appointment to interview him for the magazine, and Auden set a date for Saturday, April 8, believing that Chester would bring Miller along. The handsome Miller, tall, blond, Anglo-Saxon, and heterosexual, probably reminded Auden of the schoolboy chums of his youth with whom he had been infatuated during boarding school years. Miller later recalled his own reaction to the events of that evening: "We all knew Auden was homosexual," he said, "but I never thought about it much in relation to myself. I was terribly naive. I made it quite clear that I was in love with a young poetess, so I must have become somewhat of a bore." At any rate, when Kallman arrived for the appointment with Auden, he arrived alone.

The young man who appeared at Auden's door on April 8, 1939, had just turned eighteen. He was the type who appealed to adolescent girls, and, had his intellectual bent not yet put its traces upon his features, he could easily have been taken for an actor. Indeed, had he followed the natural inclination of his maternal ancestors—his mother and his grandfather had both been actors—he would have found his place upon the stage.

He was naturally blond, about five feet eleven in height, slender, weighing 145 pounds, with gray-blue eyes, a pale, flawless skin, a Norse skull, Latin lips, and a straight, narrow nose. He had a touch of the gamin in his expression, and Auden would later describe him as an *ange gauche,*[1] an awkward angel. Chester Kallman was a combination of an angel and a satyr, with the physical attributes of both: the coloring of a Florentine angel; the full lips of a satyr. Strictly speaking, Chester resembled, rather than the angels of Botticelli or Fra Angelico, the Florentine Bronzino's "Portrait of a Young Man," even to the expression of the mouth, the hauteur of the eyes, and the cast and gesture of the body—"a portrait of pure pride," as Auden himself often said.

But Bronzino liked to paint dark subjects against bright back-

---

[1] One evening at dinner in 1944, Wystan said to me, "Don't you think Chester is a typical *ange gauche?*"

grounds. Chester Kallman's effect upon the world was quite the reverse. Chester always appeared, with his blondness and bright wit, as a creature of light against the backgrounds in which he found himself. Apparently Auden was not blinded by this first burst of light upon his life, for a moment after Chester Kallman arrived at his door, Auden walked into another room where Christopher Isherwood was now working and said to him: "It's the wrong blond." Auden had expected to see Walter Miller. But if at first Chester was perceived to be the wrong blond, by the end of the afternoon he became the only right one.

It never occurred to this junior at Brooklyn College that he would not be entirely acceptable in Auden's world. Kallman considered himself on an intellectual footing with the great man, for he had a self-confidence beyond his years. He had always been selected for the highest division in his classes, and, at the age of sixteen, he had been admitted to Brooklyn College, which, in the days before open enrollment, was considered by many to be on a par with Harvard. Chester's father, Dr. Edward Kallman, had encouraged his son's love of art, literature, and music—and good living; and he had introduced Chester also to a number of people prominent not only in New York society but also in the arts. It never occurred to Chester Kallman to question his own superiority. Auden, who did not like to be treated with artificial ceremony, was to be attracted to this self-assurance and to accept Chester's evaluation of himself.

However, the first moments of the interview did not go well. Auden seemed restless and bored. He was expecting some friends from England for tea and was preoccupied with the preparations. Having asked his usual one-question-prepared-in-advance-for-social-occasions (this time it was "How do you like being on a literary magazine?"), he did not pay attention to the answer but fell silent and simply responded with grunts. Chester began the interview cautiously. He asked as many questions as he dared, and eventually he and Auden began to talk about English literature. Chester made a casual reference to a Renaissance poet called Thomas Rogers and his "Celestial Elegies." Auden was fond of Rogers and came alive at once. Then everything started, for Wystan recognized a kindred spirit. He stopped being restless and bored, forgot about his tea party, and continued a lively conversation with Chester until the doorbell rang and his guests appeared to an empty tea tray. Auden invited Chester to remain for tea.[1]

[1] The author's conversations with Chester Kallman, 1943 through 1948.

Naturally, Auden did not fall in love with Chester Kallman because of a reference to Thomas Rogers. Hundreds of other boys of eighteen would have known the reference, and thousands were as handsome. Surely other forces were at work, conscious, unconscious, inexplicable. But for whatever cause, Wystan Auden was in love with Chester Kallman from that first afternoon in New York in the spring of 1939 until that last night in Vienna in the autumn of 1973.

Auden, who always kept returning to Wagner, liked to compare this first meeting with Chester to the recognition scene between Siegmund and Sieglinde in the first act of *Die Walküre*,[1] a scene which he played over and over again throughout his life. There was something in his northern nature that tied him to the legend of Siegfried. To Chester he could say at last *"Du bist der Lenz, nach dem ich verlangte."*[2] Over a period of years that included university days, Auden, like Sieglinde, had said, *"Fremdes nur sah ich von je, freundlos war mir das Nähe."*[3] Despite the many friends at boarding school and at Oxford, he was longing to find, not just a friend, but "Der Freund." His recognition of Chester as that friend, not only a lover but also a spiritual companion, paralleled in Auden's mind the recognition between Wagner's hero and heroine.

Auden fell in love with Chester Kallman, not so much because he needed to be loved as because he needed to love. Here was, for some reason, someone who he knew would absorb his life. In the past he had felt sexual attraction and had fulfilled his physical needs, sometimes mechanically, as in Berlin, but what he had felt had not been love. This was different. Now, after having lived for thirty-two years and having crossed an ocean into a new land, he had found what he had been seeking.

"The Prophets," written in May 1939, is probably his first published poem to Chester Kallman. In it he talks of his boyhood fascination with machinery and abandoned lead mines, and of how they, though unresponsive objects, silently told him to wait and he would find the object of his quest, "proof that you existed." He greets the discovery with delight and wonder:

> *For now I have the answer from the face*
> *That never will go back into a book*
> *But asks for all my life, and is the Place*

[1] The author's conversations with W. H. Auden, 1943 through 1971.
[2] "You are the spring for which I yearned."
[3] "All I had ever seen was strange, I never found a friend near me."

Where all I touch is moved to an embrace,
And there is no such thing as a vain look.[1]

He now knew that he did not have to give up the experience of romantic love as written about by the traditional poets. Enamored of
Wagner's operas, he even wore a gold-band wedding ring, bought one
for Chester, announced himself married to Chester, and sang in his
foghorn voice *"Du bist der Lenz"* as he pounded it out on the piano.
Chester belonged to him, and he rejoiced. Though in some ways Chester and Wystan were eons apart, they were in others kindred. Chester's enduring attraction for Auden was not just a physical one. Ten
years later, Auden was to write to Kallman in a letter (February 21,
1949) that he was "the one comrade my non-sexual life cannot do
without."[2] After the first moment of recognition, the happy days of
courtship commenced. Wystan, traditional by nature, was traditional
in love.

He took a lively interest in Chester's life, including Chester's friends
at Brooklyn College. Not only did he visit their office and speak at
their English Club meetings, but he also invited them to his apartment for tea and drinks. He read and criticized their poems, essays,
and short stories, finding in these lively, intelligent youngsters a pleasant reminder of his own college days. Samuel Exler, a new member of
the staff, happened to be in the *Observer* office when Auden arrived
one day. His reaction gives one an idea of Auden's effect upon others.
"I just sat there awestruck when he came in," said Exler, "so para-
lyzed I couldn't say a word. But he just came in and sat down on the
window ledge quite at home and was very friendly and pleasant. I
was struck by his handsome face, and it suddenly struck me how much
he resembled Chester."[3]

Both Walter Miller and Exler believe that Auden was genuinely interested in the work on the magazine. When in Oxford he himself had
edited such a publication and later had founded *The Badger* while he
was a teacher at the Downs School in Colwall, England. He believed
that the opportunity to publish caused students to improve their writing technique and that student publications performed an important
educational purpose. "Wystan was interested in us," said Miller. "He
read the *Observer* from cover to cover, not simply because Chester

[1] Auden, "The Prophets," in *Collected Poems,* p. 203.

[2] The unpublished letters of W. H. Auden to Chester Kallman.

[3] This and subsequent quotes from Walter James Miller and Samuel Exler from
their conversations with the author, June 23 and 30, 1982.

was on the staff, but also because he found it interesting and worth-
while."

In the spring of 1939 Auden had to leave New York to teach at St.
Mark's School in Southborough, Massachusetts, for four weeks. The
letters he wrote to Chester during this time have all been lost, but
since Chester read portions of them aloud to his fellow classmates in
the student cafeteria, one can glimpse the substance of one or two. "I
remember," said Miller, "that Chester had asked Auden the inevitable
question: 'Do you think I have talent?' Wystan wrote back from Southborough: 'You know as well as I do that there are hundreds of young
poets sitting in attics writing poetry, and most of them are not going
to make it. But the established poets like me look upon this as a wave
coming toward us!' " Apparently at this time, Wystan was not going to
commit himself about Chester's talent.

Besides Chester's friends at Brooklyn College, Auden took an interest in Chester's family—his father, Dr. Edward Kallman, a dentist who
had an office in Manhattan, and his grandmother, Rosalia Kallman,
whom Chester called Bobby, and with whom he and his father lived.
After having finished his writing for the day, Auden would take the
Brighton subway to Flatbush, Brooklyn, jotting down lines of poetry
along the way, and spend the afternoon with Chester in Bobby's apartment. He would sit in the kitchen drinking coffee and talking to
Bobby while petting the family cat, Boogit.

Once a week Wystan and Chester would go to the opera at the old
Metropolitan Opera House, and afterward they would dine and drink
champagne at the most expensive restaurant Wystan could afford.
Wystan took up all of Chester's enthusiasms and all his prejudices.
Chester taught his companion to laugh more than he had ever done
before, even with Isherwood. Some felt that Wystan had taken up
with Chester too readily, and his old friends from England were not
entirely happy about this new chum. But Chester and Wystan convinced themselves that Wystan's old friends were envious and went
right on making up their own private jokes and vocabulary all the
time, laughing at the world.

When Dr. Kallman discovered that Chester and Auden had become
friends, he had no doubt about the nature of the relationship. He
asked only that Chester not be careless and reveal anything to Bobby
and his Aunt Sadie, or to other members of the family. Eddie Kallman
was nothing if not a man of the world. A pragmatist, he knew that one
must make the best of what cannot be changed. He realized it would
be to his son's advantage to have a friend like Auden, whom he regarded

as "noble and honorable," and if Chester had to be homosexual, it was better that he be so with Auden than with someone else.

Wystan was welcomed warmly and affectionately into the family circle and seemed to enjoy calling Bobby by Chester's name for her. He liked to visit and make himself generally useful. He took pleasure in the ambiance of the Kallman household. Dr. Kallman was having marital problems with his second wife (Chester's mother, Bertha, died in 1925), and Wystan found it diverting to offer advice, to take sides, to gossip, and to behave in every way like a real in-law.

Bobby, still the matriarch of the family, had not lost her inclination to rule. Her sharp, sardonic wit, like that of her son and her grandson, could destroy you with a word. She was a strong woman with bright snapping eyes and a large frame, and age had not withered her charms. Wystan was very much attached to her. Indeed, Bobby's house in 1939 must have been a genial place, redolent of good cooking and full of laughter, with neighbors and relatives running in and out. Bobby gave advice to the entire community, enjoyed a bit of gossip, and always served you something good to eat. Wystan came frequently to the house to drink a glass of wine, eat, and listen to Bobby's philosophy. They liked each other, and if Bobby sensed anything different about the relationship between Auden and her grandson, she said nothing.

In the summer of 1940, Auden decided to take Chester to the Southwest. They remained a month in Taos, New Mexico, on a honeymoon. Situated between the Rio Grande and the Sangre de Cristo Mountains, Taos was founded in 1615 by Spanish adventurers. It became an art colony in the late nineteenth century and, because of its breathtaking and varied beauty, attracted artists and writers of every description in the twentieth. D. H. Lawrence lived there with his wife, Frieda, before his death in 1930.

Wystan sent postcards and letters back home to Chester's father and grandmother. In one he spoke of Chester's homesickness and begged Eddie to write. Before Eddie set himself down to answer, Chester and Wystan had returned to New York and were filling the evenings with uproarious stories about Mrs. Lawrence and her circle back in Taos. Wystan had indeed found in Chester someone with whom to laugh.

When Benjamin Britten, the English composer, and Peter Pears, the tenor, came to the United States later in the summer, Chester and Wystan were visiting near Williamsburg, Massachusetts. The two Englishmen joined them, along with Chester's father and his younger brother, Malcolm, aged eleven. They all took rooms in an old shaded inn that had been standing since the Revolution. The meals were lavish and inexpensive in those prewar Depression days.

Peter Pears had an old Ford Model T flivver he had picked up for twenty-four dollars in which he, Dr. Kallman, and Malcolm roared all day through the New England countryside while Wystan and Benjamin worked on *Paul Bunyan* and Chester wrote poetry. From time to time Wystan would join the driving party and himself take the wheel. His particular brand of driving was mad at best, wild, and impulsive, partly because he needed distance glasses and was too vain to wear them. He was continually taking them off and mislaying them, so that much of the driving was guesswork.

By October 1940, Wystan had moved into an old house on 7 Middagh Street in Brooklyn Heights. He shared the house with a number of literary and artistic figures, including George Davis, the editor of *Harper's Bazaar,* and Carson McCullers, the novelist, the original tenants. Wystan was manager and paterfamilias. Gypsy Rose Lee, a popular striptease artist and the girlfriend of George Davis, wrote a mystery called *The G-String Murders* while visiting the house. Gypsy was fond of Chester, who later moved into the house, and Eddie remembered how often she asked the boy's opinion on various subjects and the seductive manner in which she said his name: "Chestah!" From time to time others, too, came to live in the house for a while: Peter Pears, Benjamin Britten, Louis MacNeice, Paul Brooks. Christopher Isherwood often came to visit. Wystan managed everything from the disciplining of the help to the finances with the precision and aplomb of a schoolmaster. Unfortunately this utopia was short-lived. In 1945 the house was bulldozed and became part of the Brooklyn–Queens Expressway.

Bobby and Eddie cooked the dinner for Chester's twentieth birthday party in the house on Middagh Street on January 7, 1941, transporting the food from Bobby's kitchen in Flatbush. In addition to the other guests, Lincoln Kirstein, cofounder of the New York City Ballet, and Marc Blitzstein, the composer, dropped in to drink Eddie's sidecars, a combination of Cointreau, lemon juice, and brandy, very popular at the time. Peter Pears sang "Make Believe" from *Show Boat,* and Wystan wrote a poem for the occasion.

TO CHESTER KALLMAN,
b. Jan. 7, 1921

There's wine on the table, and friends and relations
From all over the city collected here;

So, Chester, let's open our gay celebrations
    By wishing you luck in your twentieth year.

What is the first thing I'd get for a poet
    If I could importune the gods, which I can't?
A technical gift? But you have that, and know it.
    The first thing I ask is an adequate rente.

Not very much—say 500 a quarter—
    But enough to enable the boy to resist
Becoming a Sunday reviewer, reporter,
    Scenario writer or novelist.

Stalin and Ford are strangely united
    In a common scorn of the rentier;
Yet could I become one, I should be delighted;
    So hurrah for the small private income, I say.

But money alone is of course no solution,
    The sick and the dead have no use for their wealth;
So I wish you, dear Chester, a tough constitution:
    The artist today must take care of his health.

So early to bed and few amorous antics,
    And some moderation in eats and drinks;
The race is too tough to be run by Romantics:
    You mustn't die young like Kelly and Sheets.

So much would occur to a sensitive stranger,
    But friends must get down to the Particular:
O what are the needs and O what are the dangers
    For the Thinking-Sensation Type that you are?

Thought can be led to dogmatic abuses;
    A theory's a tool to reject when it's broke:
So consider them all as just gifts from the Muses
    Who are charming but fond of a practical joke.

Sensation that in the Gestalt of a city
    Can see the Concrete in its multiple parts,

You can train it on music, but I think it's a pity
If it's quite untrained in the Visual Arts.

In harness the Two are a fine combination
But a little too fond of the mirror—Beware
When you look in one then of the fair fascination
Provided by that ingenious pair.

Remember that poor old Lame Shadow, that other
Neglected child in his jealousy;
Must he always be conscious of missing his mother?
O learn Feeling from Elsie,[1] Intuition from me.

And for all of us here, let me ask in conclusion
That our wishes be horses and do as they're bid;
Success to the happy and loving, confusion
To Political Parties, Policemen, and Sid.[2]

And a message to all in the States where they're apt to
Believe in the Tough and The Real—I say NERTS:
Considering the world that we have to adapt to
We can thank our stars if we're introverts.[3]

Frequently Wystan and Chester would stop at Dr. Kallman's office at 130 West Fifty-seventh Street in order to dress before going to the opera. Not particular about haberdashery for any other occasion (Wystan frequently went about in bedroom slippers even then), they were punctilious about being dressed *en habit* for the opera. The only difficulty was in keeping the shirtfronts white, because neither Chester nor Wystan ever could get the grime of the city off their hands. When they had donned their rented evening clothes, had slicked back their hair, and were ready to leave, Eddie's nurse, Frances Kydd,[4] had to chase them about with a gum eraser in order to clean the finger smudges from their shirtfronts. During the opera Wystan took off his

[1] Elsie Trainen (not her real name), one of Chester's friends from Brooklyn College.
[2] Syd Herman Kallman, Chester's first stepmother.
[3] This is the first time the above poem has been published. It was discovered posthumously among Chester Kallman's papers in Greece.
[4] Not her real name.

shoes and sat in his stocking feet, much to the consternation of the glittering world around him in the orchestra. But he was properly dressed for the opera: His English sense of propriety had been satisfied. Chester and Wystan were, despite it all, a stunning pair.

Although Wystan had always loved Mozart and Wagner, he had little feeling for the opera in general before he met Chester, having been brought up with the idea that opera was musically inferior to other forms such as symphonies and concertos. By the time he had known Chester for a short while, however, he became an Italian opera enthusiast and enjoyed almost as much as Chester not only the operas themselves but also the gossip about the private lives of the singers, about which Chester was an authority. They heard everything: the operas of Monteverdi, Rossini, Bellini, Donizetti, and especially of Chester's favorite, Verdi. They also enjoyed the operas of the *verismo* school of Italian opera and went as often as possible to hear the works of Mascagni, Leoncavallo, and Puccini. They loved the lighter opera of Vienna, too, and when they returned from an evening at *Der Rosenkavalier,* Chester would act out all the scenes. Chester's favorite bit of gossip was the tragic love affair between Ezio Pinza and Elisabeth Rethberg, which he would describe in great detail time after time.

The years from the spring of 1939 to the summer of 1941 were happy days for Auden: He loved and he believed himself to be loved. When in 1940 he wrote "In Sickness and in Health" he was really writing about himself and Chester Kallman. He took seriously the words from the marriage service which say: "Forsaking all others till death us do part." He still believed unromantically in romance. What he did not know in 1940, however, was that Chester Kallman was burning with a fever different from his own.

CHAPTER 3

The Red Man

BY THE TIME of his death there were few people, even on the fringe of the intellectual world, who did not know something about the works of W. H. Auden and something about his life. His easier poems were taught in high school English classes and college survey courses, and by 1970 his rugged face, now heavily lined and handsome no longer, was already recognizable by ordinary people in lobbies of apartment houses where he went to visit his friends. He was truly a man of his time, and he spoke intimately to it. Even the name for his century, the Age of Anxiety, was taken from the title of one of his poems.

Auden was six feet tall, slender, blond, and somewhat narrower in the shoulder than wide in the hip. His large plump fingers, which one of his friends referred to as yams, stained with tobacco and ink, had the close-bitten nails said by psychologists to indicate the devourer. He was ungraceful in his physical movements; indeed, he always appeared to be uncomfortable in his body, and when he walked, usually at full speed, he reminded one of nothing so much as a huge gander. Until he was fifty he was pale, smooth skinned, and handsome, and his eyes were beautiful. In their amber depths I always detected a profound sadness. They held you at bay, but now and then, for a moment, they would reveal themselves, and then you knew their temper and their color.

Despite the pallor of his skin, his color was red. When Auden spoke from the stage of the Horace Rackham School of Graduate Studies at the University of Michigan in the summer of 1941, it seemed to me at the time that he emanated shades of red. Even the white suit he was wearing took upon itself the glow, not of the blue-lit auditorium, but of his red aura. The color suited him; it is the color of winners.

Wystan Hugh Auden was born to parents of the English middle class on February 21, 1907, in York, England, approximately fifty miles from Haworth, the home of Emily and Charlotte Brontë, and until his death he was to love the bleak northern landscape. His father, George Augustus Auden (1872–1957), was a practicing physician, the school medical officer in Birmingham. From his father, Auden inherited his blond, Scandinavian appearance, his interest in science, and his love of books and learning. Besides being devoted to science, Dr. Auden was a classical scholar and a skilled amateur archaeologist, interested in Norse sagas and Anglo-Saxon lore.

Dr. Auden's interest in Saxon history accounts for the unusual first name of his youngest son. The poet's patron saint was Wystan of York, a Mercian prince, whose shrine was in Evasham Abbey, but whose remains are to be found, it is said, in Wistow in Leicestershire, where he was murdered in 850 by his uncle because Wystan upheld the marriage laws of the church. The devout young prince objected, as did Hamlet, to the marriage of his widowed mother to his father's brother. Dr. Auden discovered a church in Repton dedicated to Saint Wystan, whose feast day is June 1, and decided to dedicate his son to the saint as well. Auden was much attracted to his name and to the legend of his patron saint, and he liked to believe that he alone of all people was chosen to carry it in its original Anglo-Saxon spelling.

The person who had the greatest single influence upon Wystan Hugh Auden was his mother. Constance Rosalie Bicknell was born in 1869, the youngest child in a family of eight. Her father was the vicar of Wroxham. Orphaned at the age of twelve, she was brought up by her Uncle Charlie, a bachelor. When Constance was eighteen, Uncle Charlie took her on her first trip abroad, and he died one night when they were in Bordighera on the Italian Riviera, leaving his young, inexperienced but obviously capable niece to handle all the arrangements for funeral and burial. One glimpses early the forthright nature of this admirable woman.

Constance was striking and might easily have posed for the portrait of the typical Edwardian lady, with her narrow waist, her classic profile, her soft brown hair piled high upon her head, and her large wide-brimmed hats. She must have been exquisite in the starched uniform and headdress of hospital nurse, which indeed she wore, for after obtaining an honors degree in French from London University, she took nurses' training at St. Bartholomew's Hospital, London. Her ambition was to become a Protestant missionary nurse in Africa.

At St. Bartholomew's she met a young intern, three years her junior. Dr. Auden was devoted to science, but he was also interested in things cultural, particularly music, and they became friends. Soon they fell in love and were married. They settled in York, the cathedral city in the north. George was successful as a general practitioner, and soon the Audens were to move into a fine home and to employ a coachman, a cook, and scullery and parlor maids. They had three children: first Bernard, in 1900; then John, in 1904; then, last of all, Wystan, in 1907. Constance was already thirty-seven when her last child was born.

When Wystan was one year old, the family suddenly moved from York. Dr. Auden gave up his lucrative practice, his coachman, his cook, and his maids in order to take the position of school medical officer in Birmingham. Though Dr. Auden was forced to sacrifice some income with this new post, his wife was relieved he accepted it. While in some ways modern, she was in others Victorian and did not approve of her husband's previous work in gynecology.

Constance was a strict but loving mother, and her influence upon her youngest son in particular was strong. Years later he was to say, speaking on her behalf, "Mother would never approve" or "Mother would be cross" about one or another matter of decorum that came up later in his life. When Dr. Auden joined the Royal Army Medical Corps and went off to World War I to serve in Gallipoli, Egypt, and France, it was mother whom the boys saw on their vacations. It was his mother with whom Wystan spent his time during his preschool years. She taught him to read, to appreciate books and music, and to love animals. There is a charming photograph extant of Wystan as a small boy lovingly holding a calico cat. Years later, when living at 77 St. Mark's Place in New York, he was to say, "I just got a calico cat. I used to have a calico cat back in England. They're good luck." Wystan loved all animals, particularly cats. "I believe they have souls," he said more than once. "The church is wrong, you know, to say they haven't."

Constance had a gift for music, and she often played the piano and sang with her little son. She was particularly fond of the love duet from *Tristan und Isolde,* her little five year old in his high treble voice taking the part of Isolde. When Wystan and his brothers, Bernard and John, were away at boarding school and their father was off to war, they looked forward to their summer vacations with their mother, who, now staying with friends and relatives, would rent rooms for the summer for herself and the children in various parts of England so they could become acquainted with the land of their birth.

The little chubby towheaded Wystan, with his sharp intelligence and eager inquisitive ways, was Constance's favorite, and her relatives and other children believed she spoiled him. However, a devout woman with a good deal of common sense, she disciplined him too, and on occasion showed a flaring temper. Wystan, later in New York, once said, "There were times when I was sure that my mother would kill me." He never explained what he meant, and no one dared ask.

Mrs. Auden was intensely religious. Not able to become a missionary, she saw her vocation in being a good wife and mother, and she did her best to fulfill daily what she regarded as the will of God for her. As members of the high Anglican church, she and her husband attended two services on Sunday, the boys serving as acolytes and choirboys. There were family prayers before breakfast each morning, with the servants in attendance. From time to time Constance would go to an Anglican convent for a religious retreat. When Wystan was at St. Edmund's she presented a handsome crucifix to the school. Her sons were inspired by her example. Even during his rebellious years, Wystan had a respect for the church, and through most of his adulthood he attended church regularly. Each Sunday in New York would find him up early ("Especially if I have a hangover") and sitting either in Grace Church or in St. Mark's Church in-the-Bowery. Wystan's brother John became a Roman Catholic in 1951.

Constance Auden disapproved of low church, believing that chanting, incense, and ritual were an integral part of the religious experience, incomplete and fragmented without them. Wystan always regretted the changes in the Roman ritual and later in the high Anglican, regarding them as "blasphemous," "schismatic," and "banal." "My dear, it's so lowbrow," he used to say. He never forgave Rome for abandoning Latin. He disapproved of the changes made by Vatican II.

The precept and example given him by his mother trained Auden's nature, eccentric and wild though it was, to accept early the discipline and routine of a daily schedule. Each morning of his life he arose at six and wrote until noon. Each night throughout his life he retired before ten. He lived on a monastic time schedule, and he was never late for an appointment. Though he left his home, even his country, which he considered restrictive, it was just such restrictiveness imposed early that channeled the talent that might otherwise have been diffused. Without it he would not have become the great poet he was. To his mother, who was with him daily during his most formative years and who trained him early, he owed his later position in the world of the twentieth century.

When Wystan was eight years old, in 1915, he was sent to boarding school at St. Edmund's, Hindhead in Surrey, and in the fall of 1920 he entered Gresham's School, Holt, in Norfolk, for his college preparatory. His education was the traditional classical education given to English boys of the upper classes, and it included Latin, Greek, and French. Auden always believed it to be the only true education and the background for all vocations and professions, scientific and military as well as literary, legal, and religious: the only civilizing education.

In 1925, Wystan was ready for Oxford. He entered Christ Church college with a scholarship and decided to study for a career in the natural sciences. He was to graduate from Christ Church in 1928, but not with a degree in the natural sciences.

While attending Christ Church he met again his old friend from St. Edmund's, Christopher Isherwood, when both were in London. Isherwood was attending Cambridge at the time, but he finally left university after a year, giving up the study of medicine for a career in writing. Auden and Isherwood, despite their separation, immediately became close friends. Auden accepted criticism and suggestions from his old school chum readily and good-naturedly, and throughout his life thought of Isherwood as perhaps his closest friend. When Auden sublet an apartment during the middle 1940s in a building next door to a large Congregational church on West Fifty-seventh Street in New York, he thought it something of a good joke. "I must tell Christopher," he said. "He's the only one who would appreciate my living next to a church. There are some things one can share only with old friends." Every now and then during the 1940s and 1950s, Isherwood would appear in New York, fresh faced and elegant from California, bestowing a beatific if slightly amused smile upon the guests, who lounged about his friend's rooms.

At university Auden met those friends and poets who were to remain devoted to him for life: Stephen Spender, Louis MacNeice, and C. Day Lewis. Auden, flamboyant and exhibitionistic, was a natural leader.

Having entered Oxford with a scholarship in the biological sciences, Auden changed to English literature during his second year. Wystan, aggressively brilliant and well read, found his tutor, Nevill Coghill, sympathetic. Coghill's mild personality allowed Wystan to guide himself into the career of his choice. He is said to have told Coghill the first day they met that he intended to be "a great poet." He also told the same thing to one of his classmates when taking a walk in the woods at Gresham's.

From the time of his days at Gresham's throughout his undergraduate life at Oxford, Auden had been a practicing homosexual. It was not surprising that Auden should have been a homosexual in those days. What is surprising is that he should have made a cult of it. It was not unusual for English boys in boarding school—or American boys in public high schools, for that matter—to have had these experiences, and they were thought of as a stage one went through. Most of the boys when they became older led reasonably happily married lives and had families as most men do anywhere. Those who were genuinely homosexual remained so.

Auden was a creature of his class and his generation, and, despite his eccentricities, he fully expected to marry and raise a family as most of the friends of his youth eventually did, whatever their sexual experiences at boarding school. Thus it was that in 1928, the year Wystan graduated from Oxford, he announced his engagement to a young woman named Sheilah Richardson, who later became a nurse, though little more is known about her. However, one evening in New York, when having dinner with friends, Auden mentioned that in his youth he had gone out on a date with a girl. "I couldn't think of anything else to say, so I asked her to marry me," he remembered, much to the amusement of his friends. His intentions seemed serious enough at the time, however, and the marriage was to take place on some day in the indefinite future when he returned from abroad.

From the time Wystan graduated from university, and even before, he began to travel. In 1925 his father had taken him to Kitzbühel in Austria, a country that he was later to make his home, and from that time on he harbored a fondness for all things Germanić. In July 1927, he and Dr. Auden visited Yugoslavia. After his graduation from Oxford, Wystan went to Berlin to live for a while, and, in the manner of the English upper classes, to broaden his education. Later he was to visit Iceland, Portugal, Spain, China, and then the United States.

His days in Berlin had a profound effect on his life and his poetry. It was here, first living in the middle-class suburb of Nikolassee, then in the blue-collar section of Hallesches Tor, that he enjoyed a freedom he could not have had at home. Here he also met John Willoughby Layard of King's College, Cambridge, who had been cured of hysterical paralysis by the unorthodox methods of Homer Lane, an American psychologist now dead, to whom Layard had been devoted and whose theories he promulgated.

Lane believed that human beings were essentially virtuous and that lack of inhibition and complete freedom of expression, especially sexual expression, must lead inevitably to goodness. If you suppressed your desires, you would become neurotic.[1] These theories, familiar and somewhat naive as they appeared to a later generation already disillusioned with them, attracted the young Auden, who saw in them a joyful liberation for himself from what he regarded as his own repressive and restrictive childhood. He avidly studied not only Lane's doctrines as spoken by Layard but also the writings of the German psychoanalyst Georg Groddeck.

Wystan began his hoped-for liberation by engaging in frenetic sexual activity. His theories about repression, together with his sudden freedom from restraint when away from England, may account for his sexual behavior while in Germany. When he moved to Hallesches Tor and drank at the Cozy Corner bar, which he referred to as his brothel,[2] he engaged in a number of encounters with different boys (he later made a list), and his appetite was voracious. However, it was merely an appetite, for his many encounters were usually with boys of the street whom he paid, rather than with equals for whom he felt a romantic passion.

The schoolboy chums of his early days with whom he fell in love were often essentially heterosexual extroverts and of an active, athletic nature quite different from his own. Sex and romance were not necessarily connected in his mind, and his attitude toward sex was practical

[1] Humphrey Carpenter, *W. H. Auden: A Biography* (Boston: Houghton Mifflin, 1981), pp. 89–93.

[2] Carpenter, *Auden: A Biography,* p. 96.

and experimental. He was young; he believed himself to need sex, and he had it. Now and then he would have an encounter with one or another old school friend whom he met again, but there was no talk of everlasting love.

Wystan had already read Freud, encouraged by his father to read the latest in scientific thought, and he had once toyed with the idea of becoming a psychiatrist. When Layard came along with Homer Lane's theories, he felt that he had met a kindred soul. Wystan had also been reading D. H. Lawrence, whose ideas he considered similar to Lane's, and he began voicing theories that the human being could avoid all the misery of illness by what he called "purity of heart," defined as the absence of repression. "To those brought up on repression, the mere release of the unconscious is sufficient to give a sense of value and meaning to life,"[1] he said more than once. "Be happy and you will be good."[2]

Throughout his life Wystan was to practice cures. If a person had rheumatism or arthritis, Wystan thought his problem to be stubbornness; if he was deformed, he was in a struggle between instinct and will;[3] if he had boils, he was frustrated in love, and the frustration was coming out as pus. An abnormal tallness was an attempt to reach heaven, and the presence of cancer was the result of the frustration of the creative urge. When he heard that Freud had died of cancer of the jaw, he said, "Who would have thought he was a liar."[4] Constipation, Wystan insisted, was the result of not valuing a creative talent. Bad breath meant a desire to withdraw from society and thus set up a mechanism to keep people at a distance.[5] (Almost a direct quote from Georg Groddeck.) Diabetes, he once told his friend Dr. David Protetch, who was afflicted with it, had something to do with "the sweets of sin." He had cures for asthma, tuberculosis, ulcer, diabetes, allergies, and every other affliction, and he would keep you occupied for hours explaining them and discussing his many successes.

Upon Auden's return to England at Christmas, his mother was outraged at her darling's disheveled appearance and fought with him continually to mend his manners, comb his hair, keep his room tidy and himself clean. Wystan now found life with his parents unendur-

[1] Carpenter, *Auden: A Biography*, p. 89.

[2] Ibid., p. 86.

[3] Ibid., p. 92.

[4] Ibid.

[5] Auden's theories, when not quoted from Carpenter, are those he told the author in conversation.

able and he left the family home to stay with one or another of his friends, visiting his parents only upon occasion.

In those days, however, Wystan seemed unable to remain long in one place and wanted the stimulation and sense of independence he had achieved on the Continent, so after his Christmas visit to England, he returned to Berlin. A few months later Christopher Isherwood joined him. Their association became productive as always, for they wrote together an unpublished poetic drama, *The Enemies of a Bishop*. It was at this point that Auden broke off his engagement. Nothing more was said about Sheilah. However, later in New York he told his friends that the girl whom he had asked to marry had entered an Anglican convent. His friends found the story a charming one, but they suspected that Wystan was not above supplying a dramatic ending to his romance in order to enliven the evening.

Wystan's twenty-third birthday, the date at which his father would stop supporting him, would be approaching the following February, so by the summer of 1929 he found himself back in England ready to look for a job. The only occupation for which he was prepared was teaching school, and eventually he found a position at Larchfield Academy, Helensburgh. To his surprise, teaching suited him. It gave him an outlet not only for his inclination to lead but also for his impulse to be dramatic. Further, teaching at Larchfield gave him an opportunity to continue his experiments in healing. He remained at the school for two years, entering into the life around him and writing poetry in his spare time. At this time Faber & Faber accepted some of his poems for publication. The poems submitted reflected his days in Germany and the theories of Homer Lane. Wystan had now gained the attention of T. S. Eliot, a director of Faber & Faber.

A few months after spending a fortnight in Berlin with Isherwood, Auden's book *Poems* (1930) was published. He received some favorable reviews, and the poems created excitement among young intellectuals. His was a new voice in a new age, calling upon the vocabulary of science and modern life and using a telegraphic economy of words. Many young poets on both sides of the Atlantic found in him their inspiration. The publication of *Poems* (1930) was a landmark, and Auden's fame began to grow.

Auden left Larchfield in the summer of 1932 and got a job at another boys' preparatory school, the Downs, at Colwall. There Wystan taught English and French as well as arithmetic and biology, and he clumsily went about supervising games. He started a magazine called *The Badger* in order to encourage his students to write poetry, and

he directed dramatic performances. The students called him Uncle
Wiz. He smoked continuously, bit his fingernails, wore a large black
Flemish hat, and puzzled everyone with his capricious temperament,
now bright, now sullen.

During the early 1940s, Wystan was given to expressing his educational theories, particularly to me after I had just received my teaching license in New York. "Men make the best teachers," he was fond
of saying. "That's because they're lazy. Then students have to find out
things for themselves. Women do too much for students." He then
gave me a drill book he had used in his classes at the Downs. "Just
give them some of these exercises and let them work them out for
themselves. It will give you a bit of a rest, you know." The name of
the book was *Common Sense Texts in English,* by Robert Swann,
B.A., published by Methuen & Co., Ltd., London, in 1931. The exercises took various forms. Some were in accepted usage and diction, the
student having been given sentences or a paragraph to correct. Sometimes the student was asked to substitute a more imaginative synonym
for a given word. Other exercises required the student to write a
story, to describe an experience from memory, or write a poem in a
given meter.

Taking Wystan's advice, I tried one of the easier exercises with my
classes in a New York high school. The American students, children
of a more permissive culture than Auden's at the Downs, could not
even comprehend the directions, let alone do the assignment, except
after much explanation and discussion. When told about my classes'
inability to grasp the exercise, Wystan responded, "I don't see why
not; they're really very simple drills, my dear."

Every now and then while at the Downs, Wystan would escape for
a weekend to Oxford, where he would meet an undergraduate he
knew and have sex. Later on he was not above having brief affairs
with his students. On vacations he would go to the Lake District to
see his parents, who had a cottage there, stay a month or so, and then
be off to Berlin and Isherwood.

In June 1935, while still teaching at the Downs School, Auden
married Erika Mann, daughter of Thomas Mann, the novelist, and
sister of Klaus, a friend of Christopher Isherwood. Though Auden
had never met Erika Mann, he agreed to marry her so she might escape from Hitler's Germany. They were married on June 15, 1935,
at the Registry Office, Ledbury, Hereford. Although he visited her
and her family from time to time while in America, and while he
facetiously referred to her occasionally as "my wife," his contact with

her was never close. Yet she remained legally married to him all her life and was to leave him in her will a sum of three thousand dollars.

During his days at the Downs School, although he had rejected the religion of his childhood, he insisted later he had had a genuine mystical experience. He was not to return to the Anglican church for almost a decade, but that experience, which he describes in his essay on the Protestant mystics,[1] was prophetic of how he would change spiritually within the next ten years.

The job that Auden took after his happy days at the Downs was one working for the producer John Grierson, who was making documentaries for a film unit attached to the General Post Office. Auden wrote commentaries on two films intended to present the life of the average worker. One was *Night Mail;* the other was *Coal Face.* The man selected to furnish the original music was Benjamin Britten, then twenty-two, who was to become Auden's good friend for many years. Auden remained in this job until February 1936, when he decided to quit the film industry and give all his attention to his writing.

He was encouraged by the success of a play he had written with Isherwood, *The Dog Beneath the Skin,* which opened on January 30, 1936, at the Westminster Theatre and received favorable reviews. It ran for six weeks. In fact, the authors were asked to write another play for the Group Theatre. Auden thus went off to visit Isherwood, now in Portugal with an expatriate German friend, and the two authors set about writing another play, *The Ascent of F6,* about mountain climbing. John Auden, Wystan's brother, had been a mountaineer for some time and had given his younger brother a great deal of information about the practical business of climbing mountains and about mountains themselves. The book is dedicated to him.

When Auden returned from Portugal, he asked Faber & Faber to give him a contract to do a travel book on Iceland, which he believed to be the home of his forebears, and the publishing house advanced him enough money to make the trip. It became a wild camping trip eventually, for he met Louis MacNeice and some boys from the Downs there. During the stay in Reykjavik, on the way home, and back in England he wrote the delightful "Letter to Lord Byron." Louis MacNeice, his old friend from Oxford, and he collaborated on *Letters from Iceland* (1936). Wystan often made the comment that he had found almost no homosexuality there.

---

[1] W. H. Auden, *Forewords and Afterwords,* ed. Edward Mendelson (New York: Random House, 1973), pp. 69–70.

As Auden's interest in the theories of D. H. Lawrence and Layard began to fade, his attraction to left-wing political theories revived. At the same time, the war in Spain, which had started in 1936, intensified. He decided to work there on the side of the Loyalists as a stretcher bearer or ambulance driver. He departed for Spain in January 1937, full of idealism and courage, but when he arrived, things were so disorganized he found little to do. Although he seldom spoke at length about his experiences during the Spanish Civil War, he lost his enthusiasm for left-wing politics because of what he had witnessed there.

Auden left Spain in March 1937. That year he wrote his poem "Spain," with its arresting refrain, "But today, the struggle." He later rejected the poem. It was Chester's father's favorite poem, and he was disappointed when Wystan banished it from the canon of his work.

"Why, Wystan?" Eddie would ask. "It's such a beautiful poem."

"No," Wystan answered, his jaw set in a stubborn line. "It won't do."

In the early fall of 1937, plans were made for Auden to travel to another war, this time in China, in order to write a travel book about the Far East for Bennett Cerf at Random House, New York, and for Faber & Faber of London. The result was *Journey to a War,* which he collaborated on with his old friend Christopher Isherwood.

In the meantime he had won the 1937 King's Gold Medal for Poetry given to the best book published in 1937 by a poet under thirty-five. The book was *Look, Stranger!* Later, Wystan told Chester's father that when he was presented to George VI on November 23, 1937, he had asked the King, "Did you like my book, Sir?" Auden had been oblivious of the rule that, when presented, one never speaks to a reigning monarch unless first spoken to. The King, sensitive and intelligent, but a stammerer, was so shocked by the breach of protocol that he suffered a severe spasm that prevented him from speaking. Gracious by nature, however, the King tried to answer. Only noises issued from his throat. Wystan, embarrassed, bowed, and walked back, glad to have the entire affair ended.

Auden and Isherwood arrived in China in January 1938. The two of them spent much of their time in British enclaves, councils, and embassies, drinking tea and gossiping with officials. Young and adventurous, Auden and Isherwood longed to see some action, so they walked some miles to the front at Meiki. Although they also saw bombs falling on city streets, they spent most of their time interviewing Englishmen. Once, however, they had an opportunity to talk in Hankow with Madame Chiang Kai-shek, the beautiful wife of Chiang, who had been educated at Wellesley in the United States. Chiang himself appeared toward the end of the interview looking "like a country doctor."[1]

After what they called "a tourist's acquaintance with China"[2] they took the ship the *Empress of Asia* first to Japan for a brief visit, then to Vancouver. They next boarded a train for New York City. Though their first visit was brief, the New World made a lasting impression upon them. They both decided to return to the United States and eventually chose to make it their permanent home.

According to Auden's biographer Humphrey Carpenter, Auden had decided to emigrate from England as early as 1938.

> He was trying to find the personal ideals for which he had been searching ever since the collapse of his Lane–Layard–Lawrence beliefs; these he had failed to replace either with Gerald Heard's[3] view of personality or with Marxism, with which he had only toyed. Each of his foreign trips had been in its different way an attempt to "make action urgent and its nature clear." Iceland, he had hoped, would allow him to distance himself from European culture and view it objectively. . . . Spain was an attempt . . . "to gamble on something bigger" . . . This, too, had failed, because the Spanish war was not the clear-cut set of issues he had hoped to find. As to the China trip, it had done no more than strengthen his belief in universal human failure. . . .[4]
>
> So he turned to America, not because he had any dream of it as the perfect society, but because he regarded it as a place where the options were still open, and where no set pattern of civilization had yet been developed. As he put it in 1939: "What England can give me, I feel it already has, and that I can never lose it. America is so vast. . . ."[5]

Auden and Isherwood departed for New York in the middle of January 1939.

[1] Carpenter, *Auden: A Biography,* p. 236.

[2] Ibid.

[3] Gerald Heard, an eccentric friend of Auden, believed that the suppression of the inner personality would lead to neurosis in the individual and to revolution in society (see Carpenter, p. 136).

[4] Carpenter, *Auden: A Biography,* p. 243.

[5] Ibid., p. 244.

CHAPTER 4

L'Ange Gauche

WHEREVER CHESTER KALLMAN went and in whatever company, everything became more exciting or more funny—or more terrible; it all depended upon how he saw it, or how he reacted to it. He made you feel what he wanted you to feel. He created his world around you and manipulated you with his will.

It was not without reason that Auden called Chester *l'ange gauche,* the awkward divinity—half angel, half changeling. He even looked like an *ange gauche.* His face with its luminous skin, classic features, and fine blond hair also had the perpetual rings under the eyes and pouting mouth of a spoiled child that has just been weeping. His tall, sturdy body, slender as a wand in the early days, with its wide shoulders and perfect legs, had just the suggestion of a curvature along the spine, a condition that became worse with time. His pale gray-blue, sometimes violet, eyes and their long straight blond lashes were topped by the peaked eyebrows of a satyr. He could be generous, gallant, and compassionate; he could be quixotic, scathing, and cruel.

Everyone feared his scorpion wit. But he was irresistible, though it became clear to everyone who knew him that to love him was to court disaster. It became clear as well that he had an uncontrollable tendency toward self-destruction, and that those who loved him would have to stand idly by, for they could do nothing to save him.

When Chester's father, Dr. Edward Kallman, met Igor Stravinsky in the spring of 1965, the first question the composer asked him was, "How does one get a son like Chester?"

A remarkable son, he was the child of an equally remarkable mother. Bertha Dorothy Coopersmith, Chester's mother, was born on May 6, 1896, to an actor father, who was always on tour, and a pretty, but simple, mother. When Bertha was a child still in elementary school, she acted in the Yiddish theater then flourishing on Second Avenue in Manhattan. She was intelligent and had such a good memory that she could read a page of script through once and have it letter perfect. It was a skill that was to stand her in good stead later on. When times became bleak, as they usually did in the Yiddish theater, and when Papa Coopersmith allegedly ran off with an exotic dancer, Bertha, her mother, and her sister, Suzie, moved to Brooklyn, where rents were cheap, and fended for themselves. The girls took part-time jobs in a dry-goods store while going to Eastern District High School, and the mother took in sewing. Bertha, tired at twelve years old of *la vie bohème* and all that went with it, decided to become a nurse. She met her future husband at Eastern District High School.

Edward Kallman was born at 12:01 A.M. on January 1, the first minute of the year 1892, to Herman and Rosalia Kallman, who had come to America from Courland, that section of ancient Latvia ruled for centuries by German barons. Rosalia always said that she had cheated the steamship company out of a fare, for she was pregnant with Eddie during the voyage. Since Herman and Rosalia were first cousins, all their relatives—sisters, brothers, cousins, and second cousins—were related by blood as well as marriage. Through the years ahead, almost everybody in New York seemed somehow related to the Kallmans.

Eddie grew up to be a handsome lad—tall, blond, high-spirited, full of fun. Bertha, along with a number of her other classmates at Eastern District, fell in love with him at the age of fourteen. Eddie had seen Bertha playing the role of Portia when the school produced *The Merchant of Venice,* and was attracted not only by her acting ability and copper hair, but also by the high grades he saw on her report card. Eddie admired intelligent women. He also admired women who, like

his mother, could somehow dominate him. Eddie's family liked
Bertha, too, and welcomed her into their home.

Eddie and Bertha were engaged to be married as early as 1911, but
as the years went by, Bertha had her problems with him. Why—his
attitude seemed to imply—did he have to have just one girl when he
could easily please many more? They were eventually married on October 27, 1919, after Eddie returned from France, where he had spent
eighteen months in the army during World War I.

Chester Simon Kallman was born on January 7, 1921, at 9:30 in
the evening in Brooklyn Jewish Hospital. He was born in the hospital
where his mother had taken her nurses' training and had won a gold
medal for excellence in scholarship. His father, who had graduated
from Columbia's College of Dental and Oral Surgery, had just set up
his dental practice at One Union Square, Manhattan, as partner to
the uncle of the actress Nazimova, a successful immigrant from
czarist Russia.

As a boy, Chester Kallman was well-behaved, jolly, and reasonable.
But he could also be mischievous. When his mother spanked him, he
would say, "I'll go to live with Aunt Sadie." (Aunt Sadie, whom Chester adored, is Eddie's younger sister.) He was intelligent; he adored
words, the longer the better, and he learned to read before the age of
five. The center of his life, however, was the Victrola. Dr. Kallman
collected the classical records popular at the time, and Chester, who
had already fallen in love with music, fell madly in love with Amelita
Galli-Curci and could place the needle on the exact groove of the
record that contained the fioritura passage or the cabaletta nearest his
heart. Throughout his life Chester was to fall in love with divas.

The marriage of Bertha and Eddie was happy enough, but it was to
be short-lived, ending in tragedy five years after it began. Bertha developed a varicosity in her right leg and died of an embolism suddenly
on August 10, 1925. After her death, a change took place in Eddie,
who had never before faced personal tragedy. He could not make himself go back into the house where he had lived with his wife. He could
not look at her photograph again. He moved with his son, age four,
into the house of his parents, then in Flatbush, leaving the funeral
arrangements and the estate to be managed by his in-laws.

After the death of his mother, Chester did not seem to change per-
ceptibly in temperament or interests. Things might have gone on
pleasantly enough for Chester during his childhood and adolescence
despite the early death of his mother had it not been for two other
events. Between 1926 and 1927 two marriages took place that were to

color his entire life thereafter. One was the marriage of his aunt; the other was the remarriage of his father.

The aunt's marriage occurred first. Sadie Kallman Jacobs was one of those rare women who are natural-born mothers. She did by instinct what other women try to do by the book and fail. When he was four, Chester had made his aunt promise that when he grew up she would marry him. She foolishly said that she would, not realizing in her naiveté the profound feelings of the boy.

Chester knew that she had a friend named Irving who called upon her twice a week, but he was not aware of the full significance of the friendship until the week came in which they were to be married. When Chester found out that Sadie was to marry Irving and not himself, he cried, he screamed, he kicked at everything in the house. The storm lasted until the hour of the wedding, when Chester was finally pacified by being told that he, too, would be marrying Sadie. Chester stood with Sadie and Irving under the wedding canopy all through the ceremony. He danced with her—and Irving—all evening long. He went to sleep exhausted but peaceful, only to find when he awoke the next morning that she was gone. The realization of the awful truth overcame him. He did not recover soon, if at all, despite continued efforts on the part of his family. When he later wrote poems about his lost mother, they must in part have been addressed to his aunt.

His father's marriage the next year was a different matter but no less traumatic. Eddie's second wife was a woman of twenty-eight named Sadye, or Syd, Herman.

Although Chester had tried from time to time to live with his father and stepmother shortly after the birth of his brother, Malcolm, on July 29, 1929, he always went back to his grandparents' house, then in Brighton Beach. In 1932, however, when he was eleven, his grandfather was ailing, so Bobby took him with them to New Bedford, Massachusetts, and then Chester finally went to live permanently in his father's house.

By this time Eddie and Syd had moved with Malcolm into a new apartment building, the Del-Mar, which, before the landfill, faced directly on the boardwalk and the Atlantic at Brighton Beach. The Del-Mar, considered a marvel of 1930s architectural innovation, had salt baths in the basement and a garden on the roof. All the apartments looked out on the ocean, and all the tenants paid what seemed to them an exorbitant rent: $90 a month for three large rooms and $135 for four.

Chester had just been enrolled in the junior high school on Boody

Avenue South and West Fourth Street, a school that, before the egali-
tarianism of later generations, had a class for bright children that was
unabashedly called "rapid advanced." So rapid was it that Chester
was to be a sophomore in Abraham Lincoln High School at thirteen,
as was his brother, and a freshman in Brooklyn College three years
later. Chester's academic advancement was allegedly a source of annoyance to his stepmother.

Indeed, from the day of Eddie's marriage, the recurring problem in
Chester's life was his stepmother. Syd had told Eddie before the marriage that she would know just how to be a stepmother to Chester
because she herself had had one. Her first suggestion after the marriage was that Chester be sent away to boarding school. Apparently
Syd's experience with her own stepmother, whom she detested, had
taught her how to fill the traditional role, for Chester hated Syd until
the day he died. He hated her with a mortal loathing—so great, in fact,
that one doubts whether so simple and so unimaginative a creature as
she could have been worthy of it. He regaled his protesting friends,
already tired of hearing about Syd, daily for years with stories of his
persecutions, and Wystan later took up the battle. In fact, Wystan
used to say that his idea of purgatory was to be forced to spend an
eternity tied to Syd and never to be released until one learned to
love her.[1]

In writing about Chester Kallman, one is confronted with the fact
of Syd, because her influence upon him was great, though not happy.
It was she who was present in his home during many of his formative
years, and it was her influence, at least in part, to which Dr. Kallman
always attributed his son's preference for men. She was an important
enough influence for Wystan to mention her from time to time in
letters and to keep Chester discussing her for many years. But one
is faced with a dilemma. In an attempt to find the truth, one is left
with only one truth, Chester's; for Syd's side of the story, if indeed
she had one, is shrouded in the past and died with her. In all fairness,
one must suppose that the young Chester, precocious and spoiled,
was not easy for his pedestrian stepmother to handle and that, even
if she had no cause for resentment against him other than her intensely jealous nature, she would have been put off by him.

Chester was soon back in the home of his grandparents, for he had

---

[1] He was to say the same thing about Frances Kydd, Dr. Kallman's nurse,
later on.

become unusually nervous living with his stepmother. The jealous streak in Syd became worse as time passed. It was directed, of course, at other women and, perhaps, with some justification; but it was also directed at Chester. According to Eddie she interfered with Chester's interests, making fun of his musical and literary pursuits. He said she clapped her hands when told that Chester failed to win a prize in English.

Chester's stories about her left out no detail. According to him she was mean: She watered his milk; she turned on the vacuum cleaner just when the symphony was about to begin; she turned off the music programs to play her everlasting soap operas; she took the meat from his lamb chops and left him the fat; she struck him; she was maniacally jealous. She called him a sissy and a hothouse flower. She soured his life. Chester's grandmother hated her; his aunt hated her; his first and second cousins hated her; finally his father hated her.

Yet, despite the antagonism between stepmother and stepson, Chester loved the brother eight years his junior. Chester and Malcolm were to be devoted to each other throughout their lives. When Malcolm spoke of his brother, one was always aware of the deep affection between them, despite the dissension in their home life. Chester used to baby-sit for his brother and would supervise, correct, and punish Malcolm with all the authority of an old-fashioned patriarch, dispensing favors or withholding them according to whether Malcolm drank his milk and took his nap at the appropriate time.

The term before Chester enrolled in Brooklyn College, he and his father left Malcolm and Syd. When his father returned to the Del-Mar from a pleasure trip to Europe in July 1936, Chester had an attack of appendicitis and had to be taken to the hospital for an emergency operation. Eddie decided to take the convalescent Chester to the Vermont summer home of an old friend and patient, Leonid Shostakovich, for a rest. Syd had a tantrum because she wanted her husband to remain at home or at least to take her along, and, in an ill-considered ultimatum, directed him not to come back to his home alive. He took her at her word, for she had provided the excuse he had been seeking. He went off to the country, and when he returned, he returned with Chester to the home of his mother.

Bobby had come back from New England after the sudden death of her husband to an apartment near Brooklyn College at the Flatbush Avenue stop of the Seventh Avenue subway line. Chester was to live with his father and his grandmother during his last term in high school and until he graduated from Brooklyn College in January 1941. Eddie Kallman never went back to his wife. Syd always refused to give Eddie a divorce, for she hoped he would someday return.

Chester was happy enough with his grandmother and his father in 1936. He went to the opera at least once a week; he saw his friends from college; he was taken out to plays and concerts by his father's nurse and later his girlfriend, Frances Kydd; he visited his father's office in Manhattan and enjoyed his father's freedom along with his own.

Perhaps the most outstanding quality about Chester's early life was the love—almost the tenderness—his fellow classmates felt for him. Fifty years later they remembered his brilliance and gentleness. When asked for information about Chester's school days, they responded with enthusiasm and generosity, eager that Chester be presented to the world "as he really was, not as some appendage to Auden."[1] They thought that he ought to be "brought out of the shadows."[2] "He was," they said, "a brilliant, beautiful boy."[3]

Brooklyn College, opened in 1930 by merging the Brooklyn branches of City and Hunter colleges, was tuition-free to New York residents who qualified. An oasis of green lawns and eighteenth-century red-brick buildings in the Jeffersonian style, with airy windows and white cupolas, the college spread out in a large irregular oval eight blocks from east to west. The campus in the thirties was the more pleasant because of its vistas of space (later cluttered with buildings) that contrasted happily with the metropolis that teemed around it. It held only four elegant buildings: the library, the science building, the arts building, and the gymnasium.

The students who attended during the 1930s were especially academically active, for they were perhaps more intelligent than the average college student, having been selected from among those having the highest grades (and the highest IQs) in the senior classes of the borough. They were also the poorest. In those days before open enrollment, it was often said that while not every student at Brooklyn College would have been accepted into Harvard, at least half of the students in Harvard would not have qualified for Brooklyn.

The group of students who were Chester Kallman's companions from 1937 to 1941 belonged to the mainstream of college life. They were, for the most part, heterosexual and middle- or lower-middle

---

[1] The author's conversation with Joseph Wershba, October 23, 1981.

[2] Letter to the author from Dr. Nathan Kravetz, October 28, 1981.

[3] The author's conversation with Charlotte Weisman-Lew, October 25, 1981.

class. They lived at home, traveled to school by subway if they did not live in the neighborhood, and took part-time jobs to support themselves, often contributing money to the family purse. The Great Depression had inflicted its pain and trauma upon everyone, and it was not yet over. Politics at Brooklyn tended to be leftist or Democrat; FDR was perceived to be the true friend of the man in the street; all capitalists were suspect.

Chester went about with the crowd from the literary magazine, the *Observer,* and later became one of its student editors. It was a sophisticated group that loved poetry, art, and music and was actively interested in politics, particularly the politics of the left. They would all gather in the tiny *Observer* office, which, with the office of the school newspaper, *The Vanguard,* was lodged in the gym building, as was the cafeteria. It was a nucleus of activity and a center of college life. It was here you talked politics, gossiped, told jokes, and met your girlfriends. It was the one place relatives could be sure of reaching you in an emergency. It was for these young intellectuals a bulwark against what they considered to be the madness of the world; it was a haven. Almost every one of them eventually became a professional writer of one kind or another, and throughout their lives each remembered the *Observer* office with affection and gratitude.

A frequent visitor to the *Observer* office was a girl named Elsie Trainen. Elsie was Chester's girl. Walter Miller, Chester's college friend who later became an English professor at NYU, knew her well and described her as

> . . . a red-haired girl with alabaster skin and circles under the eyes. I could not imagine a girl that young having circles under her eyes unless they were caused by losing sleep over Chester. She followed him around all the time, and she would never allow anybody to say a word against Chester, not even a word criticizing his poetry, she was so loyal. I remember one night Nina Camden had several of us up to her country house and I criticized one of Chester's poems. Elsie got up and went away from the table. She and Chester were passionate friends; she was in love with him.[1]

It was in 1938, when Chester was seventeen and a sophomore at Brooklyn College, that he began to change. He was still managing editor of the literary magazine, and still meeting in the *Observer* of-

[1] The author's conversations with Walter James Miller and Samuel Exler, June 23 and 30, 1982.

fice with his classmates; yet according to his father, "Chester was taking up with odd characters on the fringe." He was still bringing Elsie home to his grandmother's apartment for lunch, but he was distracted and seemed to be concerned with other matters.

One day in 1938 a man named Robert King[1] made a dental appointment with Dr. Kallman. King was a small gray man of middle years who wrote a financial advisory newsletter on Wall Street. He claimed to be a descendant of an old aristocratic family that had, over the centuries, lent money to the Roman pontiffs. He himself had inherited a fortune, was making another on Wall Street, and was living in a penthouse on West Fifty-sixth Street. When asked who recommended him as a patient, he said that he had met Chester at the opera from time to time, needed a dentist, and decided to call his father. King was an amiable patient and invited his dentist to dinner on the Astor Roof.

It was on the Astor Roof that the lightning struck. "I want to adopt Chester," King said forthrightly to an astounded Eddie. "I can do a great deal for him. Send him to Harvard, my old school. Take him to Europe."

"I don't understand," said Eddie, choking on his champagne. "Why Chester?"

"I just want to be near him," said King candidly. "Travel with him. Sleep next to him. You see," continued King, "I know what he is, because I'm one, too."

"What do you mean?" asked Eddie.

"He's homosexual. Now please! I know what you must be thinking. And I'm sorry, but there's nothing you can do about it any more than there was anything my family could do about me."

"How can you say such a thing? How can you make such a statement that you 'know'? You say you saw Chester at the opera. Well, you must have seen him there with a girl. He always takes a girl," said Eddie, dangerously calm.

"I've been watching him every week at the opera, and I know that that girl doesn't mean anything to him. She's a friend, nothing more."

"I know for a fact," said Eddie with conviction, "that Chester has affairs with women. Married women," he added, for good measure. King merely smiled ruefully and said nothing. Eddie, angry, looked down at his plate, too furious to meet King's eyes.

"Look," King said finally, his voice gentle, "I'm rich. I can do

[1] Not his real name.

everything for him. He's going to find another man anyway. Why shouldn't it be me? Let me adopt him. He's young enough. I want Chester. You won't be sorry. In fact," continued King, "one day when Chester was visiting my apartment with his friends, my second cousin Elliott came to visit and Chester began flirting with him. I could see that my cousin was attractive to Chester. Well, the next day I saw my lawyer. I took my cousin out of my will."

Eddie was speechless and from that moment regarded King as no more than a lunatic. Suddenly Eddie's anger abated. He was not thinking of Harvard for Chester or of trips to Europe. He was thinking of the words said impulsively about his son some years ago by his second wife, and they ate into him like a cancer: "He's a hothouse flower."

Like most heterosexuals he never thought about homosexuality in others and would not have recognized it had he seen a thousand examples, let alone that of his own son. In Eddie's world, men loved women. Yet the words of his wife came back to him again and again, and he knew that when she said them he had been angry, because he half believed them to be true.

The next evening Eddie returned earlier than usual to Flatbush Avenue and had dinner at home. As soon as he could get Chester out of his grandmother's earshot, he told him to come with him into the bedroom because he wanted to talk.

"I had dinner last night at the Astor Roof," Eddie began.

"Oh?" Chester responded amiably.

"With Robert King."

"Robert King?" Chester asked, turning pale.

"He said he had something to tell me. Do you know what he told me?" Chester turned paler, and for the first time in his life could not think of anything to say. "King says that you're a homosexual and that he wants to adopt you. I told him that it wasn't true. Is it true?"

"What right did he have to talk to you? What right did he have to go behind my back?" Chester was glaring with anger.

"The point is that he did. Is it true?"

"Dad, everybody has these experiences," said Chester, confused and embarrassed. "I mean, everybody goes through these stages. Sometimes it's a part of growing up."

"*Getsail mir nicht kain meisse,*" which, roughly translated, means: Don't try to con me. "Is it true or not?"

"All right, Dad. It's true," Chester said finally. "I'm sorry you had to find out this way. I'm sorry you had to find out at all. What business was it of King's to speak for me?"

"I just don't understand. I thought you had a girlfriend, lots of girlfriends."

"I have."

"I thought you had real experiences with women."

"In a way, but that's not important, Dad. What King told you is true."

Eddie had to face the truth. The great irony was that the son of this intensely masculine and heterosexual man, this lover of women, should have turned out to be homosexual. Eddie never ceased to ask himself why. It would have stunned him if someone had suggested that the answer might possibly have lain partly in Eddie himself—that Chester, loving his father, and having only one parent, resented the women he knew to be in his father's life, looking upon them all as rivals, as they themselves had regarded him. Eddie would probably have been even more stunned if someone had suggested that the cause lay somewhere in a mysterious biology, and that the die had been cast even before Chester was born. Who would ever know the whole truth?

If Chester was attached to his father, Auden had been attached to his mother, who had been with him almost exclusively during his early formative years, when his brothers were at boarding school and his father was in the British army during World War I. However, Auden had had little cause for jealousy with his mother, who presented no rivals for his affection. Interestingly enough, Auden in his early life expected to marry eventually; Chester never did.

Chester was sent to a psychiatrist who was highly recommended by one of Eddie's patients, also a psychiatrist. Dr. Rex could not help Chester, for Chester would not be helped. When Chester discovered that Rex had not read T. S. Eliot, he refused to go back to see him.

Chester loved his father, and the knowledge of Chester's homosexuality did not dampen Eddie's love for his son. However, it was the fate of both Eddie and Chester to inspire jealousy, and if the women in Eddie's life looked upon Chester as a rival, the men in Chester's were later to look upon Eddie as such. Auden eventually was to drive a wedge between father and son, a wedge that was always present for the remainder of their lives. From the days in Brooklyn on the Flatbush Avenue stop until the early 1940s, Chester and his father were especially close. Wystan Auden had not yet succeeded in separating Chester from everyone but himself.

CHAPTER 5

The Blue Man

THE FRENCH, WHO understand love so well, not only its bright but also its bitter side, give romantic love four years at best, as one of my French teachers used to say. Wystan's halcyon days, which began with such promise in April of 1939, ended in a nightmare two years later. The miracle was that they lasted that long.

In July 1941, Wystan found out that Chester had taken another lover. It was this incident that prompted him to write: "I was forced to know in person what it is like to feel oneself in the prey of demonic powers, in both the Greek and Christian sense, stripped of self-control and self-respect, behaving like a ham actor in a Strindberg play."[1] Chester, who by nature sought variety and sexual liberty, had betrayed what Wystan considered his marriage vows.

To Chester, who had never experienced a lasting love, despite his protestations to the contrary, and whose approach to love itself was

---

[1] Carpenter, *Auden: A Biography,* p. 311.

frankly lighthearted, not unlike that of his father before him, it
seemed that the fuss Wystan was making was peculiar and tedious, if
not evidence of temporary derangement. But a fuss it was, and at one
point Wystan was sure he could have murdered Chester, as Verlaine
had attempted to murder Rimbaud.

It was a man named Jack Lansing[1] who came between them. Lansing, despite his Latin eyes, was as English as cricket. He could trace
his maternal ancestors back to the Saxons in the *Domesday Book,*
while his father claimed a distant kinship to William the Conqueror.
His great-great-great-greatgrandfather had taken refuge in England
during the French Revolution, married an Englishwoman of his class,
and settled down permanently in the country. His father, a patriot
and a general, died heroically in battle during World War II. Jack
was born in Derby, near Bakewell, on the family estate in 1915. He
went to Harrow and then to Oxford.

In 1939, Jack Lansing was young, bonny, and yearning for adventure. He was also bisexual. By nature a soldier of fortune, he had
fought in Spain for the Republicans. When his own country went to
war with the Nazis he found himself aboard a British merchant ship
in 1940, in waters filled with German mines, carrying mysterious car-
goes to top-secret ports. In late 1940 he was in New York harbor. New
York was to Jack then, in fact, a haven and a paradise: "I was shot
out of the gloom of the London blackout and the cannons of war,"
Jack wrote me in a letter, "into the bright lights, the glitter, glamour,
and excitement and for me the fascination of New York."[2]

Jack had literary ambitions along with his love of adventure, and
when he found himself in New York, he bore a somewhat crumpled
letter of introduction to W. H. Auden from a mutual friend at Oxford. The poet put him up for his stay on Middagh Street, a generous
impulse that Auden lived to regret. Jack continued:

> For me, Wystan was the greatest English-speaking poet alive. So I
> felt rather as you might have felt if invited to ring the doorbell of
> Keats in the celestial halls of yonder. I was uneasy. How could I
> possibly live up to the great poet? Why would he bother with a
> stranger? But I needn't have worried. Because when I finally
> called him, he was marvelous and immediately invited me to
> dinner. Then he was incredibly hospitable and promptly invited

[1] Not his real name.
[2] Letter to the author from Jack Lansing, June 21, 1981.

me to stay. . . . I liked him enormously, one of the most fascinating people I've met.[1]

Chester was staying off and on at 7 Middagh Street, and he must
have found the tall, athletic Englishman, with his dark, almond-
shaped eyes, public school manners, Oxford accent, and perfect body
attractive at first sight.

Jack was equally fascinated by Chester. "He had the face," wrote
Jack, "of an unblemished angel, sensual but infinitely appealing. Even
when you first knew him, the effects of dissipation had etched their
perhaps intriguing traces, with the bags under his eyes and the hint
of the lascivious and self-indulgent to his ever warm and generous
mouth, suggesting rather more the gamin than the choirboy."[2] The
account Jack gives of the seduction throws light not only on life on
Middagh Street but also on the relationship between Chester and
Wystan, for the affair seems to have taken place a good while before
the knowledge of it came to Wystan.

> I was fascinated by Chester's scintillating and witty conversation.
> He and Wystan obviously enjoyed tremendous intellectual rap-
> port. But the fact that Wystan and Chester had pledged their eter-
> nal troth I had no earthly way of knowing. This was, in fact,
> Wystan's Achilles' heel. He had consummated a marriage *dans les
> yeux de Dieu* and was not even living with his partner for life. He
> was so blindly in love with Chester that he believed implicitly in
> his "innocence" and fidelity to his marriage vows. I was staying
> with Wystan; yet he never hinted to me or confided in me that
> Chester was his lover who must not be touched. Certainly I
> thought that there might be an affair, but scarcely a very active
> one.
>
>   A day or so later, I had to go to *The New Republic* to type up
> an article I'd written (Wystan had given me an introduction to
> Malcolm Cowley). Chester very sweetly accompanied me and typed
> the piece to my dictation. As before, which you will recall as one
> of his charms, he enveloped me in that aura of sensual sympathy
> which was almost tactile, like being caressed by silk. He also made
> advances to me and, since I thought him immensely attractive, off
> we went to Brooklyn with Harold Nivens to the house of Walter

[1] Ibid.
[2] This and subsequent quotes from Jack Lansing from a letter to the author,
June 27, 1981.

Matthews [two of Jack's friends, not their real names] and—you
can envision the rest.

I then sailed for England and returned to New York a couple of
months later. . . . I now think of myself as in love with Chester,
but obviously I hadn't had time thus to fall or else had some in-
stincts about Wystan, as I remember having to pull the wool over
Tony's [Jack's lover at the time] eyes when I finally returned to
Brooklyn with Chester.

It was as we were crossing the road together that Chester used
what I can only describe as his extraordinary emotional powers,
the like of which I have not encountered in anyone else, to bind
me irrevocably to him, so that I was suffused with love for him.
So back we went to Walter's. This was serious. . . .

On the day I sailed for Glasgow, I met Chester in a bar. He
told me he was united with Wystan, who must never find out
about our affair. I was very upset and horrified to think that I
had been two-timing Wystan. I told Chester that either I must
tell Wystan of our love for each other, since at least this might not
destroy the bond between him and Chester, or else I must bow out
and never see Chester again. Chester, understandably frightened of
losing Wystan, begged me not to tell Wystan—and I sailed away.

Jack left for Glasgow en route to Derby, probably in early 1941,
and did not see Chester until some months after the crisis in July.
How Wystan finally found out about Chester's involvement with Jack
has never been clear, but Chester probably told Wystan himself one
way or another. When Chester Kallman fell in love, it was always for
the first time, and now he was in love for the first time with Jack
Lansing. Like his maternal grandfather before him, he dramatized his
emotions, probably to prove to himself that he had them, and when he
was in love there were few who did not know it. The knowledge of
what had happened did not escape Wystan, who could be fooled but
not forever, and who brought matters to a showdown in early July
1941—at which point Chester retired to his room in a fit of pique,
threw himself on the bed, and went to sleep.

After an hour or so Wystan again insisted on a showdown, but he
could not remember afterward very much of what took place. He was
aware only of a violent impulse to murder, if not Jack Lansing, then
Chester, or perhaps both; and during the night that followed he put
his large, thick fingers around Chester's throat and pressed hard. Only
a miracle stopped him in time. Chester awoke in a rage, his face

flushed and his eyes bright with anger. He pushed Wystan away and
fled from the room.

Chester, of course, eventually won, as he would always win. Terror
at his own violence quieted Wystan, and he was determined to come
to terms with the demon in his soul. He took a different tack. He
would always love Chester, but he would now be his friend if he could
not be his lover. He only asked that Chester not leave him, for he
could not bear a life without him. He tried to convince himself that
all he wanted was Chester's happiness, and he was prepared to recon-
cile himself with the presence of Jack in Chester's life. He prayed to
the God of his childhood that he might have *agape* if he could not
have *eros*. Yet he never recovered from what happened on that afternoon in July, and forever after he was to see Jack Lansing increas-
ingly as the cause of Chester's betrayal and of his own deep sorrow.
Chester never went to bed with Wystan again.

The truth was that Wystan had fallen under the Kallman spell. Having myself fallen victim to their charms, and having received the confidences of a number of women connected romantically with Eddie's
brother, sons, and cousins, I can testify that the Kallman men were
sorcerers. They could change the gray world of everyday into a place
of romance and excitement. Going for a walk with them down Lexington Avenue or around Gramercy Park, or taking a ferry ride to
Staten Island was more fun than going to Paris with anyone else. They
made you laugh at everyone and everything. The world was created
for their amusement. They seldom made advances of a sexual nature;
in fact, they seldom touched you except to hold your arm when crossing a street. But when they fell in love it was always for the first time.

The only trouble was that the love seldom lasted. They needed the
challenge of other hearts. As time went by, you realized that you could
be just so close and no closer; yet you wanted to possess this man as
he possessed you, for he was the best of lovers, and you knew that you
would never again meet anyone who could take his place. But beyond
a given point a door closed and you were outside, as Wystan suddenly
felt himself outside when he discovered Chester had found someone
new. If you kept pounding at the door, you made a mistake. The more
you pounded, the more secure the lock that held the door.

What the elusive Kallman men possessed they ceased to want.
Wystan was so enchanted with Chester that once he had met him he
even neglected his family and old school friends. Once he thought he
had lost him, he nearly fell to pieces. For him, no one else would do.

Despite his rigid upbringing and strong will, he never could free himself from the spell that held him in thrall until the hour of his death.

When Jack and Chester were seeing each other in secret, Jack made dental appointments with Chester's father, arrived early, and met Chester in the office when Dr. Kallman was out to lunch. One afternoon Dr. Kallman returned and found his operating door locked and his two o'clock patient, also early, restively waiting in the reception room. Jack and Chester were in the operating room engaged in a heated discussion that lasted at least an hour. An irate father banged on the door and demanded that his son and Jack choose another place for their rendezvous. Dr. Kallman was annoyed with his son. Although he did not condone his son's homosexuality, he believed Wystan estimable and worthy of love. He approved of Wystan, but he did not approve of Chester's relations with Jack or anyone else. He liked Jack well enough, but he did not want to see the relationship between his son and the poet end, for he knew of Chester's promiscuous inclinations and feared for him. "Wystan is an honorable man," he advised. "Go back to him, Chester."

Whether his father's promptings or his own attachment to Wystan persuaded him, Chester did not break off relations with Wystan, though their sexual life together was ended. As a matter of fact, Chester rarely broke off relations with anyone, for he needed the human contact of his friends, even those with whom he had had feuds or violent differences. After a short time of absence, they were always welcomed back. Surely he realized how Wystan had been injured, and his father's words must have given him pause for thought: "You will never find a friend like that again."

Although Chester did not go with Wystan to Olivet College in Michigan, where Wystan was invited to lecture for a week or so in mid-July, he did agree to accompany Wystan later in the summer to the home of Caroline Newton in Jamestown, Rhode Island, where Wystan wanted an opportunity to think things over. Caroline Newton, rich, single, and infatuated with Wystan, gave him time and sympathy. She also gave Wystan money and an original Blake print that was to hang in Chester's rooms wherever he lived from that time on. It was the picture commonly known as "The Ancient of Days," portraying a bearded figure kneeling in the heavens and measuring the universe with a gigantic set of calipers.

The money that Caroline gave Wystan was used to finance Chester's graduate school at the University of Michigan in Ann Arbor. Wystan was to be a visiting professor at the university for the aca-

demic year starting in autumn 1941. Dr. Kallman believed it was now
time for Chester to earn his own living and not depend upon his father. He also believed that Chester would be better off with a job, and
he was not about to finance another year of what he believed would
be Chester's inactivity. Apparently Caroline was to fill in the gap.

The next time Chester saw Jack seems to have been in the winter
of 1941, although Jack's memory here may be hazy after more than
forty years; for Wystan in the fall of 1941 speaks of Chester's being
with his British sailor. Possibly Jack was back and forth during the
late summer and autumn of 1941. At any rate, Jack described the
meeting as follows:

> I thought it safe to return to New York. Chester being so young
> would long since have forgotten all about me. So back I came to
> find that anyhow Chester and Wystan were in California. It was
> Christmas Eve, and I was visiting Dr. Kallman, who insisted that
> I send along with him a greetings telegram to Chester and Wystan.
> There was no way that I could get out of it, and I sent off one of
> my crazy effusions addressed to Wystan—"Hallelujah to you and
> Chester." Desiccated-at-your-non-materialization-type-of-thing. The
> next thing was a telegram from Chester announcing that he was
> winging his way three thousand miles to see me. . . . And Wystan,
> of course, knew all about it. However, I gathered from Chester
> that he didn't reveal all to Wystan when the telegram arrived,
> which he might have felt bound to do, unable to contain his feel-
> ings, but some time previously.

The "some time previously" was most probably that July day in 1941.

Having by this time apparently resigned himself to the affair, Wystan returned to Ann Arbor in early January of 1942, leaving Chester
to New York and the arms of Jack. However, Chester, who was to en-
roll at the University of Michigan as a graduate student in English,
was to try for one of the Hopwood awards, which offered a first prize
of money and the promise of publication, for which the university is
well known. He had to be in Ann Arbor by early February, so his
time in New York could not have been more than a month. In fact,
in a letter from Ann Arbor to Caroline Newton in Rhode Island in
January 1942, Wystan mentions that "Chester is in New York where
there is an English sailor. They are both very happy, which makes me
so." All this was, of course, pious hogwash. Wystan was not happy
about Chester's affair with Jack or with anybody. Rather, this reflects
Wystan's heroic attempt at self-mastery and Christian virtue.

L'affaire Jack probably lasted the whole of the next summer into the autumn of 1942, for Jack wrote that Wystan sent for him from Swarthmore in Pennsylvania, where he had gone to teach in the autumn of that year:

> Meantime . . . Wystan asked me to see him in Pennsylvania. We both behaved in a positively Kiplingesque manner, very English. Wystan was kind, gentle, and forgiving. In the most civilized way, he was prepared to make the sacrifice for Chester's happiness, and indeed for a year or so, until the final bust-up, he seemed to accept me as one of the family and we remained firm friends. However, it was I who made the fatal blunder that most probably led to the fatal misunderstanding. For Wystan asked me the question the answer to which was absolutely vital for him. He urged me to tell him if he was right in thinking that Chester was "innocent" and had been before he met him, meaning that he had only slept with him and me and did not indulge in . . . sexual adventures with pick-ups, etc. I was flabbergasted, because already Chester was far more sexually sophisticated and had had more experience probably than both of us put together. I realized that, if I told Wystan the truth, it might have the most serious repercussions on their relationship, and I felt that I must protect Chester at all costs. So I told Wystan that, as far as I knew, Chester had remained "innocent."

Jack's theory may be at least partly true. Perhaps Wystan did view Chester as an "innocent" and Jack as the grand seducer, and for this reason Wystan was later to see Jack as Mephistopheles. Perhaps had Jack told Wystan the truth, Wystan would have seen Chester not as an innocent but for the freewheeling young man that he was. However, many would believe the theory unlikely. Wystan would not see what he did not want to see.

To Jack, in recalling those frenetic days, Chester was ultimately responsible for the disintegration of the relationship between himself and Auden.

> After I was back with Chester he intimated his displeasure that two rivals for his hand (Wystan and myself) should remain close friends, when we should be enemies battling for possession. Chester fancied himself as the all-consuming flame, and, with this extraordinary power of attraction he could exude, could out-Dietrich Marlene. In this case Chester evidently liked men to fight for his

favors, not cozy up in a friendly alliance. Living with Chester, I learned a lot about him. . . . To put it mildly, Chester's passions ruled his head. . . . It was Chester's nature to create jealousy, misery, and rage in his lovers. This may sound ruthless, but he would cuckold them to their faces. The reason was a longing to be mastered. He was thrilled when I threatened to throw him out of the window and [another time] walloped him in the face. But even when he was tired of his lovers, Chester wanted to continue to bind them to him and had this incredible magnetic capacity of doing so, even after he had lost his looks.

However convinced Jack may still be of Chester's sadomasochistic tendencies—and no one who knew him would doubt that Chester had them—much that Chester did was for effect. He admired Marlene Dietrich at the time and may very well have found it diverting to imitate her ways, which were themselves a kind of camp, as he enjoyed imitating the scenes of all his favorite divas in all the operas he adored. Chester was playacting much of the time. One often was not sure whether he deeply meant what he said and did at a given moment, or whether he was using camp to conquer ennui.

Jack's trouble with Wystan had other causes besides Chester's desire that they be rivals. Chester returned from Ann Arbor in June 1943, and that winter Jack ran off with one of Wystan's temporary boyfriends, Royce Wagoner.[1] Wystan had met Wagoner, an adorable brown-eyed native of New Orleans, through a friend of Chester when Royce was a freshman at the University of Michigan in 1941. In the winter of 1943 Royce was in New York visiting Chester, as did crowds of Ann Arbor students when they were passing through, and there met Jack. Jack insists that the affair was engineered by Chester and that he, Jack, knew nothing, at least at first, of Wystan's relationship with Royce. Jack related what happened the day after he had met Royce:

> Chester informed me that he had told Royce that I was in love with him, Royce. I was flabbergasted. . . . With Wystan in Pennsylvania and Royce in [Louisiana], the former could hardly mind if I tried to make the latter happy, or so I thought. Perhaps if I visited Royce, I might fall in love with him. So I went to [New Orleans] for a few days and did duly form a strong attachment to Royce. On my return, Wystan invited me to visit him in Pennsylvania. He said that I simply could not go on being the great,

[1] Not his real name.

romantic figure, that I was once more usurping one of his lovers. Again we spent a very pleasant evening. Though I may have been on probation, Wystan had not then turned against me. Once more, though, I made the fatal error of protecting Chester (as Chester knew I would!) by not telling Wystan that Chester had set up the whole thing with Royce as I by now fully realized. I did though feel that it was imperative that I write to Royce. The next few times I saw Wystan, to my horror, he was extremely rude and disagreeable. I realized that either Royce or Chester must have poisoned him against me. . . . Later, I found out that Wystan was telling people that I was a fringe personality who was incapable of a real relationship, so specialized in ruining other people's.

Through Jack, Wystan was forced to see Chester's nature for what it really was: essentially promiscuous, for all its other virtues. Wystan could never forgive the English sailor for that revelation. Wystan had been willing to share his lover with someone who offered the same kind of love that he himself could give. He had made the noble gesture of forgiveness—all high-minded and Christian—to Chester and his sailor, only to find that Chester and the sailor both were no more capable of eternal love than of flying to Jupiter. Wystan could not forgive Jack for making pointless Wystan's own sacrifice. Jack's affair with Royce must have seemed to Wystan an undistinguished, if not shoddy, sequel to the crisis of July.

It is hard to say who was innocent in *l'affaire* Jack, as it was often called, but, if anyone was, it was probably Jack himself. If anyone was not, it was Chester. As Jack regularly confided to all who would listen, it probably was Chester who made the first advances to him, and Jack naturally assumed, as he put it, that the coast was clear. Having taken sex casually during his young life, it never occurred to Jack at first that "Wystan would make so great a fuss about fidelity, my dear." But Chester did know Wystan. Chester knew that the relationship Wystan had been seeking went deeper than simply casual sex, and Chester, even at the age of nineteen to Wystan's thirty-three, must have had some idea of what one false step on his part would do. Yet both Chester and Wystan finally condemned Jack for what had happened.

At any rate, *l'affaire* Jack had run its course, and by the next year or so, Chester was again in love for the first time, this time with another sailor, an Irish-American boy whom he had met in Ann Arbor. Although he avoided Wystan—and with good reason—Jack was still in and out of New York throughout the war and after. He would visit Chester's apartment on East Twenty-seventh Street, making friends with all of Chester's friends, both male and female. Chester, who never liked to relinquish his friends or lovers, never really forgave Jack for the affair with Royce. However, though Chester made ravishing fun of Jack and the young man from New Orleans, he could never carry a grudge for long. Yet Chester accepted Wystan's version of Jack as essentially evil, and was glad to be through with the whole thing.

In moments of clearsighted recollection, Wystan must have viewed all the fuss he had made about Jack as droll and ironic. A year or so later Jack meant no more to Chester than the man in the moon. Chester replaced Jack with one lover after another, a process that continued for the remainder of Chester's life. Yet for Wystan Jack continued to be a symbol of his own failure at marriage and love.

Why did Auden permit himself to endure what amounted to a second-best position in Chester's love life? Would it not have been better to cast the young man out and look for somebody else? Auden was, after all, an intellectual, a writer growing more famous with the years, and he surely possessed interests and spiritual resources that would have permitted him to live a rich interior life without the need for a constant companion. The answer to such a question does not exist. Wystan wanted Chester, and no one else would suffice. A landscape without Chester was too dreary for Wystan to contemplate.

From time to time Wystan would try other lovers, women as well as men, and all different from Chester. If Wystan experimented with heterosexuality from time to time, it was experiment only. What he wanted was the steady continuity of marriage. Perhaps he thought he could find this with a woman. He never could. Unfortunately, the only person he ever wanted to marry was Chester, and Chester was not the marrying kind. Wystan always went back to Chester, for Chester, unfaithful and sexually cold to him, was the only one he loved.

Wystan, it must be remembered, was the Red man. He was essentially a winner, an achiever of goals, and he never gave up. Wystan would put up with Chester's sexual vagaries, which he knew were fleeting. He felt certain he would not have to fear a rival for friendship among any of Chester's lovers. Who could rival himself in the vast wasteland that confronted them both? He said many times that spiritual love and companionship, or *agape,* was more important than *eros,* or sex, and, in fact, he eventually achieved with Chester a marriage of *agape.*

Wystan was an achiever, but Chester was not. His color was blue, passive, symbolic of the receptivity of Venus. He was not a setter of

goals or a winner of them, because no goal seemed sufficiently important to him. He was fond of Wystan. Once he could establish a kind
of sexual liberty, he was also fond of the life he had with Wystan. For
the first time someone had offered him financial as well as emotional
security, and he did not disdain either. His father, after all, expected
him to earn his own living; Wystan did not. Chester knew that he
could not with honor depend upon his father, and he wanted to depend upon someone. The truth was that Chester did not want to go
out and look for a job. If Chester ever contemplated how he would
earn a living, he honestly always believed he would someday be able
to earn it as a writer. That someday was always just around the corner, but it was never now. Chester made no effort to achieve a future
of any kind. As long as he had Wystan, he drifted—into writing books
of poetry, into writing librettos, into doing translations—and Wystan
was there to catch him after each spill.

However, to suggest that Chester planned to use Wystan as a source
of financial support would be unfair. Chester never in his life planned
to use anybody. In fact, he had no plans of any kind. He drifted into
life with Wystan as he drifted into everything else. He allowed things
to happen to him; he did not make them happen. He was the pro-
verbial ship without a rudder. He belonged in another, more pampered culture—perhaps in the corridors of Versailles. His nature was
not in tune with the hustle and bustle of the century in which he
found himself.

Although Jack Lansing barely lasted longer than the rise and fall
of the tides, he was a landmark in the relationship between Wystan
and Chester; because of Jack nothing would ever be the same again.

The summer of 1941 was a cruel one for Wystan, for it was also the
time of another trauma. As if the crisis of July in what he considered
his marriage had not been enough, later on that summer, when he
was visiting with Chester at the home of Caroline Newton in Jamestown, Rhode Island, his mother died. When the telegram came, Chester was the one to give him the news. According to reports, Wystan
had previously accepted a dinner invitation he did not want to keep.
When Chester told him they would have to break it, Wystan, not realizing the reason, said, "Goody! Goody!" When Chester then told him
why, Wystan sat for a long time without speaking. Then he said,
"How like her that her last act on earth should be to get me out of a
social engagement that I didn't want." He then burst into tears. Not
long after, he received a letter written to him by his mother just before her death. He could not bring himself to read it.

Wystan told Anne Weiss,[1] one of his and Chester's friends, that he did not know how he could have endured the days after his mother's death if Chester had not been with him. Anne herself described some years later Chester's sympathy when her own mother died: "After the funeral I came to New York and went to see Chester at St. Mark's Place [the apartment Wystan retained in New York from 1953 to 1972], and I don't know what I myself would have done without him. He didn't say a word, and he didn't let me talk about it. He just made me comfortable. He brought me tea, actually. Then he made me dinner and took me to the opera. He had the subtle gift of sympathy."

By December 1941, Wystan seemed to have found some equilibrium. It was then that he wrote the following letter, which was discovered in the laboratory of Dr. Kallman's office sometime in 1946. It tells, as no biographer can, the real story of Chester and Wystan.

Christmas Day. 1941

Dearest Chester

Because it is in you, a Jew, that I, a Gentile inheriting an O-so-genteel anti-semitism, have found my happiness:
As this morning I think of Bethlehem, I think of you.

Because it is you, from Brooklyn, who have taught me, from Oxford, how the most liberal young man can assume that his money and his education ought to be able to buy love;
As this morning I think of the inn stable, I think of you.

Because, suffering on your account the torments of sexual jealousy, I have had a glimpse of the infinite vileness of masculine conceit;
As this morning I think of Joseph I think of you.

Because mothers have much to do with your queerness and mine, because we have both lost ours, and because Mary is a camp name;
As this morning I think of Mary I think of you.

Because the necessarily serious relation of a child to its parents is the symbol, pattern, and warning of any serious love that may

[1] Anne Weiss and her husband, Irving, who was one of Chester's classmates at Brooklyn College and the University of Michigan, were close friends of Wystan and Chester. The Weisses and their children lived on Ischia during the period when Wystan and Chester summered there.

later depend upon its choice, because you are to me emotionally a mother, physically a father, and intellectually a son;
As this morning I think of the Holy Family, I think of you.

Because, on account of you, I have been, in intention, and almost in act, a murderer;
As this morning I think of Herod, I think of you.

Because even *les matelots*[1] and *les morceaux de commerces*[2] instinctively pay you homage;
As this morning I think of the shepherds, I think of you.

Because I believe in your creative gift, and because I rely absolutely upon your critical judgement;
As this morning I think of the magi, I think of you.

Because it is through you that God has chosen to show me my beatitude;
As this morning I think of the Godhead, I think of you.

Because in the eyes of our bohemian friends our relationship is absurd;
As this morning I think of the Paradox of the Incarnation I think of you.

Because our love, beginning Hans Andersen, became Grimm, and there are probably even grimmer tests to come, nevertheless I believe that if only we have faith in God and in each other, we shall be permitted to realize all that love is intended to be;
As this morning I think of the Good Friday and Easter Sunday already implicit in Christmas day, I think of you.[3]

[1] Sailors—Chester often picked up sailors at bars.
[2] Pieces of trade—camp name for pickups (usually heterosexual) in tough bars.
[3] Courtesy of the Humanities Research Center, the University of Texas at Austin.

CHAPTER 6

"Star Dust" and "Frenesi"

IN THE AUTUMN of 1941, Auden went to the University of Michigan at Ann Arbor to be a visiting professor for a year. The university had always attracted young writers because of the Hopwood awards, and Auden already had a clique of admirers among them. In the summer of 1941 Auden acted as one of the judges for the Hopwood awards in poetry, but he later confided to Peter Hansen that he had "not found a true poet" in the lot. He had lectured in Ann Arbor the January before, and his immense popularity had encouraged the English department to invite him as a guest professor for the next year.

The Avery Hopwood awards consisted of a sum of money and assured publication for the winner of the first prize in each of the divisions: poetry, drama, fiction, and nonfiction. Wystan's plan was for Chester to have not only the opportunity of earning his M.A. degree at Michigan but also of entering the Hopwoods in poetry, and Wystan had no doubt that Chester could win first prize. In addition, Wystan could have Chester near him during the spring term in Ann Arbor. Chester was to graduate from Brooklyn College at the end of the fall term of 1941, just before his twenty-first birthday.

The University of Michigan at Ann Arbor was one of the great schools of the Middle West, and it was a school that preferred men. There were four men to every woman. It was dear to the hearts of all its students, nevertheless. It was Artie Shaw, Beethoven, and the last dance to "Star Dust." It was green lawns, gray Civil War buildings, and modern laboratories. It was Wordsworth, Walt Whitman, Edna St. Vincent Millay, and T. S. Eliot. It was girls in pageboy bobs wearing sweaters, skirts, bobby socks, and polo coats, along with the omnipresent string of pearls. It was boys in porkpie hats and bright flannel shirts like those of the lumberjacks up North. It was faculty teas, Sunday dinners, and early curfew for girls. It was Friday night rallies and Saturday afternoon games. It was quarterback Tom Harmon and homecomings. It was as distant from New York as the moon. It was also more transient. Little did we guess in the autumn of 1941 that in a few months it would all be over and that nothing would ever be the same again. America entered World War II in December of that year.

I had just graduated that June with a B.A. from the University of Michigan, had attended the summer session of 1941, and was now back in Ann Arbor for the fall term of 1941 to continue work on my M.A. in English literature. One evening in September I was sketching at the fountain outside the Women's League when a young man about seventeen came up to me and began to criticize my drawing. He was red haired, with bright brown eyes and freckles, and extraordinarily good looking. He told me that a sum of money had been given him by a stranger for his education and that he was in Ann Arbor early for the orientation period, which he considered silly. I took a liking to him immediately. He told me that he was a fine poet and began to expound his theories about poetry, theories I later discovered resembled those of W. H. Auden, whom he had been reading. The boy's name was Peter Hansen. Later in the term he was to become Auden's first lover in Ann Arbor. He was to become as well my introduction to the world of W. H. Auden and a constant source of information and gossip about the poet. Peter was to live in both of Auden's houses in Ann Arbor and to replace, or so he told me, Charlie Miller, Auden's first houseboy, after Miller left for a peace farm. Peter himself was to leave a month or so later.

Through Peter Hansen I was to meet Auden later on in the fall term, and, later still, Chester Kallman briefly after he arrived—young, blond, and deliciously arrogant—from New York. I left Ann Arbor to teach school out of town in February 1942, however, and when I returned to the university in the summer, Auden had already left, and Peter Hansen was in the army. Chester was still in Ann Arbor, when he was not in New York on holiday, and I saw him occasionally through Mary Valentine, my best friend, who went with a boy named Royce Wagoner to visit Chester at his place on Ann Street from time to time.

It is hard to imagine two natures less in sympathy with the atmosphere of this midwestern college town than Chester and Wystan's. If it was no place for refugees, now rooming in dorms, it was less a place for two iconoclasts whose favorite play was *Hellzapoppin,* who hated Edna Millay, and who made up obscene words to the tune of "Star Dust."

The first lecture that Auden gave at the University of Michigan was in January 1940. Chester was still in New York with his father when Wystan arrived in Ann Arbor alone in the early summer of 1941 to deliver another lecture, the topic of which was "The Loneliness of the Individual." Dressed in a wrinkled white linen suit that accentuated his complexion and rusty blond hair, he confounded the full auditorium in the Horace Rackham School for Graduate Studies, a florid Egyptian building, new at the time; and nobody past the first row, where all his special cult was gathered, could understand a word of what he said. His Oxford English fell as a foreign language on midwestern ears, but they all braved it to the end. When he arrived again in the fall, undaunted students rushed to register for his class, for it was said that Auden was the greatest living poet next to Eliot.

Brief though it was, the Auden visit to Ann Arbor in the 1941–42 year was still alive in folklore forty years later, and there is no question that some of the stories were true. Whatever the faculty, particularly the Literature, Science and the Arts English faculty, imagined an English poet would be like, Wystan Hugh Auden did not fit the description. Whether the same faculty would have reacted with the same disappointment and shock had Wordsworth or Browning, or, indeed, Keats, come back from the dead offers a beguiling moment of speculation. It is sure that no scholarly head bowed over Shelley's manuscripts in the rare-book room would, in its wildest fantasies, have expected the subject of its research, if resurrected from the dead, to shock the world of 1941 in quite the same way as W. H. Auden was to shock it. Even Lord Byron or Oscar Wilde would have been expected to show some respect, at least for the chairman of the English department.

Although the idea of Wystan in a 1941 Ann Arbor is droll at best, he showed a great deal of courage in telling the deciding mentors at his first interview that he was homosexual. He wanted the job because he needed the money, and the University of Michigan offered the best terms. "I think it only fair to tell you," he blurted out during what was intended as a friendly get-acquainted conference, "that I am queer, you know. I like boys." At this he crossed his long, rumpled trouser legs, moved his awkward body to the side, and stomped out his cigarette on the saucer of his Limoges teacup with big soiled fingers, the nails of which were bitten to the quick. The dean of the graduate school, the chairman of the English department, and the three full professors said not a word. When Wystan gleefully told the story later to friends in New York, one had the impression that if the Ann Arbor faces fell, it was not because they did not know that their prospective resident poet was homosexual. They just did not expect him to say it out loud.

However, everyone expects a poet to be a bit odd; and Auden was, after all, Auden. He got the job.

Chester was unable to join Wystan immediately because he was finishing his B.A. at Brooklyn College, but he was expected to arrive in February 1942, in time for the beginning of the spring term. Wystan took rooms in the Men's Union building while waiting for a faculty member to go on leave and vacate a house for his use. It was there that Peter Hansen, a freshman aged seventeen, wrote him a note and asked to show him a sheaf of original poems. Whether it was the poetry or Peter that caught Wystan's fancy, a brief sexual affair began. Though Peter was intelligent, there was nothing about him of the *ange gauche,* none of the élan, and none of the candor that was Chester's. Wystan suspected later that Peter was set to make use of everyone he met, including Wystan himself, and what promised in the beginning to be a pleasant interlude turned sour quickly.

Peter told me that the day after he had met Auden for the first time, Auden had said he was in love with "a Jewish boy from Brooklyn" and therefore he could love no one else; however, that the problem of physical infidelity did not bother him, because emotional and spiritual fidelity were more important. And he would always be emotionally and spiritually faithful to the boy from Brooklyn. He also mentioned something about Chester and a British sailor. Wystan played the love duet between Siegmund and Sieglinde, *"Du bist der*

Lenz," from *Die Walküre,* as the background for this new amatory
adventure, and one cannot help feeling it was a pathetic attempt to
recapture those first blissful hours in the spring of 1939 when he fell
in love for the first time. The attempt, of course, was a failure.

Peter had not been generous about sharing his famous friend, but
I finally met Auden by accident. I was sitting with Peter having coffee
in a campus drugstore when Auden appeared, it seemed, from no-
where. The moment he saw Peter, he came toward us. When he was
introduced to me he did not smile but nodded and grunted in a way
that later became familiar. It struck me then, however, as uncivil. He
made no effort to put me at ease, sitting down at the table as if he had
been the host. When Peter mentioned that I had won a minor Hopwood award in poetry that last summer (of which Wystan had been
the judge), Wystan turned to me and said: "You must read *The Alle-
gory of Love* by C. S. Lewis. All young writers should read it, especially poets. It gives them the correct approach to romanticism. Romantic love was never heard of, you know, in the days of the early
Church Fathers. The Romans would have laughed at it. So would St.
Thomas Aquinas." These were the first words Auden ever said to me,
and already he had taught me something of value, even though I had
never really aspired to be a poet. He also kept insisting that I call him
not Mr. Auden but Wystan, "to rhyme with Tristan."

I noticed that he kept looking at his watch and seemed to be in a
great hurry. Then he announced that he wanted to go to the music
shop around the corner to purchase a recording of Beethoven's Fourth
Piano Concerto. He could not decide whether to buy the Gieseking
recording or the Schnabel, and he wanted Peter and me to help him
make up his mind. He hurried us with our coffee and we followed his
long strides to the shop, where we listened to both recordings. Wystan
and Peter thought the Schnabel to have more power than the Gieseking, which I preferred, but that Gieseking had a more brilliant technique. "But it's cold," said Auden. "Anyway, Gieseking is a Nazi. I
shall buy the Schnabel." He looked at his watch again, made a sotto
voce appointment with Peter, and vanished.

It was Peter Hansen who told me about Auden's interest in the occult. Although it is clear that Wystan disapproved of that sort of thing
in later years, he must have done some experimenting and reading in
esoteric subjects, for Peter's reports had the ring of truth. According
to Peter, Wystan's interest in occultism had been stimulated by his
study of William Butler Yeats; and Peter reported stories of strange
happenings at Auden's. Yeats had helped to found the Hermitic

Order of the Golden Dawn, a group of Kabbalists that had members in England, Ireland, and Scotland, and Wystan, under their influence for a time, studied the Kabbala. (Both Eddie and Chester later reported to me Wystan's interest in the Kabbala.) According to Peter, who claimed to be his companion when the two were sure to be alone in the house on Pontiac Trail, Wystan contemplated the tarot and experimented with ritual magic. Apparently Wystan's interest in the symbols on the face of the tarot cards had been stimulated not only by Yeats but also by T. S. Eliot's *The Waste Land,* and he had bought a pack in New York. One evening Peter came back from Wystan's with a tarot pack that he said Auden had given him and began telling fortunes to my friends.

Wystan's studies may or may not have been serious, but they had a frivolous side, and it is possible that his experiments were just for fun. At the time, Peter had borrowed not only a sum of money from me to finance his board bill but also my polo coat, in which he was cavorting all over campus. Finally I realized that Peter did not intend to return my coat or pay his debt, so I threatened to tell the dean and to write my father, who was an attorney. Piqued, Peter persuaded Wystan, or at least said he persuaded Wystan, to put a curse on me, and less than a week later Peter, who could not keep secrets, told me it had been done, Wystan's having used the high priestess of the major arcanum of the tarot to symbolize me. I pretended not to care, but I was horrified. I am Irish and superstitious, and, despite my Roman Catholic upbringing (or perhaps because of it), I believed in curses. Someone had told me once that curses created a karmic tie. For years I secretly attributed to Wystan's curse not only any ill luck that may have befallen me but also the way Wystan himself kept appearing and reappearing in my life, seemingly by accident. I was convinced he had established a karmic tie with me and he was propelled against his will in my direction, something like the flight of the Red Queen and Alice. Peter never paid back the debt, but he returned my polo coat, the worse for wear, two years later in New York. Chester's arrival put an end to ritual magic.

Wystan's first house in Ann Arbor was an ultramodern affair of wood slats that looked at first glance like a Michigan cattle shed or a horse barn, except that it had a huge picture window in front, a long, narrow window on the side, and sat on 1223 Pontiac Trail with the aplomb of an ugly woman *en grand décolleté.* Jean-Paul Slusser, one of the professors in the School of Architecture, had unwisely razed a charming Greek Revival house and built this new one on the foundations with the theory that it would resemble the structures of Frank Lloyd Wright. However, most of the townspeople in those days, who were more familiar with cattle barns than with Frank Lloyd Wright houses, considered Slusser's house a monstrosity. Its landscaping was a studied wilderness, but its interior was the last word in modern comfort.

During the second month of his residence in Ann Arbor, when Wystan finally acquired a house, he asked a heterosexual midwestern farm boy called Charlie Miller, who belonged to a group of college poets, and who had met Wystan briefly during his first lecture in Ann Arbor in January 1940, to be his cook and factotum. The first thing Wystan did was purchase a green car. Wystan had driven when he was in Oxford and also when at Williamsburg, Massachusetts, with Chester and Eddie, but his driving was always erratic, for he still refused to wear distance glasses. How Auden survived on the midwestern highways is one of the mysteries of his lucky life.

For some reason having to do with my being a graduate student, I was not permitted to take Auden's class, which was supposed to be limited to twenty-five students in undergraduate junior honors, though some exceptions were made for faculty wives. I knew a number of people who took the course, however, so was apprised from day to day about what went on there. According to Angelyn Stevens, the wife of one of my favorite professors, "the work in the class was tremendous, if you did everything: the *Divine Comedy* for a textbook, papers comparing two works of art; writing poems to a given scansion outline . . . it was mental food for a lifetime."[1] Wystan Auden believed in the old-fashioned curriculum that stressed the classics; he would not take class time for modern works.

In spite of Wystan's taste for the traditional in the curriculum and his disapproval of using class time for modern literature, his teaching methods were original, or at least more English than American. He would have his class of twenty-five students in English 135 to an "At Home," a tea, once a week at Pontiac Trail. He had to stop serving liquor because of a complaint by the dean of girls. He believed in memory work as an excellent training of the mind, and he assigned for the final examination six cantos of Dante's *Divine Comedy* to be memorized letter perfect. The students, surprised he did not wish them to take notes, and excited and titillated by this famous poet who dressed for the classroom in blue jeans, were not thinking in early

---

[1] From Angelyn Stevens's notebooks (unpublished).

October about the final examination in June. Its full impact was to strike them later.

Despite his efforts to acclimatize himself to America, Americans, the Middle West, and his new teaching post, Wystan was depressed during his first months in Ann Arbor. The crisis of July 1941 had taken its toll. His dreams of love and romance with Chester had been savagely dashed. He was now stranded in an alien town, middle western, dull, provincial—all those qualities that Chester was quick to ridicule and his own background quick to despise. He was also lonely. Then, at one of the At Homes he gave once a week, something happened to brighten his soul. He heard five words that changed his mood: "I am allergic to everything." They were offered by Angelyn Stevens.

Then in her late thirties, Angelyn Stevens, though the mother of three, was still youthful looking and golden haired. Her rosy skin, high cheekbones, and slanted blue-green eyes betrayed her Dutch ancestry. Angelyn had been an admirer of Auden for some time. As a faculty wife (her husband, Dr. A. K. Stevens, was an instructor of English literature at the university) she was permitted to audit Auden's class, and she attended regularly. Today she was sipping tea, but when one of the other girls offered her a plate of sandwiches, she said, "No, thank you. I'm allergic to wheat." When someone else offered her a plate of cakes, she said, "I am allergic to cake flour." When offered a dish of grapes, she said, "I am allergic to everything." That was when Wystan overheard her and, as if summoned by a bell, rushed to her side. He did not leave it for the remainder of the afternoon. The old spark that had ignited him in Berlin had now been refired. Wystan had finally found someone to cure.

Wystan was to become fond of the Stevens family, their three children, Bradley, Grace, and Mary, and their comfortable bungalow on Olivia Street, where he, Charlie Miller, and even Peter Hansen were invited to Sunday dinner. The Stevenses were happy and proud to entertain the famous young poet, who often refused invitations to the teas and other social functions given by the wives of the full professors, including the chairman of the English department. Angelyn was a good cook and served the hearty meals with potatoes that Wystan liked. But best of all, he was included into an authentic family and was in the process of curing Angelyn.

Wystan had only one class to teach, so in the afternoons when he had finished his writing, he would begin the healing sessions, using then what are now the familiar techniques of psychiatry and psychosomatic medicine.

Apparently there had been a lifelong struggle between Angelyn and her younger sister,[1] who had been born prematurely with rickets. In order to care for the sick baby, the mother had put Angelyn in the care of a nurse for the first few months. "Wystan," said A. K. Stevens, "tried to make Angelyn believe that the allergies resulted from the rivalry between herself and her sister."[2] He said that her problem resulted in not wanting to face realities that life presented, and he put her through exercises that, though painful and difficult, the force of his personality was able to make her perform.

Said A. K. Stevens:

> Part of his prescription for cure was that she should keep her promises. She had promised her sister a couple of sofa pillows. To make them (and to keep her promise), she had to open a bed pillow and by hand divide the feathers into two piles for the two pillows. Sure that she would fall in a dead faint, she undertook the task, and, of course, survived.
>
> When Wystan discovered that she had been using contraceptives, he pointed out that this, too, was retreat. Upshot, we had two more children.[3]

The first of the two was their second boy, born February 12, 1943, after Wystan left Ann Arbor, and the Stevenses named him Wystan Auden Stevens, the poet's first godchild. Since Wystan did not have to support five children, he could sound his theories with conviction and work his treatment with equanimity. Apparently the Stevenses did not mind, either, for they accepted the additions to their family with the same loving welcome as they had accepted the first three.

At the end of the fall term, Chester arrived in Ann Arbor to enter graduate school. Wystan was about to move from the modern house on Pontiac Trail, for Jean-Paul Slusser had returned from his leave. Angelyn's treatments were temporarily interrupted until Wystan could settle himself and Chester in his next faculty house. The house that Wystan rented during the spring term was at 1504 Brooklyn and more to his liking. It was, as he called it, "divinely Victorian," with its

1 The author's conversation with A. K. Stevens, April 8, 1983.
2 Ibid.
3 Letter to the author from A. K. Stevens, April 10, 1983.

gables and stoop and its graceful nineteenth-century lines. It was known as the Knott house.

Wystan and Chester enjoyed their social life with the Stevenses and with another young instructor, James Rettger, who taught linguistics, and his wife, whom they had recently met. What a social conquest it must have been for these young men to have been singled out above their older and more ambitious colleagues, now green with envy, for the favor of the Great Man.

The Stevenses and the Rettgers were invited to tea, to drinks, and, later, to dinner after dinner. They ate snails and eels and all the exotic food that Chester could convince his father to send him from New York. They drank champagne, Southern Comfort, Napoleon brandy, and German wine. They adored Chester, his cooking, and his ribald jokes—many of which he got from his father. "Send me some more jokes, Dad," Chester wrote in one of his letters home. "I'm the life of the party."

Year after year, long after that memorable year in Ann Arbor, Wystan and Chester would receive letters and Christmas cards from the Stevenses and the Rettgers, and always they would ask particularly about Chester and invite him to visit them in Ann Arbor. After Chester returned to New York in 1943, he never once went back. Nonetheless, the contact with these two men undoubtedly influenced both couples for the rest of their lives.

This influence also touched others at the university, especially the students who sat in Auden's class. Wystan disapproved of progressive education by whatever name it was known, and he insisted that American youth was schooled but not educated as a result of its pernicious influence. Just as he viewed intensive phonics (not gradual phonics) as the one and only way of teaching reading, he viewed the study of the classics as the one true education; and he believed memorization, particularly the memorization of great lines, to be part of the classical discipline. Thus it was that he announced on the first day of class that for the final exam each student would be required to write from memory six cantos of the *Divine Comedy*.

The assignment was taken at first by these awestruck students with dumb shock. Not a word was spoken. They had not thought in early October that he had been serious. After a few hours had passed, however, and cantos had been scanned, there were rumblings in the offices of the chairman of the English department, the dean of studies, and all the full professors. The rumblings grew louder. A distinguished delegation of gray-haired men (to whom Chester referred as "the corpse corps") approached Wystan armed with logic, psychology, pedagogy, and sweet reason. Nothing availed. Wystan insisted that his students memorize or fail, and memorize they did. Sorority, fraternity, dormitory, and League house burned the midnight lamps. Students walked about the campus lips moving, book in hand, as in a trance. But Wystan's students were able to write six cantos of Dante, all punctuation perfect, by the end of that year.

Georg Groddeck's *Das Buch vom Es* was another of Wystan's enthusiasms that caused a stir in Ann Arbor. If Freud was considered risky, he was at least solidly accepted into the academic circles of the day. Groddeck, with his frank discussions of human motivation as related to the sex drive and the ills of the body, was not widely known and thus suspect. Wystan, who had discovered Groddeck during his days with Layard in Berlin, now was recommending it as outside reading to his class, composed primarily of undergraduate students. The library grudgingly put it on the reserved shelf "For graduate students only," because the authorities considered it obscene.

Word about the book spread around campus like wildfire. Everybody wanted to read Groddeck's *The It,* as it was commonly known, but nobody could get hold of it. Everybody on campus from Martha Cook House to the locker room in the football stadium was looking for a graduate student to convince, cajole, bribe, or threaten into taking out the book when it became available.[1] Since there were only four copies, the graduate students, viewed most of the time as dull drones by the chic undergraduate set, became the rage of the campus. But louder rumblings from the offices of the deans finally caused the librarians to remove the book from the shelves, and a number of unkind remarks could be heard about Wystan if one visited the Hopwood Room or attended faculty teas.

Perhaps the most publicized bit of scandal surrounding Wystan and Chester's stay in Ann Arbor involved Thomas A. Knott, editor of *The Merriam-Webster Dictionary,* now working on the *Middle English Dictionary,* whose house Wystan had rented. The Knotts loved their pretty Victorian cottage, the pastel walls, the polished hardwood floors, the bright chintz-covered furniture with drapes to match, and the pale rugs. They were especially proud of the newly painted white kitchen,

---

[1] I myself was able to provide a number of undergraduates with the book, since I had heard about it early from Peter and was one of the first to procure it.

the purity of the tile floor, and the white café curtains with the emerald satin piping along the edge; and Mrs. Knott did not deny she was pleased when you said that you could eat off her floor.

Thus it was with some relief that the Knotts discovered that the university had found them as a tenant not just anyone. They were not reluctant when they discovered their house would be let for the term they were going away to a young English poet. They had always been given to believe that poets were finer than other men somehow, more sensitive to beauty and more appreciative of lovely things. They had never met a poet, of course, not a real one. Perhaps their home would be the subject of a famous poem, and people would visit it years later as a historic landmark.

Chester and Wystan settled into the house in early February to begin housekeeping. In this context, however, "housekeeping" calls out for some defining. To Chester the word housekeeping meant cooking. To Wystan, it meant somewhere to sleep, eat, and work. To both it meant entertaining friends with caviar and champagne (whenever one could obtain these goods in this backwoods of the world) or fried eggs and cheap red wine when money ran out. Wystan, physically ungraceful by nature, insisted that inanimate things threatened him—"Things conspire against me," he used to say—and thus was not about to confront vacuum cleaner and scrub mop. Chester saw his cooking obligation as primary, and had no idea whatsoever about how one cleaned a house. Nor did they hire anyone who would, or, perhaps, could perform the menial duties for them: Both Peter and Charlie were long gone.

Wystan and Chester's apartments and houses alike always had the appearance of a carpenter's shop gone awry or a public building about to be vacated. Guests of all types would come and go, spilling wine on the rugs, if there were rugs; filling ashtrays that were not emptied from one week to the next; walking with hobnailed boots on rugs and hardwood; leaving cigarette ashes to alight where they listed. Phonograph records were strewn about on end tables, coffee tables, eating tables, bookshelves, empty chairs, beds, bureau tops, desks; as were manuscripts and galley sheets, doctors' prescriptions, utility bills, letters, receipts, and money. The rugs were never vacuumed; the floors were never swept. If one took up a broom to help out, Chester would raise his wrist to his brow in a pained expression and say, "Pul-eeze! Do not raise the dust." On the walls and drapes was the visible evidence of each party. Dirty dishes were everywhere, including the bathtub, unless it was filled with cold water and used to chill cases of champagne. Books were absolutely everywhere.

The kitchen walls bore evidence of every meal Chester had cooked. They were grimy within a week. On the stained stove were pots piled upon dirty pots. The larger the kitchen, the greater the mess. Dirty dishes were in the sink, on the floor, on the table, on the drainboards, on top of the refrigerator. Someone, probably Chester, frequently used the kitchen curtains to wipe the grease off of his hands. No one ever bothered to clean the kitchen floor, take out the empty bottles, or pack up the garbage. Wystan and Chester were not in the least upset by the prospect of rodents. In the past Wystan had set out food at night for his favorite mouse, and he soon had an opportunity to do the same thing in the Knotts' house in Ann Arbor.

If Professor and Mrs. Thomas A. Knott returned after their trip rested and still high of heart, terror struck them when they walked into their little house, now vacated by the poet and his circle but bearing unmistakable evidence of their occupancy during that recent term. The lovely hardwood floors were marred by what appeared to be dungeon chains. The once pristine walls were spotted by ink, by grease, by wine, by lipstick, by unidentifiable substances of mysterious origin; the pastel rugs and living room furniture had cigarette burns; the lovely white kitchen curtains with the green piping on the edges were pulled down from their rods and lay limp and sullied across the back of a chair. There were cigarette burns on the table, on the sideboards, on the seats of chairs. There was even a blotch of red upon the ceiling from a can of deteriorated tomato paste. Mrs. Knott at first thought it to be blood.

With dispatch, Professor Knott made a call to one of his friends who was a full professor in the law school, and within fifteen minutes the law quads were buzzing. Within another fifteen, Auden, already established at Swarthmore in his next teaching assignment as poet-in-residence, was contacted by a legal authority and asked to pay a sum sufficient to restore the Knotts' devastated house. Auden refused. He said that he could not see that the house had undergone any change since his tenancy began, and he probably honestly could not. Chester was furious and insisted to friends years later that the house had been left in perfect order; in fact, he himself had spent at least an hour cleaning the bathroom. It was not the last time that Chester and Wystan were to have trouble with landlords.

The next year Chester was to announce in his New York apartment that "Some lunatic from Ann Arbor is suing Wystan." The case finally came to trial and Auden lost. Knott received sufficient money to rehabilitate his house. The rumor, substantiated by no less an authority than Dr. A. K. Stevens, was that Wystan, in town for the christening of his godchild, Wystan Auden Stevens, paid Knott in bags of pennies he personally obtained from the local bank and delivered to the doorstep of 1504 Brooklyn. From that year on Knott was uncomfortable about poets and was said to have chilled his relations with the English department, keeping close and warm attachments to persons in the law quads.

With Wystan gone from Ann Arbor to earn money at Swarthmore, Chester at twenty-one was at last free to enjoy college life, and he did. He set up his particular brand of housekeeping in a basement studio apartment on lower Ann Street, later to become a place of fascination to the student body for its alleged wickedness; and he was now free to entertain, not so much the Stevenses and the Rettgers, thirty-five and middle-aged like Wystan, but all his newly made friends, most of them young like himself.

They were varied and legion. There were undergraduate girls with crushes on Chester; there were undergraduate boys with crushes on the girls; there were fraternity brothers and sisters taken "to see Chester's place" as tourists are taken to shadowy sections of Montmartre; there were assorted graduate students; there were medical students, soldiers, sailors, marines, football heroes, waiters, and taxi drivers; there were professors of history, doctors of philosophy, instructors of English and mathematics, some destined to become famous. There were heterosexuals, homosexuals, bisexuals, and celibates. Wystan would not have permitted most of them into his house.

Here, as always, Chester was the attraction, and he gathered about him a circle of friends whom he dominated, as always. He cooked for them (after they bought the groceries), amused them with his father's jokes; he exasperated them, he entertained them, he instructed them. They, of course, adored him, and his actor's heart was happy with such adoration. They followed where he led them like the Pied Piper: to concerts at Hill auditorium; to plays at the Lydia Mendelson; to Flautze's Beer Hall; to the opera in Detroit. He was the arbiter of taste, like a French monarch of the *dix-huitième*. They loved Beethoven and Stravinsky because Chester loved Beethoven and Stravinsky. They hated Brahms and Shostakovich because Chester hated Brahms and Shostakovich. They laughed when he laughed. They were partisan against his enemies. They actively took his side in every feud, and there were always feuds.

He rallied them against the latest work of a modern composer the same way he summoned up support for one student actress in his circle against another who was not. Wherever they went they made a commotion and let their opinions, his opinions, be felt. Even in the local moving picture houses they grouped themselves *en masse* and laughed out loud at all the serious love scenes between Jeanette Mac-Donald and Nelson Eddy. They would die of laughter as Chester imitated a professor whom he had taken a dislike to, and his imitations were acidly accurate, if dangerous to himself. They laughed with delight when he composed obscene lyrics to the latest Dinah Shore record. They loved him and they feared him. Compared with Chester, the opinions of their parents, their professors, even their erstwhile idols, were provincial and *démodé*. The children of the Middle West took to him like parched earth to water.

Chester had further opportunity to extend his influence as music critic on the college newspaper, *The Michigan Daily*. Every week he would write his articles, full of all the musical insights and prejudices he had already passed on to Wystan, and he made the preferences between Brahms and Beethoven a *cause célèbre*. Never were the intellectual faculties of the music school so much in demand now that Chester Kallman had insulted Brahms. But Chester wearied of his fight about Brahms the moment other news reached him.

He discovered that the Philadelphia Orchestra was going to play Dmitri Shostakovich's Symphony No. 7, *The Leningrad,* Shostakovich's latest work, at the Hill Auditorium in Ann Arbor. Whether Chester disapproved of his father's friend and Dmitri's cousin Leonid, or whether because he simply did not care for surging tonal music, Chester lashed out against the Soviet composer who had done him no harm. He warned his readers not to take the upcoming concert seriously, displaying for their edification what he considered to be all of Shostakovich's musical flaws.

The music school, now up in arms against Chester, writing vituperative letters daily to the editor about the boy from New York who thought he knew it all, was for the first time in history of the same conviction as the Young Communist League—ready for revolution. Half the campus joined forces against Chester Kallman. At the tables of the Michigan League and the Michigan Union, in the bedrooms of the sorority and the fraternity houses, in the halls of Betsy Barbour,

Mosher-Jordan, Stockwell, and even Martha Cook, brother and sister
were fighting brother and sister. The pro-Shostakovich and the anti-
Shostakovich were everywhere.

Finally the night of the concert arrived. Never had so many students
attended a concert; the faculty was almost crowded out. Hill Auditorium was filled to the rafters and there were students standing in the
wings of the orchestra and sitting on the steps of the top balcony, all
glowering at each other and throwing remarks at anyone they knew
to be in Chester's group. Chester was in his glory as he sat in his critic's orchestra seat, blond and sardonically smiling. The next day he
wrote a scathing article about Shostakovich but also about tasteless
people who liked to listen to him. As for the music school, Chester's
final remarks were later to be repeated by Wystan: "Everyone knows
that musicians know nothing about music."

Chester was having the time of his life. This was better than Brooklyn College, or even life with Wystan, because now he had nobody to
restrain him and he had a place of his own. He even permitted himself to enjoy the established middle-class forms of social play: He
dressed up in a tuxedo ("Dad, please send me $10 to rent a tuxedo.
I'm taking a girl to a dance.") and took the beautiful Tamara Hendel
to her junior prom, the social event of the season. He danced all night,
looking like a matinee idol as he twisted and turned to the tunes of
the big bands: "Deep Purple," "Frenesi," "Marie," and all the rest,
ending with "Star Dust." At other times he played his phonograph
through all hours of the night until the neighbors upstairs yelled from
the darkness, "Can't you at least keep it down to a dull roar?" Still,
the apartment on Ann Street, replete with garbage, bottles, dust, dirty
dishes, and the smell of delicious food cooking, remained a now-
accepted institution until the summer of 1943.

Enjoyable as Chester's time was at Michigan, the prime purpose for
his stay after Wystan had left was, of course, to get his master's degree
in English and to win an Avery Hopwood Award. In this plan the
hearts and minds of Wystan and Chester's father were in complete ac-
cord. The money sent to finance Chester's college life might not have
been so generously and freely given had the truth been known. The
truth was that Chester was not making much progress toward his M.A.
In the beginning, when he first came to Ann Arbor and lived with
Wystan, things went quite well. His father received a report of his
courses at the end of the first term in graduate school; Chester had received all A's as he had done before at Brooklyn College. Then came

the boredom, the usual professor that Chester did not like and for whom he refused to do work. The term paper remained unwritten. A resentful Chester received an incomplete mark.

Chester's experience with the Hopwood awards was similar. He took a violent dislike at first sight to the professor who supervised the Hopwood awards and presided in the Hopwood Room. Chester made up a scatological name to rhyme with the surname of the professor. This gave many moments of hilarity to his circle, who could not resist repeating it, and Chester never dared to submit a manuscript to the Hopwoods. However, since names were anonymous on work submitted at these awards, and since the head of the Hopwood Room did not judge manuscripts, Chester still could have submitted his poems without fear of recrimination. Why did he not? Perhaps for the same reason he did not write his term paper—the pattern of self-destruction that later would etch itself so deeply into his life. Or was it simply that he was bored and even indolent, preferring the good times and his freedom to the harshness of academic life or the austerities of artistic creation? Or was it that now that he had Wystan, he had all the fruits of fame without the work it entailed?

In 1943 Chester fell in love again for the first time. One of the sorority sisters who had been taken along for a lark one Saturday night to "see Chester's place"—a Theresa Mary McInerney—had brought with her her fiancé, Michael Joseph Demarest,[1] aged twenty, a handsome, strapping Irish-American boy with black hair, blue eyes, and a ravishing Irish smile. Micky Demarest had met Theresa Mary when they were both students in St. Thomas's High School in St. Thomas Parish, Ann Arbor, and they were members of St. Thomas's Church off campus, where they had pledged their troth—Micky, after having had a heart-to-heart talk with his Irish father—and where Father Carey had already read the banns. Theresa Mary was preparing to be a teacher, but, despite her Irish ancestry, seemed to bear within her nature little of the traditional Irish style. Her smile was rare; her laugh even rarer. When she looked upon you with her light brown eyes, even if she were meeting you for the first time and you were a girl, she looked at you as one who had mortally wounded and betrayed her.

Throughout the usual Saturday night at Chester's, Theresa Mary's sorority sisters (Theresa Mary belonged to the new Catholic sorority)

---

[1] Not their real names.

noticed that she was watching Micky Demarest a bit too closely, and, as one girl put it confidentially to another, "Now that she's finally got her hooks into him, I suppose she wants to be sure they stay."

At 12:45 most of Chester's female guests departed with their escorts, but the party continued with intimate members of Chester's circle hardly noticing that the girls had gone. Theresa Mary was glad to go and said so. She also said that she did not feel comfortable in Chester's place and that the wine had made her ill. Thus it was with some surprise and no little satisfaction to Chester when who should return to the party a half-hour later alone and fancy-free but Micky Demarest, bearing a bottle of Bushmills Irish Whiskey, stolen from his father's cellar. They drank the whiskey, talked and laughed until three, when everyone left to go home—everyone, that is, except Micky Demarest, who remained on until late the next day.

For Chester, the encounter with Micky Demarest was not a one-night stand, whatever it was for Micky. In fact, it was love at first sight. He threw himself into the emotion with Wagnerian abandon. He took a sudden interest in the little town of Ann Arbor, where Micky was born. Its old gray frame houses and tacky stores on Main Street were beautiful to him now. The English sailor was soon forgotten. He longed to enter into the life that Micky lived and even showed a distinct tolerance for Theresa Mary. It was probably because of Micky as much as for any other reason that he decided to take the most beautiful girl on campus, Tammy Hendel, to the junior prom, where Micky was also taking Theresa Mary.

The prom night was a success. Chester invited a few of his friends to his apartment for drinks beforehand, including Tammy, Micky, and Theresa Mary. He served the rare black caviar he had been saving from the package recently sent him by his father from New York. He spent the entire day before the prom taking foam baths and putting on mudpacks and preparing for the great event, for he was really going to the prom with Micky Demarest. And he cut a fine figure, his blond hair in its cloudlike pompadour above the austere black and white of the tuxedo. He danced like a prince to "Frenesi" and finally to "Star Dust," and he did the hop and the boogie-woogie in between. They were a striking foursome. Even Theresa Mary managed to look less hazel in a green duchess satin, and in white chiffon, Tammy Hendel was a dream. Micky was magical as always, and the effect was heightened by a draught from a flask of Bushmills that he carried in his hip pocket.

When it was over, the boys took the girls for champagne and then to the sorority houses and said good night. Chester even kissed Tammy. Then Chester and Micky in their tuxedos sauntered like a couple of boulevardiers back to the apartment on Ann Street. Life was beautiful and the world was good and the war seemed far away. But all good things come to an end eventually, and the war was to touch the lives of Micky and Chester as it had touched the lives of thousands of others.

Not long after the prom Micky was called overseas and Chester was lonely without him. Before Micky left, there were sad farewells and Micky allowed Chester to make plans for the future. Theresa Mary by this time was looking more betrayed than ever, and the girls in the Catholic sorority house noticed that she was often without a date on Saturday nights. But before he left, Micky must have permitted her to make plans, too, as she seemed content to put off the wedding for a while.

Chester, of course, had the impression that Micky had put it off permanently. Indeed, Chester carried that impression with him to New York and into the next two years. He even sent Micky letters and food packages regularly, sometimes even begging money from his friends and his father to do so. But toward the end of the war Micky's letters did not come frequently, even in response to Chester's packages. Soon they did not come at all. Chester worried that he had been killed in action and wrote to friends still in Ann Arbor. Whether it was the Stevenses, the Rettgers, or someone else, a letter came telling him that Micky Demarest had returned unharmed, and that he had married Theresa Mary McInerney in St. Thomas's Church on the third Sunday after Easter. Chester never heard from him again.

Chester left Michigan in the spring of 1943 without his master's degree as he had left Brooklyn College with his B.A. but without his diploma a year and a half before. In one case it meant completing a term paper; in the other, it meant paying the college authorities two dollars for a lost key. He would not write the term paper for the professor he disliked at the University of Michigan; he would not pay Brooklyn College for a key. Chester was depressed. His friends had either graduated, gone home for the summer, or had been drafted. The war was on full force by this time, and Ann Arbor was filling up with people Chester did not know and did not care about: wives of soldiers taking rooms there to work in the Willow Run Bomber Plant on B-24 E's; enlisted men taking training courses at the university; odd people called in to fill teaching posts vacated temporarily, one hoped, by professors drafted into the army; assorted army and navy personnel. Besides, money was running out, and Chester was beginning to miss his father and New York. Peter Hansen was the only one left of the old crowd. He had returned from the army for some reason in the fall of 1942 and had remained on as a marginal member of Chester's circle now that Wystan was gone.

In the late June of 1943 Chester and Peter took the Wolverine Express train for New York.

CHAPTER 7

"My Mary and Dorothy Period"

CHESTER WAS KNOWN to refer to the years between 1943 and 1946 as "my Mary and Dorothy period." The war was raging in Europe, and his friends and lovers were in the army or navy, fighting overseas. Wystan, too, was absent most of the time, working at Swarthmore and teaching occasional courses at Bryn Mawr and Temple University on the side. Chester, just back home from Ann Arbor, had a warm place in his heart for the little college town that had lionized him and was happy to see Mary Valentine and me, waif-like and forlorn as we were, when we approached him one rainy November evening in 1943 as he sat over coffee in the old Waldorf Cafeteria on Sixth Avenue. It was clear to him that, having arrived from Ann Arbor less than a week before, we were already receiving New York's baptism of fire, or, in this case, a baptism of water: It never stopped raining.

We were midwestern girls who wanted to get out of the Middle West. We had decided to leave Ann Arbor and university life "where there was no future for a woman" and seek our fortunes in New York. Exactly what these fortunes might be, we had not yet decided. In any event, we took all our worldly goods, which consisted of two suitcases between us and two one-way coach tickets on the New York Central Railroad, to the Big City. The one-way tickets were bought "so we can't come back, even if we want to." We also had two twenty-five-dollar war bonds.

By the time we met Chester Kallman in the Waldorf, we were so broken in spirit that we were ready even to go back to the Middle West. We had spent six nights in the grubbiest of hotels and rooming houses, had run out of money, and had taken shelter in the lodging house of the Travelers' Aid Society on East Thirty-sixth Street. In addition to having been robbed once, suffering turned ankles and wounded feet, and having no rubbers or umbrella, we were plagued by constant rain. The rain poured down in torrents, stopped for a half-hour or so and then fell again, heavy and wet and nastily cold. It was like the curse of locusts. In later years we were to say that it had never rained in New York again as much and as long as in November of 1943.

Chester had come to New York a few months before us, but he missed Ann Arbor, and we probably brought it back to him suddenly like messengers from the past. He always remembered the happy times he had spent among the friends he had made there. Indeed, he could even be sentimental about his enemies and the feuds and the sham battles he always fought wherever he went. Chester was friendly by nature. Though he carried grudges, he was quick to forgive when his antagonist made the least show of penitence. He liked people; what is more, he needed them. His actor's nature required their presence in order for him to express himself. The only person he never forgave was Syd.

When the time came for Chester to leave Ann Arbor, Auden had already been teaching in Swarthmore for a year. Left to his own resources, Chester was running out of funds, so in the spring of 1943 Chester returned to New York in the company of Peter Hansen, the boy with whom Auden had taken up in the fall of 1941, and as quickly abandoned, but who had returned to the Kallman circle when Chester lived on Ann Street in Ann Arbor. Chester and Peter arrived at the office of Chester's father on Fifty-seventh Street destitute and asking for funds to tide them over. They had rented an apartment but said they needed money to go shopping for what they referred to as things to start a household. They came back proudly displaying a porcelain teapot. The apartment was eventually furnished in Chester's haphazard fashion, with a folding cot, a few kitchen chairs, a large shipping crate that served as a table, a record player, thousands of records, and a trunk load of dirty clothes. Peter and Chester stayed in that apartment for barely a month.

Chester's enthusiasm for opera arias played as loud as possible "so that the music can inundate one; so that one can be drunk with glorious sound" was not shared by the other tenants, particularly when Chester's desire to become drunk with glorious sound occurred late at night. The landlord appeared at the door soon after the young men bought the porcelain teapot and asked them to leave as soon as possible. He was even willing to give them back their month's security. It was then that Dr. Kallman found Chester the apartment that he kept for two decades and in which Auden stayed from time to time. What happened to Peter Hansen is not clear—he was looking for more elegant surroundings as he vanished uptown, still in my polo coat.

Chester and his father shared the top floor of a building at 129 East Twenty-seventh Street, owned by an Armenian entrepreneur in the Greek-Armenian section on lower Lexington Avenue, not far from the old George Washington Hotel. In 1983 the building was still standing, almost as it had been in 1943, untouched by the wrecker's ball. Dr. Kallman, hiding out with his nurse, Frances Kydd, from the importunities of his second wife—who, it will be recalled, told him to get out "and not come back alive" but now bitterly regretted her words—found the place in 1942, with the help of an Armenian restaurant owner. He rented the back apartment on the top floor. When Chester again needed a place to live, his father discovered that the front apartment on the same floor had been abandoned. He paid the landlord the month's rent, all of $13.50, and Chester moved in alone. He was to live there from 1943 until he left for Europe in 1948, at which time an odd assortment of friends and lovers took over the apartment from year to year, or from season to season, until late in the next decade. Auden stayed there, too, when on vacation, and until he settled himself in his own apartment.

Mary and I always said later that if we could choose one event that changed the course of our lives, it would be our meeting with Chester in the Waldorf Cafeteria on that November evening. When he invited us to his apartment for drinks the next day, we felt we had found a haven. We felt that maybe everything would be all right after all. We went back to Travelers' Aid in the rain that night with a lighter step and happily helped peel the hundreds of hard-boiled eggs that were served for dinner. In the meantime, Chester told his father about us. "I've just met two girls I knew in Ann Arbor. I've invited them over tomorrow, so let them in if I'm not there. They're crazy as March hares. They'll probably arrive early because they're afraid to be out after dark."

The next day we did arrive early because we were indeed afraid to be out after dark. We knocked at Dr. Kallman's door by mistake, because it was at the head of the stairs. We had passed the smoke-filled Democratic Club on the second floor and the somnolent men in black hats who leered at us from the doorway; we had managed the rickety stairs that wound upward alongside bleak, scarred walls. "Do you think we're in the right place?" I asked Mary.

When Dr. Kallman appeared, good-natured and portly in athletic shorts, his upper body bare, smiling while leaning against the door sill, panic seized us. "Is Chester Kallman here?" Mary asked weakly. When he said, "Won't I do?" I grabbed Mary's arm and said, "Let's go," and started down the stairs. Dr. Kallman, often a tease, realized he had gone too far. He told us he was Chester's father and invited us in. "Excuse the way I look. Friday afternoon is my painting day. I never paint with my clothes on." That was our introduction to the ménage Kallman.

Dr. Kallman, a double for General Eisenhower, served us a drink and some hors d'oeuvres we had never heard of, and we waited for Chester to return. We were surprised to know that Chester *had* a father, so much did he belong, in our eyes, to another world where, like a bright colored bird, unfamiliar with the drabness of the real world, he inhabited an exotic clime. We discovered, nevertheless, that Chester had a middle-class background and a family with a grandmother who lived with an aunt in New Bedford, Massachusetts. Bobby had returned to Sadie's house in New England a year before.

Chester finally returned home with two friends he had known from Brooklyn College days, a married couple, Rhoda Jaffe and Milton Klonsky, and everyone went into Chester's place. Rhoda, who would later play an important role in Auden's life, was a large-boned blonde of about Chester's age. She was working as a waitress in order to pay her psychiatrist, while Milton, together with Chester, was writing a radio script. Rhoda talked fluently about everyone's psychological problems as well as her own, and Chester and Milton were occupied with making fun of radio. Later on that evening more people arrived. There was a tall sailor with an English accent whom everybody called

Jack and some girls in WAC uniforms, one of whom was Tammy Hendel from Ann Arbor. Suddenly a boy came in called Royce Wagoner, whom Mary had known at the University of Michigan. He was visiting New York with his mother and was trying to escape her for the evening. Later other people from Ann Arbor also appeared. It was like a football homecoming.

Chester's apartment was dim and dusty blue. The skylight in the living room had been blackened because of the air raid regulations, but there were two windows thick with grime facing Twenty-seventh Street. A makeshift mattress-bed was under the windows, a working fireplace on the east wall; a sofa of a color undistinguishable because of the dust and cigarette burns, was on the west wall. In front of the sofa on a coffee table stood a broken porcelain teapot, now used as a coffeepot, put together with a can used as a drip-type top. There was a dirty flat green ashtray, filled to the brim with cigarette butts, and a large expensive book of the shiny Christmas variety, of Daumier's sketches. Here and there on the coffee table were dried wine-colored rings where glasses of burgundy had once stood.

To the left of the fireplace was the music center, so-called. It consisted of a broken phonograph, the arm of which was tied together with a string, and thousands of breakable records. These were the days before the long-playing plastics, and one was always having to change records. There were records everywhere. There were records in stacks on the bed, single records propped against the wall, on the shelf above the fireplace, among the hundreds of photographs; there were records on the box tops that served as end tables. Most of the records, though, were stacked in albums on boxes around the phonograph. Hanging on the wall above the music corner was the Blake print "The Ancient of Days," of God creating the world. The mystery was how, when Chester wanted to play a particular record, he could always reach out and find it, and how that rickety phonograph could produce so grand a sound.

About the floor were a number of scatter rugs, also of an indeterminate color, which, because the apartment depended on the Balkan Restaurant for its heat, came in handy when the restaurant closed and the rooms chilled at night. Auden was known to sleep nightly, when he returned to New York during one of the vacations, wrapped in all the scatter rugs, with a bottle of red wine and a plate of boiled potatoes on the floor by the side of the bed.

The apartment had a windowless kitchen off to the left and a small bedroom off the living room to the right, with yet another grimy window. This room was seldom used except for a random overnight guest and usually served as a storage space. Piles and piles of laundry could be found on the raised mattress.

From that night on began the "Mary and Dorothy period" in Chester's life. Heartened and fortified by Chester and Milton, who were native New Yorkers, we found the city less formidable. We decided to remain after all, leave Travelers' Aid as soon as we could find jobs, and confront the city on its own terms. Chester continued to make appointments to see us and continued to encourage us to make New York our home.

As for Chester, it is hard to say what he saw in those two girls from bourgeois families and orthodox Christian homes of the Middle West. But he enjoyed being the big brother; he enjoyed showing off his city; he enjoyed introducing us to the opera and to his favorite records; he liked the adoration he saw in our eyes. Chester, in fact, liked women, but he feared complications with them. Mary and I offered him, at least at first, the company of women of his own age without any of the complications. We were simply his girlfriends and that was all. Perhaps he found our backgrounds, so different from his own, as interesting and as curious as we found his. He listened with fascination to the stories we told about various members of our families. At any rate, we seemed to fill a need in his nature at that time that no one else was able to fill. He was a benevolent despot; he ruled our lives. In turn, we also relieved the loneliness he must have felt, now with his close friends away at war and Wystan also gone.

Chester himself had received his "greetings," as we called it, from Uncle Sam and had appeared for his medical examination at the induction center in New York shortly after having returned from Ann Arbor. However, he had two problems that prevented his being drafted into the army: a heart murmur as the result of a childhood case of rheumatic fever, and a spinal curvature sufficient to cause the army to reject him. Thus he carried a 4F card, indicating excuse from service. The card was stolen once and lost from time to time, and he was continually applying for a duplicate, much to the annoyance of the bureaucracy.

Mary and I finally found jobs in the George Washington Hotel, a small family hotel in those days, on Lexington Avenue at Twenty-third Street, two blocks north of Gramercy Park and four blocks south of Chester's place. When I asked Chester's advice about working there, he said, "It's a nice hotel. Wystan used to live there and he liked it very much."[1] We took the jobs.

Mary worked as a cashier in the bar and the restaurant, and I worked alone in a small, hidden office on the second floor, facing Twenty-fourth Street and a haberdasher. A large statue of a painted dapple-gray horse equipped with red harness greeted me from my one window every morning at nine o'clock. The horse was still standing there forty years later. I was never certain what the purpose of my job was, except that it was sent to me from heaven in order to provide daily bread. All I knew for sure was that I was expected to type endless alphabetized lists of names and addresses, apparently of past and present patrons of the hotel. The typing kept me busy for months, from November 1943 until the spring of 1944, in fact. By that time I had passed my examination to be a substitute teacher of high school English and was about to launch upon the career for which I thought I had been trained. There were many times later I wished I had remained at the George Washington Hotel.

The George Washington Hotel was, in the mid-1940s, probably very much as it had been when Wystan and Isherwood lived there in 1939, except that it had a different manager. Auden's poem about it, discovered years later, accurately portrays its ambiance. It was clean, inexpensive, and respectable.

ODE

In this epoch of high-pressure selling
  When the salesman gives us no rest,
And even Governments are yelling
  "Our Brand is Better than Best";
When the hoardings announce a new diet
  To take all our odor away,
Or a medicine to keep the kids quiet,
  Or a belt that will give us S.A.,
Or a soap to wash shirts in a minute,
  One wonders, at times, I'm afraid,
If there is one word of truth in it,
  And how much the writers were paid.

[1] Auden and Christopher Isherwood lived in the George Washington Hotel for a few months after they arrived in New York in January 1939. They then moved to an apartment in Yorkville on the upper East Side of Manhattan.

O is there a technique to praise the
  HOTEL GEORGE WASHINGTON then,
That doesn't resemble the ways the
  Really professional men
Convince a two hundred pound matron
  She's the feather she was in her youth?
Well, considering who is the patron,
  I think I shall stick to the truth.
It stands on the Isle of Manhattan
  Not far from the Lexington line,
And although it's démodé to fatten,
  There's a ballroom where parties may dine.

The walls look unlikely to crumble
  And although, to be perfectly fair,
A few entomologists grumble
  That bugs are exceedingly rare,
The Normal Man life is so rich in
  Will not be disgusted, perhaps,
To learn that there's food in the kitchen,
  And that water comes out of the taps,
That the sheets are not covered with toffee,
  And I think he may safely assume
That he won't find a fish in his coffee
  Or a very large snake in his room.

While the curious student may study
  All the sorts and conditions of men,
And distinguish the Bore from the Buddy,
  And the Fowl from the Broody Old Hen;
And presently learn to discover
  How one looks when one's deeply in debt,
And which one is in search of a lover
  And which one is in need of a vet;
And among all these Mrs. and Mr.'s,
  To detect as each couple arrives,
How many are really their sisters,
  And how many are simply their wives.

But now let me add in conclusion
  Just one little personal remark;
Though I know that the Self's an illusion,
  And that words leave us all in the dark,
That we're serious medical cases
  If we think that we think that we know,
Yet I've stayed in hotels in most places
  Where my passport permits me to go
(Excluding the British Dominions
  And Turkey and U.S.S.R.),
And this one, in my humble opinion's
  The nicest I've been in so far.

To the Manager of the George Washington Hotel
Mr. Donald Neville-Willing
and to all the staff with gratitude
and good wishes from
W. H. Auden
1939[1]

In early 1944, Mary and I moved into an unfurnished apartment on the top floor of a six-flight walk-up building in Chelsea on West Twenty-fourth Street and Eighth Avenue. We bought a secondhand studio couch that opened into a double bed, which we placed in the living room, and a vanity dresser with a high mirror, which we placed in the bedroom. Together with my phonograph from college, Mary's typewriter, and some wooden carting crates for tables, the apartment was furnished, except for dishes, which we bought from the ten-cent store on the corner. There was, of course, no telephone, for no one could get a telephone during the war, so visiting friends, young and dauntless, braved the six flights and simply knocked on the door to see whether we were at home.

Through it all, Chester was like a big brother, advising and guiding. He helped us move what furniture we had up the six flights, stopping at every other landing for a moment to rest or to have a ciga-

---

[1] This poem, one of Auden's numerous odes, does not appear in his books. It was published for the first time in *The New York Times Book Review* on March 8, 1981. The original is in the Berg Collection of the New York Public Library. Courtesy of Edward Mendelson.

rette. Chester also moved his social headquarters to our apartment, since it had regular steam heat, so David Protetch, Billy Vinson, and other Ann Arbor friends on leave from the army and navy would eventually find themselves trudging up the six flights of stairs to have one of Chester's dinners and try on our colorful hats, cavorting about the living room, winding the veils around their faces in mock seduction, and drinking gallons of wine.

In spite of the struggle to earn a living, these were happy days. Chester took us everywhere. He took us to Staten Island on the ferry, to Hoboken on the ferry, to the Empire State Building, to Central Park and the zoo. He took us to see the Rousseaus and the Cézannes at the Museum of Modern Art, where we also saw all the old movies. He took us to Jones Beach in the summer, where Mary and Chester swam out too far and left me anxious and worrying on the beach. He took us to the Cloisters on the Fifth Avenue double-decker bus that cost ten cents. He took us to the Metropolitan Museum of Art to see Crivelli's "The Virgin and Child," one of his favorite paintings. But most of all he took us to the old Metropolitan Opera House.

Each week during the opera season, whether the night was mild or the snow was deep and the wind chill, we stood in our fragile shoes at 5:00 in the evening on the standing-room-only queue outside the old building, waiting for the doors to open at 8:00. Then we rushed in to find a place near the orchestra and stood for the entire performance, seeing the golden horseshoe and the glittering crowds, all in evening dress, as the lights dimmed and the orchestra conductor—Leinsdorf, Szell, Toscanini—entered and made his bow. We heard all the favorite singers of the day: Bidù Sayão, Ezio Pinza, Eleanor Steber, Zinka Milanov, Nadine Conner, Jarmila Novotna, Lotte Lehmann. We saw *Don Giovanni, Falstaff, La Traviata, La Bohème, Madama Butterfly, Tosca, Aïda, Rigoletto, Die Meistersinger, Die Walküre, Tristan und Isolde, Così fan tutte, The Abduction from the Seraglio, The Magic Flute,* and many more.

If Chester had changed Wystan's life back in 1939, he also changed the lives of Mary and me in 1943 and the years that followed. When one took up with Chester, it was not difficult to exclude everyone else from one's life. Chester absorbed not only all your days but most of your evenings, for he made everything that happened exciting.

Best of all, he made you laugh. An iconoclast like his father, he made fun of all you were bred to hold sacred, things like Irene Dunne and Charles Boyer in *Love Affair,* Bette Davis and Paul Henried in *Now Voyager,* especially the last scene with the stars looking down. He loved the movies, of course, and would often go to see the same one again and again. I think we must have seen *Naughty Marietta* four or five times. It was high camp to him. We would rock in hysterics during the most romantic love scenes at his sotto voce comments until an usher would stand over us with a stern eye, suggesting that we either be silent or leave. If Chester saw a movie he particularly liked, and you had not seen it, he would dramatize every important scene and then go to see the movie again with you. It never turned out to be so funny and so interesting as Chester's version of it.

It was at this time that Chester took delight in making up new words, which were later taken up by Wystan and began to appear in his poetry, much to the confusion of scholars. One such word was "hideola." One afternoon Mary, Chester, and I were on the Long Island train on our way to Dr. Kallman's summer house in Sea Cliff. For some reason the train stopped at a town along the way, and everyone had to disembark and wait for the next train. We were all furious as we stood on the overpass, looking down at the village below. "What is the name of this town?" Chester asked a fellow passenger.

"Mineola."

"What a hideous town," said Chester, now not in a mood to appreciate Long Island. "It ought to be called Hideola, not Mineola." And Chester, Mary, and I began laughing and chanting "Hideola Mineola," much to the delight of our fellow passengers. From then on the new adjective, hideola, was used to denote people, places, or things that Chester considered distasteful or ugly.

Chester loved New York then, and he took us to places we had never expected to see in our lives. Most of these excursions did not cost anything, except for a five-cent subway or bus ride and about thirty-five cents, if that, for lunch. He took us to the Lewisohn Stadium in summer, to free concerts in various churches on Sunday afternoons in winter. He took us to dinners at various inexpensive ethnic restaurants and to Greenwich Village bars. If we paid the check, we did not mind. When David Protetch and Billy Vinson came to town, we all went dancing on Saturday night in Village bars or in German cafés in Yorkville until the early hours of the morning, when we limped home in our high-heeled shoes, happy and warm with wine.

Chester loved to cook. He seldom had dinner in those days without us, and he usually cooked in our apartment, as our kitchen stove was slightly better than his. We would shop together, sharing wartime ration cards, on Ninth Avenue, pooling our money, and carry the groceries and wine up the six flights. There was always music with dinner. Chester would bring over his favorite records and play them late into the night. On Friday, after an evening out, all three of us would often fall asleep in our party clothes on the secondhand studio couch, opened up into a double bed. We would wake up on Sunday morning, surprised to see the sun shining on the tower of the Empire State Building, the tiger kitten that Dr. Kallman had given us curled up on the only pillow.

Visiting the sixth floor walk-up from time to time was Jack Lansing. Between his missions overseas, Jack would suddenly appear at the door of the apartment bearing gifts. One was a brown felt hat with a veil, together with a faded blue neckerchief, both thrown into a brown paper bag and presented with a courtly speech. The hat and the kerchief both were worn alternately by Mary and me, especially the hat, for many seasons after. Throughout the next decade Jack always appeared on Christmas, and he always presented a gift—usually something to wear—which he had purchased on one of his secret missions and had carried back with his sailor's gear to New York. His favorite gift was a hat.

In late May of that year when Mary and I went to our mailbox one sunny morning, we found an official-looking envelope. It contained an eviction notice from James N. Wells, Realty Agent, on West Twenty-third Street. Full of self-righteous indignation, we rushed over to the agent. We found that the neighbors on the sixth floor had been complaining for a long time about music being played at all hours of the night and about noise being made by our guests, men in women's hats, cavorting on the fire escape.

"But why weren't we warned at least? How can you just evict us without any warning?" But James N. Wells was adamant. We had to be out of the apartment by June 6. The denizens of the sixth-floor walk-up had not appreciated Chester's opera records any more than the fellow tenants in Chester's first New York apartment; these lower-middle-class laborers did not want to become "drunk with glorious sound" on weekday nights.

One block west on Twenty-fourth Street, between Ninth and Tenth avenues, across from the London Terrace, was a small apartment building that housed a bar-restaurant called the Fireside Inn, where Mary, Chester, and I had eaten now and then. It was owned by a tiny, elegant woman called Jetta Merkel, who loved cats and did not mind people with an artistic temperament. Mrs. Merkel was cultivated, had lived in Europe, had known James Joyce in Dublin, and was not averse to renting to friends of a friend of W. H. Auden. It was a small studio, also on the top floor, but only on the third floor this time. It looked out on the garden restaurant, a walled-in penthouse, and a large tree. It was a haven for cats. Although the price was outrageous, sixty-five dollars a month, the apartment was furnished, and Mary and I felt we had come up a bit in the world. We bought a secondhand phonograph (our original one had been stolen), took the vanity dresser, left the secondhand bed behind for James N. Wells, Inc., and moved with the tiger kitten into 409 West Twenty-fourth Street.

Chester was not working at a regular-paying job when we first met him in New York in the fall of 1943, and we were not sure how he made a living. He was doing some free-lance writing at the time for a patient of his father who ran a radio interview program for WNEW, but Chester found keeping to deadlines tedious, if not impossible, so his employer, later to become the head of a leading television station, had to hire someone more efficient, if less inspired. His father was some help to him, but his father insisted, to no avail, that Chester find work. Chester must have received some checks from Wystan, but how often they came, we were not sure. It was not that Chester minded the idea of having a job; he did not like being in the position of a petitioner, of asking and applying for one. His pride, not his indolence, stood in his way.

Over a period of time, Mary and I also realized that Chester did not know the first thing about taking care of money. Although he had a constant need for it, he lost it as quickly as he had it. Either he spent it in bars, or he had it stolen from him by young men whom he continued to pick up on Saturday night and who continued to rob him on Sunday morning. Chester was always in dire need of money, and yet he seemed to be making no plans for earning it. "What does Chester plan to do for a living?" his father would ask Mary and me. "He can't live on writing poetry. He isn't Wystan." If you asked Chester the same question, the answer was always the same: "I don't know."

Yet he continued to live on in the apartment on Twenty-seventh Street, scraping money together for rent, for his electric and gas bills, for his bus and subway fares, for the food in the local markets, for the change required at the bars, for his opera tickets. In spite of the dramatic crises that occurred at the beginning of each month because "Chester doesn't have his rent money," the rent was finally paid, the utilities were paid, and Chester managed to eat and go to the bars and to the opera. Then Mary Valentine became determined to interest him in permanent and steady employment.

By the time Mary and I had moved into the apartment above the

Fireside, I had received my substitute's license and Mary had persuaded Chester to take a civil service examination. He found the idea
droll and diverting, so, to be sociable, he accompanied Mary to the
test. They both received high marks and both were selected for work in
intelligence. They were assigned to the Bureau of Censorship, a large,
drafty old building on West Twenty-fifth Street. Chester suddenly had
a job, the only job he was ever to stay at with a regular salary. Since I
was away teaching during the day, Chester and Mary were together in
the drafty building on Twenty-fifth Street censoring GI letters and
examining them for possible enemy codes, a few of which they discovered. Chester seemed to enjoy his job, and he and Mary would talk of
their coworkers throughout the evening. At noon lunch breaks he and
Mary would come back to the apartment and make a meal. Sometimes
Chester would arrange a program of opera records for his coworkers
at Censorship, one of whom was a Russian prince, and he and Mary
would carry the portable phonograph and all the records to the Censorship building.

When Chester shared with you his love of music, it somehow over-
flowed from him to you and pervaded your life. He played you the
particular enthusiasm of the moment: sometimes the Chopin mazur-
kas by Horowitz; sometimes the songs of Hugo Wolf; sometimes
Mahler's *Das Lied*. But, best of all, he loved the songs sung by Flagstad. He would regale you with the opera gossip, acting in detail the
scenes as he saw them of the various love affairs of the divas. He used
to say that Flagstad was his mother. In those days of the war, when
Flagstad was called a Nazi, Chester defended her against all attacks.
But if Flagstad was his mother, Verdi was his father. He would play
the records from *Aïda*, from *Rigoletto*, from *Traviata*, from *Falstaff;*
he would pore over Verdi's biography and study Verdi's photograph.
When I painted Chester's portrait, he wanted as a background the
figure of Verdi hovering over him, rather than the rocks and the sea
at Jones Beach. One of the reasons he wanted to go to Italy was to see
the land of Verdi and to hear his operas sung and produced by Verdi's
countrymen.

The days when Mary and Chester were at Censorship were happy
and uneventful. The hours during the week were regular. Chester was
at last earning a salary. In the evening Chester, Mary, and I would
cook dinner, listen to music, talk or read. Chester was writing poetry
then; Mary was reading Henry James; I was painting or grading papers. Fridays of a work week have a special kind of excitement, fed by
the prospect of two free days to come. We three would drink wine

and listen to Billie Holiday. Sometimes Chester would take us out to his favorite bars and we would come home alone before midnight, leaving him to his own social life. But gradually things began to change.

If you associated with Chester long enough, it was inevitable that you would eventually encounter Wystan.

CHAPTER 8

The Serpent
in the Garden

WE HAD HEARD of Wystan, of course, and I had met him in Ann Arbor. We had read English literature at the university and were familiar with the modern poets. We knew that Auden was well known in literary circles and that he had inspired something of a cult. Yet we never thought of Wystan as anyone other than Chester's eccentric English friend who said "cow bath" for "cold bath"; who hated Edna St. Vincent Millay; who never took salt with his eggs; who never ate sweets; who always had to have potatoes with dinner; who went to bed just when things got started; who got up at six in the morning; who would not answer the telephone or the doorbell before one; who liked to wear secondhand clothes, sometimes even bedroom slippers in the street; who disliked the French.

Mary, who had a French great-grandmother, and I, who idolized every French saint from Jeanne d'Arc to Thérèse de Lisieux, found Wystan's attitude toward the French the most bizarre of his bizarreries; but while we were slow to approve of him, we never let Chester

suspect our true feelings. In spite of Wystan's offense to our franco-
philia, we were in awe of him, and we never felt comfortable with him
about. But our greatest objection was that he usurped Chester. "I
don't think he really likes us," we said one to the other. "I don't care
even if he turns out to be the greatest poet of the century. It's more
fun to be alone with Chester. Besides, he appropriates Chester as if it
were his absolute right. That's what annoys me. As if nobody else
counted!"

Chester, on his best behavior in order to mollify Wystan toward
Mary and me, allowed himself to be directed by Wystan, who, from
time to time, resembled nothing so much as a crotchety schoolmaster.
"Chester, no music now, please! Let us at least have some peace while
we eat." When Wystan came to New York for brief holidays from
Swarthmore, where he continued to teach until 1945, he would occupy
most of Chester's time. Either Chester would cook for him on East
Twenty-seventh Street or be invited with him to mysterious apartments uptown. "I'm sorry," Chester would say, "I can't come over
tonight. Wystan and I are invited to have dinner with some dull people who like nonobjective art. They're rich." But Chester began to
chafe at the bit.

Wystan's jealousy was quixotic: It would strike some people and
elude others for no apparent reason. One afternoon in the early 1940s,
while walking with Wystan in Greenwich Village, Chester met his
father's younger cousin, Getel Kahn Nastasi, on Christopher Street.
As a child, Getel had been with Chester's mother the day she died,
and she had always had a special fondness and sympathy for Chester,
as he for her. They greeted each other enthusiastically, hugging and
kissing and exchanging news of the family, when Getel noticed Wystan
watching them from the curb.

"Oh, I'd like you to meet a friend of mine," said Chester. When he
presented Wystan to Getel, the poet did not smile but simply grunted,
looked at her coldly, and, glancing at his watch, reminded Chester that
they were late for an appointment. They hurried off, leaving Getel,
who was not prepared to understand or to forgive Wystan's rudeness,
with a resentment that lasted for life.

Back in 1941, when Wystan was extolling the virtues of *agape,* he
did not reckon with the problems that would arise from the very
solution that he thought he had found to his jealousy of Chester's
erotic life. In 1941, Wystan had not yet seen the extent to which
Chester, attractive by nature, would attract genuine friends. After all,
in 1939, when Wystan and Chester had first met, Chester's social life

was limited. His effort to hide his homosexuality for the sake of his family caused him to approach any friendship with other boys of like inclinations cautiously. He did not make new friends at that time, and he gradually avoided his old heterosexual crowd at Brooklyn College. When he met Wystan he was a star-struck boy of eighteen, and, for the time at least, Wystan was enough. Thus Wystan had Chester more or less to himself, or at least thought he had, from the time they first met in April 1939 until the crisis of July 1941, and even after. Wystan had "put a halo around homosexuality,"[1] to quote Chester's father, and Chester was by 1942 free to be himself. Wystan had not reckoned on Ann Arbor.

Chester, extroverted and friendly like his father, attracted both men and women, not only as lovers but also as friends. In fact, most of the people Chester went to bed with were not friends at all and would never have been invited into the living room. Most of his friendships were platonic. Chester needed, wanted, and attracted faithful friends, heterosexual as well as homosexual. After Wystan left Michigan for Swarthmore, he probably had no idea of the extent of Chester's social life in Ann Arbor. Wystan, who was satisfied that Chester have a number of lovers as long as he alone could be Chester's best and only friend, was again to be disappointed. Soon he was confronted with crowds of friends issuing from Ann Arbor and other points south and north like a band of locusts. "Then Chester's fellow graduates started to arrive in droves (or so it seemed) into New York," Jack Lansing remarked, "and I soon had made more friends from Michigan than I ever did at Oxford."[2]

Wystan was soon to discover that Chester's friendships could be as exclusive and passionate as his love affairs—perhaps more so—and that these friendships could as easily take him away from Wystan as could love. Wystan, now in the spring of 1944, was to find in *agape* a dubious ally—he who had endured the fires of jealousy and the humiliation of having to accept second place in Chester's life; he, who wanted to be the center, was again on the periphery. Having endured exile at Swarthmore, where he had gone in order to earn money partly for the support of Chester, he was now to face these incursions from Ann Arbor.

The first of these incursions of a serious nature came in the persons of Mary Valentine and me. It would have been impossible to take

[1] Humanized homosexuality and made it acceptable.
[2] Letter to the author from Jack Lansing, June 27, 1981.

us seriously as rivals, were it not for Chester's seeming fascination with us. Never one to hide his enthusiasms, Chester spoke about us often, reported the things we did and said, things that he found droll and amusing. He went on about all the good times we had together going to the opera; dancing in Yorkville; cooking meals and sharing ration cards; meeting the quaint young teachers I brought home for coffee after school; giving concerts for fellow workers at the Bureau of Censorship; making friendly fun of everything and everybody; being young and happy in New York and having one's own money. To make things worse, Dr. Kallman, whom Chester saw a great deal of, now that he lived next door, was delighted with us, for he lived in constant hope that Chester would "outgrow" his homosexuality by what a psychiatrist told him was the crucial age of twenty-seven. Knowing Chester better than his father knew him, Wystan was not worried about any sexual activity in Chester's relationship with us, but he was not amused by Dr. Kallman's encouragement of the friendship. In fact, he felt the more excluded, knowing how close Chester had always been to his father. In short, Wystan was not amused by anything that was happening that year in Chester's life, including Chester's job at Censorship, but he knew that any direct approach would not succeed.

He decided for the moment to do as Chester wished and join the happy band. Of course, Wystan could not hide his true feelings, and we were immediately sensitive to his basic antagonism and froze in his company. Besides, I could never quite forget that Wystan had supposedly put that curse on me way back in Ann Arbor. Now here he was in my life again. Chester, however, was impervious to Wystan's moods and behaved as if nothing were wrong.

"I don't think you ought to make Wystan come over here for meals," I once said when Mary, Chester, and I were alone. "He doesn't like to come. We won't be offended, honestly, if you have dinner without us. We can all be together again when Wystan goes back to Swarthmore or Bennington, or wherever it is he goes. Please, Chester."

"Nonsense," Chester would respond. "He likes you both very much. He wants to come."

"But he doesn't. I'm not comfortable with him, Chester. I can sense the way he feels. He wants to be alone with you."

"You're wrong."

Nothing could persuade him to change his mind. For Mary or me to say any more would have made the situation worse, because Chester would then have scolded Wystan, and Wystan would have been more sullen than ever, grunting continually in answer to everything that was said, or putting between himself and us his long arctic silences.

Throughout the summer of 1944, every evening at about six o'clock, Wystan would appear at the door of the top apartment at 409 West Twenty-fourth Street with two fat bottles of Chianti or two slim bottles of Liebfraumilch, prepared with his two questions, one for Mary and one for me, as his contribution to the evening's conversation. Mary and I did the shopping and prepared the dessert, usually lemon meringue pie which Chester adored (but which Wystan never ate). Then Chester would make the dinner. At the end of the meal, Mary and I would do the dishes and Chester and Wystan would play records or talk until it was time to go home. Then the bills would be taken out, and each would contribute ration coupons (on Wystan's ration card he gave his occupation as "teacher") and money to the kitty for the cost of the meal and for tomorrow's shopping. The sum for each person was usually about twenty-five cents, not counting the wine, which Wystan always contributed.

Chester also arranged outings to which Wystan was expected to go along. The favorite was old Garbo movies at the Museum of Modern Art, where one of Chester's old friends, Bill Lieberman, had just found a job. Once when *Camille* was playing, Wystan was ordered to pick me up at 3:30 after school. He insisted on walking from Chelsea to East Fifty-third Street, as he did not believe it moral to ride when you could walk. I am a fast walker usually, but Wystan didn't walk; he flew like a great bird, the coattails of his old raincoat flying in the wind like wings, and he would not wait for me to catch up. He would keep saying, "You must learn to walk faster," or "Hurry up, Dorothy, don't be such a slowpoke!" It was like Alice and the Red Queen.

When Wystan and I eventually arrived at the museum and took our seats next to Chester and Mary, all sorts of people suddenly began to recognize Wystan and poke me, who sat next to him, to introduce them. He was very pleasant to the columnist Max Lerner, who sat behind us, but relieved when the lights went out and he and Chester could weep in the darkness for the hundredth time to the heartrending Garbo as Marguerite Gauthier. When the movie was over and the lights on, all eyes were red. I broke the spell by saying: "I think it's silly to make such a fuss over a prostitute."

"I agree," said Wystan.

"Why were you crying then?" Chester retorted. "I saw you crying. In fact, you were actually sobbing, you faker."

"I know," Wystan said with a smile. "One is really not rational, my dear."

Then there were times that Wystan, wanting to see some of his friends in the literary world, would, at Chester's insistence, meet them at our apartment for dinner. So all kinds of lean and forlorn-looking young men in shapeless tweeds, colored shirts, and sleeveless sweaters would arrive to spend the evening, talking earnestly to Wystan in a corner near the windows while Chester cooked dinner and played records, and Mary and I washed up the dishes afterward. Later, after the war, when Chester and Wystan were far away, Mary and I would see a review in *The New York Times* of a book, the author of which had a name with a familiar ring; or we would see a photograph of a face we recognized in a tabloid. It usually turned out to be one of the forlorn young men whom Wystan had invited to dinner in the summer of 1944, now famous in the literary world. One of these men was James Agee, smarter looking and better dressed than the others.

If Wystan had intense preferences, he also had strange prejudices, and one of them was against the playwright Tennessee Williams. No one ever understood why. Tennessee, an aspiring young writer in the middle 1940s, admired Auden and hoped to meet him in New York through Bill Cannastra, to whose loft on West Twenty-first Street Williams came as a guest when he was in town. Williams's play, *The Rose Tattoo,* would be produced on Broadway with Maureen Stapleton and Eli Wallach later in that decade, but Williams had already gained success with *The Glass Menagerie,* which had starred the legendary Laurette Taylor. Bill Cannastra, who some said was the model for the hero of *Cat on a Hot Tin Roof,* had just graduated from Harvard Law School,[1] but he had done his undergraduate work at the University of Michigan at the same time Mary and I were students there. We were neighbors of Cannastra's in Chelsea and frequent visitors to his loft. It was there we met the little man with the grin and southern accent who wanted to meet Wystan. A number of times we made an effort through Chester for Tennessee and Auden to meet, but Chester always made a sour face and refused.

"But why not, Chester?" we would ask.

"He won't do." If Chester was petulant, he was also stubborn. When he said no it was no.

Mary and I were put in a difficult position, for we liked Bill and

[1] Cannastra first met Williams while in law school, when the playwright was visiting Harvard.

wanted to please his friend, and we could not very well tell him that his friend would not do. One night when Mary and I were at one of Cannastra's parties and Tennessee was sitting at the kitchen table, a glass of bourbon in hand, grinning into space, Bill asked whether we had yet made arrangements for the meeting, and whether they all could not go up to Chester's then and there.

"But Chester doesn't have a telephone. You can't very well just go up there and knock at the door," I said.

"Why not?" asked Bill, by this time warm with wine. "Come on, Tennessee, let's go."

Sensing danger, I refused to go along, but Mary, Bill, and Tennessee jubilantly hailed a taxi and made the trip to East Twenty-seventh Street. They found Chester and Wystan alone and enjoying after-dinner coffee. Wystan was polite but cool, spoke in grunts and monosyllables, and did nothing to encourage either a visit with Mary and Bill or a friendship with Tennessee. It was clear that he wanted them to leave. The uninvited guests, taking the hint, left soon after they had arrived.

Sometime later that year, Bill decided to try a second time to establish a friendship between Wystan and Tennessee. Deciding to let matters take their course, Mary did not accompany them but went home with me. An outraged Bill Cannastra gave us reports soon enough the next day. When the party arrived at Chester's apartment and knocked at the door, the following dialogue allegedly took place:

"Who is it?" asked Chester.

"Bill Cannastra with Tennessee Williams. We want to come in."

"Go away." A pause and another knock at the door.

"Please, Chester, open the door."

"No. I said no. Go away."

Wystan, who was in Chester's apartment at the time, must have assented to Chester's decision, for he did nothing to counter it and admit the guests. Later on in Italy during the early 1950s, Chester reported that Williams again attempted to meet Wystan, this time with Truman Capote. Wystan and Chester again refused to receive either Williams or Capote. According to Wystan himself, he behaved in the same way a year or so later when Somerset Maugham asked to visit him. When asked why, Wystan answered with that half smile: "He simply won't do, you know. He really won't do."

Perhaps the Auden–Tennessee Williams episode had as its cause Chester's resentment of Cannastra, whom he probably viewed as something of a rival, for Bill too had a coterie of admirers, and he was

frankly heterosexual and looked like Botticelli's Saint Sebastian. Bill
Cannastra was killed on October 12, 1950, at the age of twenty-eight
in a subway accident at the Spring Street station of the Seventh
Avenue line. When told of his death, Wystan and Chester both remarked that the most tragic thing about it was that it had caused a
three-hour tie-up in the New York subways. Wystan and Chester, who
could be generosity itself, could also be heartless.

About the spring of 1944, Mary and I began to suspect that Chester
was self-defeating. We noticed that he spoiled things for himself whenever possible. It is a wonder that he did not spoil the relationship
between himself and Wystan. He certainly tried hard enough. It was
Wystan himself who would not permit the relationship to be spoiled;
so determined was he that it succeed that he refused to be daunted by
Chester's natural perversity, denying even to himself that their relationship caused him at least as much grief as delight. Yet Wystan was
enough of the masochist to like the perverse element in Chester. Had
Chester been docile and predictable, Wystan would have loved him
less.

Chester's continuing bent to spoil things was too frequent for one
not to notice that it had become a pattern in his life. When he was in
school there was always a teacher he thought a fool and for whom he
would not work—this was why he failed to enter the Hopwood awards
and also why he did not receive his master's degree. When at the age
of eighteen he had an article published in *Harper's Bazaar,* "I Hear
America Singing," the editor asked him to write another one on
South American music. Chester refused, saying that the music down
there did not interest him. He was not asked to write for the magazine again. When in the 1950s NBC-TV wanted to produce his translation of Verdi's *La Traviata,* the station asked him to cut a scene by
ten minutes so that it would fit into a time slot. Chester refused. The
station used a translation by someone else, and Chester was not asked
again. Later, when a leading magazine sent a writer to Vienna to do
an article on Wystan in Kirchstetten, Chester insulted the writer, who
retaliated by making snide remarks about Chester in the article, describing him as "frog-like." He was never popular with the press—he
who could bewitch anyone he chose.

During the time that Chester was seeing a great deal of Mary and
me in New York, he was writing articles for the music page of *Commonweal,* a leading Roman Catholic publication. The articles were
a success and had inspired a wide response on the part of the reading
public who loved opera. Everything was going along splendidly until

Chester was assigned to do a piece on *Die Meistersinger,* Wagner's one innocent opera: no incest, no adultery. Chester, always too brilliant for his own good, suddenly decided that *Die Meistersinger* was not innocent after all, but clearly had a strain of evil running through it. Excited by the idea and warming the more to it all the way home from the opera, he wrote his review promptly and sent it off to the Jesuit father who would read and edit it. The reverend father was not pleased. Chester was not asked again to write for *Commonweal.*

During one of his Saturday night outings with Mary and me in the spring of 1944, a day after he had received a paycheck from the Bureau of Censorship, he picked up a sailor in a bar. The sailor, named Bernie,[1] was a lean, blond macho type of about twenty with pale round blue eyes and long white lashes. Mary and I called him the Caterpillar. He went home with Chester that Saturday night. When Chester awoke on Sunday morning, the Caterpillar was gone, and so was Chester's weekly paycheck. Chester rushed crosstown to wake Mary and me, and, mad with anger and outrage, told us of his plight. We lent him enough money to tide him over the next week, hoping that Bernie was gone for good.

Bernie was gone for a week. The next weekend, the Caterpillar appeared again on payday at Chester's favorite haunt on MacDougal Street—as Mary and I looked darkly on—and again went home with Chester. Stunned by Chester's willingness to be victimized again, we were not surprised to learn that Bernie had once more taken off with Chester's paycheck. Mary convinced Chester to report his check stolen and to apply for a duplicate from the bureau. Bernie had twice forged Chester's name, it was discovered, and had twice cashed the paycheck. Deciding to find the Caterpillar and call the police, Chester agreed to prefer charges. The next weekend, Chester, Mary and I discovered the Caterpillar in another bar. However, instead of reporting him, Chester again took him home. When Chester awoke the next morning, his typewriter was gone as well as his paycheck.

Bernie would eventually go off to sea, be killed, or simply disappear, but he would be replaced by another Bernie, just as unprincipled as the last. Chester's taste had deteriorated from the year in which he had met and fallen in love with the English sailor, and his taste was to remain with the various Bernies, one much like the next, with whom he never ceased to be involved for the remainder of his life. He was continually robbed; he was often beaten. Yet as the years

[1] Not his real name.

went by he continued to return to the same bars where the Bernies were to be found, if not in New York, then in Europe.

To Mary and me, despite Chester's mysterious Saturday night forays and self-destructive tendencies (we did not know the details of his sex life), he was still the "brilliant, beautiful boy." He may have camped about occasionally and behaved with effeteness in front of his homosexual friends from Ann Arbor or New York, friends who came in now and then when on leave from the armed forces, but most of the time he was like any other boy of twenty-two or -three, full of fun and nice to be with, except that he never made passes. Of course, the very fact that he never made passes actually added to his charm. Girls in those days were not readily available, for they were expected to retain their virginity until marriage. Premarital sex was simply not accepted. Thus, boys who constantly made passes were not welcome, and it was a relief to find someone who, as we put it, appreciated you for your mind. In fact, some said that Mary, never at a loss for boyfriends, was attracted to Chester because she could not have him.

Chester was fond of both of us, but if he had had to choose between us, he would certainly have chosen Mary. And if Mary Valentine fell in love with Chester, and if she reasoned that he really was not homosexual after all, her reasoning was not so mad as Chester's Ann Arbor friends and Wystan chose to believe. Chester spent almost all his waking hours with Mary for at least two years and shared with her all his enthusiasms, his ideas, and his confidences. Further, he was physically attractive the way a man is attractive to a woman, and there was about him when he was in our company no sign of the effeminate. While he could not be called macho, he was certainly not frail. His shoulders were broad, his hands and feet were large, and he was, though slender, of a good size and height. He was also handsome, bearing a resemblance to the actor Robert Taylor, a movie hero of the day.

Of all the candidates for a prince charming to fulfill the dreams of a girl from a Michigan farm, Chester Kallman seemed the least likely, at least in the eyes of the world, including those of his friends and of Wystan. Yet to Mary that is exactly what he was. He was an intellectual in a world of fools. He was an artist and a poet in a world of dullards. He was gentle; he was funny; he was compassionate; he was sophisticated; he was attractive. He was everything that she had dreamed about on her grandmother's front porch. There was only one thing wrong. The thing that was wrong was not that he did not make passes. The thing that was really wrong was that he never seemed to want to. And there it was.

Yet, though actions speak loud, love has other, more subtle voices. The affair was Jamesian (Mary was reading James at the time), dependent for its satisfactions upon the nuances of words, of glances, of obscure references, of feelings too refined, perhaps—some would say too nonexistent—to be put into words. For example, believing Mary to resemble Zinka Milanov, the opera singer, whom Chester much admired, he would write postcards to both of us from Fire Island with the postscript, "I miss Zinka." Or he would spend the exorbitant amount of a week's salary on an album of the complete *Don Giovanni* for Mary's Christmas present. For her twentieth birthday on December 4, 1943, Chester created a chicken dish especially for the occasion, which he named *Poulet Vingt Ans* and served ceremoniously by candlelight in a darkened room to the recorded music—always music— of *Manon,* the young Bidù Sayão singing rapturously, *"Profitons bien de la jeunesse . . . nous n'avons pas toujours vingt ans."* Perhaps the words that spoke most clearly to Mary were Chester's when he said, "When I have a son . . ." He continued to tell Mary that her role in life should be that of a wife to a great man and a mother of children, and that she should indeed be married. One summer afternoon in 1945 when Mary and I were sitting in Chester's living room with Chester and David Protetch, our Ann Arbor friend just back from the navy and about to go off to medical school, David said: "I wonder which one of us will marry which one of those two girls when all this is over." If I took all this as just talk, Mary did not.

Wrote Mary in 1981:

> We were together seven days a week, morning, noon, and night except for the times when W. H. Auden came to town. I resented Auden, because I believed that Wystan wanted Chester to be dependent upon him financially, socially, and artistically. . . . I interpreted Chester's constant presence in my life to mean that he must care about me as I did about him. . . . There was a feeling of complete ease and understanding between us. Chester's feminine gestures and camping took place only when there were other homosexuals present. . . . I found it impossible to visualize Chester, who dominated every gathering and who was so forceful, as a passive homosexual.[1]

During all this time Mary had an ally. Dr. Kallman, who was waiting for Chester's transformation to heterosexuality at twenty-seven,

[1] Letter to the author from Mary Valentine, June 29, 1981.

was casting covetous eyes upon us as possible agents of his son's delivery. It was hard to convince Eddie Kallman, since he pretended
otherwise, that all those Friday nights spent on West Twenty-fourth
Street were purely platonic. Eddie, who had a sharp eye, also noticed
that it was Mary, not I, who spent the most time with Chester; and
it was Mary, not I, who looked at Chester with love in her eyes. Eddie
readily recognized the symptoms.

One spring evening in 1945, when Mary and I were having a drink
in La Maison Blanche on West Twenty-third Street, we came to a
decision. I, who suspected the Greeks were right when they said that
love was a madness, should have been more circumspect. However,
most of my days were spent teaching school in Hell's Kitchen when
Mary and Chester were decoding Nazi messages at Censorship and
cozily cooking lunch at 409 West Twenty-fourth Street, so I naturally
assumed that Mary must know firsthand things that I could know only
second. In the rashness of youth and in the interest of friendship,
therefore, I suggested a course of action to shock the unwary Chester
out of his lethargy. "Why don't you tell him that you love him?"

The next day, when I was away teaching school on West Thirty-
fifth Street, Mary, in the dusty old government building on West
Twenty-fifth, in an empty office where workers took coffee breaks, was
telling Chester that she loved him. Hoping for jubilant news when I
returned from school that afternoon, I bounded up the stairs of 409,
burst through the door, and found Mary sitting by the window, her
large soft brown eyes red-rimmed with weeping.

"Whatever happened?"

"It didn't turn out the way we thought."

"Oh, dear. Did you tell him?"

"Yes."

"Well, what did he say?" Silence. "What did he say, Mary?"

"He turned pale. He said something about not meaning to encourage me and not wanting to hurt me, and he said he was sorry. Then
he walked out of the room. He stayed out for about five or ten minutes. Then he came back. And he acted as if nothing had happened.
He doesn't love me."[1]

---

[1] A married woman among Chester's many friends insisted years later that
Chester actually did have sexual affairs with women, that he was without doubt
capable, but that he had a sharp sense of honor and would not sleep with girlfriends who might take him too seriously. "He slept with women," she said, "but
only with women who did not think anything would come of it. And he never,
never told. There were at least ten women I knew who were in love with him."

Mary's declaration did not immediately alter Chester's association with us. He still came over every day and we still went together to the opera and on other outings. We still cooked meals together. But what had been a lighthearted friendship gradually soured into the embarrassments and tensions of unrequited love. The days that Chester used to call "my Mary and Dorothy period" were over by the Christmas of 1946, never to return; but the denouement began that afternoon in the dusty office building on Twenty-fifth Street.

Most of Chester's friends who knew of his sexual habits would have found such a revelation incredible. While it was true that women fell in love with him, it seems imaginative and naive to believe that he returned that love or involved himself in any overt act. Yet Chester's nature was always somewhat more of a mystery than that of the average person. Its many facets still remain unknown.

Chester Kallman at the age of twelve, with his father and brother, Matt, in Prospect Park, Brooklyn, New York, 1933.

Christopher Isherwood and Auden leaving for China, January 1938.

"Portrait of Chester Kallman with Alonzo," painted by the author in 1946. The sand and rocks of Jones Beach were later painted over a portrait of Giuseppe Verdi, originally painted, at Kallman's request, behind the chair at right. Alonzo was Chester's cat.

Labor Day weekend, 1939, at Dr. Edward Kallman's summer house in Haskell, New Jersey. This is the first photograph ever taken of Auden and Kallman together. TOP ROW, LEFT TO RIGHT: Dr. Kallman, Auden, two unidentified friends. BOTTOM ROW: Frances Kydd is hidden behind the woman seated third from the left. The others are unidentified. Kallman is kneeling at the end of the row.

Auden, 1941. Irving Weiss, then a student, took this snapshot of Auden entering the Michigan Union on the day the poet arrived for his year's teaching assignment at the University of Michigan, Ann Arbor.

The Christmas letter of 1941, written by Auden to Kallman, was discovered by the author on the floor of Dr. Kallman's laboratory in 1946.

> Dearest Chester   Christmas 1941
>
> Because it is in you, a Jew, that I, a gentile, inheriting an O-so-genteel anti-semitism, have found my happiness:
>
>   As this morning I think of Bethlehem, I think of you.
>
> Because it is you, from Brooklyn, who have taught me, from Oxford, how the most liberal young man can assume that his money and his education ought to be able to buy love;
>
>   As this morning, I think of the inn stable, I think of you.

*David Protetch (**FAR LEFT**) and Chester Kallman in Yorkville, New York City, with Mary Valentine and the author (in black Spanish headdress).*

Kallman, Auden, and Rhoda Jaffe on Fire Island in 1946.

Auden and Kallman in Venice, approximately 1950.

Snapshot of Chester Kallman and the author, taken by Dr. Kallman on West 57th Street, New York City, in 1952.

Auden and Kallman in New York, approximately 1950.

The cast, the composer, and the librettists taking a final bow after a performance of THE RAKE'S PROGRESS. *Stravinsky, fourth from the right, stands next to Auden. Kallman is at the end, right.*

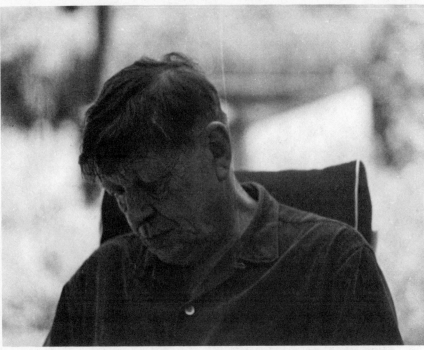

*Auden on the terrace of his home in Kirchstetten, Austria. Taken by
Peter Komadina in 1963.*

*Chester Kallman on the terrace of Auden's home in Kirchstetten, Austria.
Taken by Peter Komadina in 1963.*

Yannis Boras and Kallman, approximately 1968.

W. H.
AUDEN

Auden's grave in Kirchstetten, Austria.

CHAPTER 9

Summer Dwellings

BY AUGUST 1945, Wystan, in major's uniform and dog tags,[1] had returned from Germany, where he had held a position from April to August as a civilian research chief in the Morale Division of the U.S. Strategic Bombing Survey. After a month or so he sublet a four-room apartment from friends in a solid building on West Fifty-seventh Street next to a gray stone Congregational church. His friends found droll the image of the wild Wystan, though by now slightly subdued in his soldier's uniform, living in that middle-class apartment with its cozy chintz curtains and cozy chintz-covered overstuffed furniture. But it had a piano, and Wystan would bang out his hymns for all to hear and give soirées for his friends, all sorts of people coming over from England, enjoying some frivolity after the

[1] I had Auden's dog tags and Saint Christopher medal until 1975. The dog tags are now in the Humanities Research Center, the University of Texas, Austin, Texas. The silver Saint Christopher is now owned by Mr. and Mrs. John Peter Valentine of Georgetown, California.

war. Wystan was playing at being a middle-class householder. He liked the concept of himself in an apartment with a bedroom and real bedding regularly laundered. It was the only apartment he ever had that did not look like a carpenter's shop, and he announced loudly that a home "ought to be enveloping like a womb."

Auden was attracted to houses and enjoyed the domestic life. The summer of 1945 marked the beginning of his pursuit of a house of his own. It was as if the dust and rubble of war-torn Germany had intensified his love for structures and dwellings and increased his desire to own a home. His first one was a small summer house, more accurately described as a shack, in Cherry Grove on Fire Island, that long strip of sandy beach just off the southern coast of Long Island.

In the 1940s Cherry Grove was a mecca, as it is today, for the homosexual crowd, which spent vacations and weekends there during the summer. It was in those days quite primitive, consisting of a moderately sized frame hotel with a very active bar, a general store and post office, and row upon row of wooden shacks set on stakes beside wooden boardwalks built a foot or so above the sand. The houses were for summer use only, shingled and gabled but without insulation. Each had a kitchen, a combination living room–dining room, and two bedrooms.

The charm of the island was its fine pale sand, its sea air, and its easy life style. The charm of Cherry Grove for Wystan and Chester was its gay bar and the uninhibited homosexual ambiance. Wystan had spent a few days in the hotel during July 1944. During 1945, his friends from England, James and Tania Stern, wanted to buy one of the shacks that happened to be for sale for five hundred dollars. In September Wystan sent them the money to pay for the little house, which he planned to share, alternating his visits with theirs. In 1946 he began spending time there, and in 1947 he stayed for the entire summer. The house was named Bective Poplars, after James Stern's home, Bective Manor, in County Meath, Ireland, and Wystan's grandmother's house, the Poplars, near Repton in England.

In Cherry Grove the homosexual crowd was free to act out its fantasies without interference, and almost every member of the Auden–Kallman circle of the forties, homosexual or not, found himself in Cherry Grove at one time or another. On weekends everyone dressed up as he pleased. Often young men appeared in the latest Paris creations designed for ladies on the beach—pink silk beach pajamas and wide brimmed sun hats. There even appeared a bikini from time to time, most daring in those days. The event of the season was at least one masquerade given in July. In 1947 Wystan went as Ronald Firbank's Cardinal Pirelli, with Chester and Ann Arbor friend Billy Vinson as his acolytes.

Mary and I had less festive memories of Cherry Grove. One Friday afternoon in 1946 Chester appeared at 409 West Twenty-fourth Street and insisted that we accompany him to Cherry Grove for the weekend. "Please," he said when we first refused, "you simply must come. I'll never forgive you if you don't." Not one for overnight visits, I begged to be excused, saying that I was working on a picture. Even Mary Valentine, who usually wanted to be with Chester come what might, must have had a premonition, for she, too, was hesitant about accepting the invitation. "Does Wystan know you invited us?" she asked.

"Of course," Chester assured us. "He wants you to come. In fact, he is expecting you."

We still refused, but there was no way of getting out of it with grace. So in one hour Chester, Mary and I, carrying bags with beach clothes and sandwiches, were making our way to the old Pennsylvania Station in the heat of July. The journey was endless. First we took the slow train along Long Island's South Shore to Sayville. There we waited for a ferry, which consisted of a crowded motorboat, and, after another eternity and a hazardous voyage, we landed at the dock in Cherry Grove.

It was a different world from the one we had left—one of sand and sea, a package store, a post office, a small hotel, and then the rickety gabled shacks, one just like the next, set on stakes like African huts above the sand. We remarked that Wystan had probably paid too much for his house. When Mary and I arrived with Chester at Bective Poplars, a few shacks down the boardwalk from the package store and post office, there was no evidence that Wystan had been expecting us. Neither was there any evidence that he had been looking forward to our visit. In fact, by the expression on his face, an expression he made no effort to hide, it was plain to anyone but Chester that he was clearly furious, for he obviously had expected to have Chester alone for the weekend. Wystan was rude and cold. From the time we arrived until the time we left, he retreated into one of his great silences, answering in grunts to anything that was said. Mary and I both wanted to take the next ferry back to town, but there was no ferry until Sunday morning. To our horror, we were to be stranded for the weekend with Wystan in Cherry Grove. We spent the next two days, therefore, on the beach, going into the shack only at night to sleep in the extra bedroom or to eat without appetite the food Chester prepared.

"Chester, why did you bring us out here?" I asked, with restrained fury. "How could you put us in this position? You know very well that we are not welcome and that we didn't want to come in the first place."

"Nonsense," responded Chester. "It's just your imagination. Wystan is very fond of you. He just gets in moods." The usual answer.

"Don't, Chester. I'm not asking for reassurance. I don't want reassurance. I just want you to face facts and never do this again."

"Don't be paranoid," said Chester.

When Sunday morning came and it was time for us to take the first possible ferry back to Sayville, Wystan suddenly changed. He became friendly, almost sunny, and even loquacious. He even offered to take us to the hotel for breakfast. We refused, of course. Wystan carried our bags down the boardwalk to the package store where the little motorboat was waiting, now blessedly empty, to take us to Sayville and deliverance. Chester had decided to remain on Cherry Grove for the coming week, so Wystan and Chester waved goodbye happily from the shore.

"Why did Chester do this?" Mary and I later asked Dr. Kallman, the authority on all worldly things.

"Chester is always looking for an excuse not to be alone with Wystan. At the same time, he was getting even with him for inviting Rhoda out there."

From time to time Auden would have an affair with a woman. When in Kitzbühel with his father in 1925, he met Hedwig Petzold, some years his senior, with whom he later had a sexual experience.[1] He must have had as well some experiences with the mysterious Sheilah Richardson, to whom he became engaged the year he left Oxford. According to Keith Callaghan, one of Wystan's lovers during the forties, "Wystan did not fall in love with women; he just went to bed with them. He used sex with women as one of his cures. When he wanted to cure them, he would just pop them into bed."[2] According to Keith, Wystan had an affair during the early forties with an heiress who often went to his birthday celebrations in New York and to his bon voyage parties on shipboard long after the affair had ended.

[1] Carpenter, *Auden: A Biography*, p. 69.
[2] The author's conversation with Keith Callaghan, March 3, 1982.

In 1945 Auden was in the midst of such an affair. His relations with Chester had not improved, and perhaps he believed he could find in a woman the romantic fidelity he had sought in Chester. Someone said that he believed Chester to be having an affair with Mary Valentine and that Wystan was retaliating. At any rate, at the end of the summer of 1945 we heard that he had invited one of Chester's other girlfriends up to his rooms at 421 West Fifty-seventh Street on one pretext or another, but the girl never appeared.

A few weeks later he invited to Fifty-seventh Street Rhoda Jaffe, who, with her husband, Milton Klonsky, had been a student at Brooklyn College when Chester was there.[1] Wystan's excuse this time was that he wanted her to do some typing for him. Since he himself did not like to type, he preferred to hire someone to type his manuscripts. Apparently he was a fast worker, for, according to Chester, that very afternoon Wystan suggested to Rhoda they have an affair. It was presented just like that: "I think we ought to have an affair." She said yes, the affair was directly consummated, and Rhoda finished the typing at another time.

Fifteen years earlier Wystan had said that he was puzzled at what the attraction of women was; that it was for him "like watching a game of cricket for the first time."[2] Apparently his attitude had changed by 1945.

Rhoda Jaffe was earthy. She was a dark blonde of average height, about five feet three or four. She had an interesting face of Slavic cast that photographed well, with high cheekbones, slanting hazel eyes, flaring nostrils, and a red, generous mouth. She was more an earth mother than a fashion model, but whatever it was she had—and it was a kind of boyish charm—it must have appealed to writers, because she was the girlfriend first of her writer husband; then of a minor American poet of the New York scene; then of Auden; then of an English novelist. Eddie used to say, "Rhoda likes poets better than poetry." She had about her a candor, an innocence, and a generosity of spirit. Her consuming interest was psychology.

Only two topics of conversation absorbed Rhoda: psychology in general and her own psychological condition in particular. One learned very early that Rhoda and her sister had been in an orphanage; that they resented their father for having put them there after

---

[1] Rhoda Jaffe was living alone at 25 Grove Street during the summer of 1945 and during her affair with Auden.

[2] Carpenter, *Auden: A Biography*, p. 105.

their mother's death; and that Rhoda had been in psychotherapy ever since she could afford to employ a psychiatrist. In fact, she had worked as a waitress after she finished Brooklyn College in order to pay her analyst. The method of her therapy was Freudian, and Rhoda would analyze all her friends, acquaintances, employers, and lovers when she was not analyzing herself. She knew and used all the jargon of the profession, then regarded by many as the panacea for the ills of Western civilization. Wystan must suddenly have felt himself back in Berlin with Layard, and he took delight in mulling over with Rhoda all her dreams, all his theories about cures, and all the facets of the psyche of Chester Kallman.

Rhoda was, of course, still married to Milton Klonsky, but they had been on the verge of divorce for some time, and she was living in a separate apartment on Grove Street in the Village with a number of Siamese cats, all of which delighted Wystan, a cat lover. Thursday was the night on Wystan's tight time schedule to pay court to Rhoda, so once a week he either presented himself at 25 Grove Street or invited Rhoda to West Fifty-seventh, or, later, to 7 Cornelia. He treated her with consideration, respect, and generosity. He took her out to dinner, sometimes to the opera, invited her to his shack on Fire Island, and bought her a black silk crepe dress to wear in the evening after six. He also wrote her a number of letters, one of which included a photograph of himself, given as a Christmas present. Things must have gone reasonably well for some time, because Rhoda told Eddie Kallman, whose dental patient she was, that Wystan was "a real man in bed." She spent a great deal of energy trying to convince not only Wystan but also Chester that Wystan was really not homosexual, and she attempted to point out by profuse examples, all explained in the terms of Sigmund Freud, that she had made the difference in his life.

Chester, in the meantime, was regaling his friends with every detail of the affair that Wystan unwisely confided to him and was using it not only as a topic of general conversation but also as a new way to amuse his friends and test his histrionic skills. After he had been with Wystan and Rhoda on West Fifty-seventh Street, at the opera, in a restaurant, or on Fire Island, he would hasten to Twenty-fourth Street and amuse Mary and me as well as our guest, Gale Adams Hanlan, an old school chum from Ann Arbor, also a friend of Chester, who was staying with us at the time. When Gale was attending the Metropolitan Opera she saw Wystan and Rhoda during intermission. "He stopped," said Gale, "to say hello to me, and I was surprised to

see him with a woman, for he had been such a hot homosexual in Ann
Arbor. The girl was attractive and nicely dressed in a black suit and
white blouse. I learned later it was Rhoda Jaffe from Chester, who
used to imitate them together and make riotous fun of them to everybody."[1] Chester not only gave imitations of the couple together, but
he also made reports of the conversations that took place. According
to him they both acted like high school freshmen out on their first
date. "Wystan," he said, "is just too silly. He giggles at her and she
at him. My dear, it's just too much."

Mary and I, knowing Wystan in his more dour and stormy aspect,
and remembering him as a forthright homosexual from Ann Arbor
days, naturally found Chester's accounts highly amusing, though nothing he said could equal our amazement when he had first told us
about the affair. Fresh from the first evening with Wystan and Rhoda
together in the apartment next to the Congregational church, Chester
had run breathless up the three flights of stairs above the Fireside Inn
on Twenty-fourth Street with:

"You'll never guess what happened."

"What, Chester?"

"Wystan is having an affair, but guess with whom."

"Who is it?"

"Guess."

"I can't. Who?"

"A woman!"

"A woman? No, Chester, no. We're dying to know. Who?"

"It's Rhoda Jaffe."

"Impossible!"

And so it went.

Some said that Chester was jealous, that he wanted to be the only
one in Wystan's as in everyone else's life, and that he was especially
put out by Wystan's choice of a woman, any woman. They were right,
of course, as far as it went. But Chester, like his father, also had a
sharp sense of the comic and was enjoying himself. Perhaps he guessed
that Wystan and Rhoda were spending hours psychoanalyzing him.

Mary, Gale, and I also spent hours trying to understand the relationship between this strange couple. Although Rhoda had never
been a close friend, we knew her well enough. After all, she and
Milton had been the first people besides Chester and his father whom

---

[1] The author's conversation with Gale Adams Hanlan, April 22, 1982.

we had met in New York, and it was partly because of Milton that we had decided to remain in the city. However, from the beginning both Mary and I were put off by Rhoda's continual psychologizing and what seemed to us to be her complete lack of a sense of humor. Nobody living had ever made her laugh, not even Chester and his father. If you said anything fanciful, she would look at you suspiciously and let you know that she knew you were not telling the literal truth or try to read into your remarks some deep Freudian motive. Remembering that Wystan had always said that the people whom he loved always made him laugh and always had a sense of humor, Mary and I were sure that he did not love Rhoda. But then we remembered something else Wystan had said: "Women do not have a sense of humor." So perhaps he was content to accept her without a sense of humor as long as he had decided to accept her at all. At any rate, the affair went on for some months.

One autumn day in 1946[1] Rhoda visited Mary and me on Twenty-fourth Street and confided to us that "Wystan wants my hair to be more blond. Now that the summer is over, it will get dark again. Can you bleach my hair?"

The sensible thing would have been to send her to a beauty parlor, but girls in those post-Depression days did not think of spending money on such things. I ran down to the London Terrace drugstore around the corner and bought some ammonia and peroxide, while Mary reassured Rhoda, with unassailable reasonableness, that all would be well as long as she applied weekly treatments of castor oil.

The bleach job was most satisfactory, and Wystan was delighted with Rhoda's hair, "the lighter the better." Things went well for some time after that, apparently, for we heard no more until early winter. Suddenly, one Tuesday afternoon in late November, Rhoda arrived at 409 West Twenty-fourth Street, ostensibly to show us the new black silk crepe dress Wystan had bought her the day before. However, when she removed the red and green babushka we could see that her hair, now dry and almost white, had broken off at the ends, for it was standing out from her head like spikes.

"Rhoda, your hair has turned to straw!" we screamed, horrified.

"It's not straw," said Rhoda sullenly. "It's my hair."

"Didn't you do the oil treatments?"

"All that messy castor oil. Ick."

---

[1] Auden was in New York at this time, teaching at the New School for Social Research.

"You have to suffer to be beautiful. Well, it's too late now for regrets," I said philosophically.

"Can't you two do something? You got me into this."

"Oh, dear. I knew it. Well, the only thing to do is to put on a rinse the color of your real hair," said Mary with irrefutable midwestern logic. "Nobody will see the darker roots showing through, and your hair can just grow out by itself the way it always was."

"It has to be done before Thursday," said Rhoda. "That's the day I see Wystan."

"We know. Well, it will be done now," said Mary, and I rushed down to buy Numero Huit, an ash-blond vegetable rinse, from the London Terrace drugstore while Mary continued to reassure Rhoda.

High of hope, we applied the ash-blond rinse to Rhoda's hair. However, Mary's irrefutable midwestern logic had not taken into account some basic truths of elementary chemistry. There was a subtle green in the ash-blond rinse that took to the bleached strands of Rhoda's hair like water to a sponge. When the operation was complete, Rhoda's hair was neither blond nor ash blond; it was green. An olive green. Rhoda was hysterical. We were in a panic. We busily set about washing Rhoda's hair, hoping to modify the shade to some semblance of real hair color. But the green remained.

Wystan was furious when he saw Rhoda's hair and sent her to a beauty parlor. The next time we saw Rhoda she had the Hamlet haircomb fortunately popular at the time; the green was gone, but Rhoda was a darker blond. The Hamlet haircomb, cut close to the head as if a soup bowl had been used as a guide, was to be her coiffure until Wystan left for Europe with Chester in the spring of 1948. Mary and I did not see much of Rhoda after the day of the ash-blond rinse. Wystan always believed we had dyed Rhoda's hair green on purpose, and he was convinced Chester had a hand in it. "Why couldn't you keep it blond? You did it before," he kept saying, and no amount of explanation would satisfy him.

If at the age of thirty-eight Wystan still believed he could lead a happy heterosexual, or at least bisexual, existence, by the time he was forty he knew better. His letters to Rhoda in the spring of 1946, when he was teaching at Bennington College, had been gallant, cordial, and even affectionate, but they were forced. He still saw her when he returned to New York later that year, but by late 1947 the affair had faded. Sometime in 1947 or 1948 he introduced her to an English novelist who was in New York for the publication of his book, and Rhoda began dating him. Later Wystan was to say in a letter, "I tried to have an affair with a woman, but it was a great mistake. It was a sin. . . . It did not affect me at all. I only felt I was cheating."[1]

Rhoda took it all very well. She left Grove Street and moved uptown to live in a large apartment with some girlfriends and began taking courses at Columbia toward a graduate degree in sociology. She even left Wystan one of her Siamese cats, whom he named after an operatic character, Bastien.[2] She did not show resentment toward Wystan, and she did not hate Chester, though it was Chester, not Rhoda, whom Wystan would take to Europe. Now and then she would visit Wystan for lunch at St. Mark's Place, where he and Chester moved in 1953. They would sit and talk like old friends, and Wystan would prepare a soggy omelet in Chester's kitchen.

Much has been made of Wystan's affair with Rhoda, although it lasted little over a year. Perhaps her importance to his biographers lies in the fact that she is viewed as the archetype for Rosetta in *The Age of Anxiety*, one of Auden's most famous poems. If so, few of the people who knew her could see Rhoda in Rosetta. Perhaps Wystan the poet created Rhoda Jaffe as he created Rosetta.

Perhaps the poem that Wystan included in a letter to her in June 1947 expresses best of all the relationship between the poet and Rhoda Jaffe. He needed her for a time, if for no other reason than as a temporary resting place from Chester Kallman.

> *On and on and on*
> *The forthright catadoup*
> *Shouts at the stone-deaf stone;*
> *Over and over again,*
> *Singly or as a group,*
> *Weak diplomatic men*
> *With a small defiant light*
> *Salute the incumbent night.*
>
> *With or without a mind,*
> *Chafant or outwardly calm,*
> *Each thing has an axe to grind*
> *And exclaims its matter-of-fact;*

---

[1] Carpenter, *Auden: A Biography*, p. 349.

[2] Wystan gave Bastien to me in 1948 before he left for Ischia. "Only you and I could stand his yowl," Wystan remarked as he handed me Doris Bryant's book on the care of cats, *Pet Cats*, along with the cat himself.

The child with careful charm
Or a sudden opprobrious act,
The tiger, the griping fern,
Extort the world's concern.

All, all, have rights to declare,
Not one is man enough
To be, simply, publicly, there
With no private emphasis;
So my embodied love
Which, like most feeling, is
Half humbug and half true,
Asks neighborhood of you.[1]

During the time Wystan was having his romance with Rhoda on Thursday nights, he was having business dealings with Eddie and Eddie's lawyer, Meyer Halpern, about a house.

In the summer of 1945 Eddie Kallman fell in love with a house. He was visiting friends in Sea Cliff, Long Island, when he saw facing the cove a one-hundred-year-old house surrounded by hollyhocks—lavender, white, pink, fuchsia—and a picket fence. It had a hand-painted marine mural on the walls of the dining room and a skylight and an old spinning wheel in the studio upstairs. Eddie wanted the house. The only trouble was that he seldom had $7,000 together at one time, and the house cost $7,500. The bank had refused to give him a mortgage, not having faith in the house, even though it expressed polite faith in Eddie. Eddie, however, gave the owners a down payment of $1,000 and moved in with his girlfriend, Frances, on weekends, keeping the flat in New York for working days. The owners of the house permitted him to live there free for a year before asking for their money. He painted to his heart's content in the studio and sunned himself in the yard near the picket fence, the hollyhocks, and the Long Island Sound. The only problem now was where to get $6,500.

Wystan, whose joys and sorrows in life often began with Eddie, was invited with Chester to spend a number of Saturdays or Sundays among the hollyhocks near the sound, to drink a number of Eddie's dry martinis, and to eat his Russian caviar and his pickled brains, not to mention the gourmet meal that came later. All had a jolly time, and even Frances, who did not get along with Chester, was on her best behavior

---

[1] Auden, "Ten Songs," in *Collected Poems,* p. 215.

with him. The longer Wystan looked at the picket fence and the waters beyond from the windows in the cozy dining room, the more he liked the idea that was forming in his mind: This house would be perfect for Chester. Whereupon he decided to lend Eddie the $6,500 he needed, plus charge him interest at the going rate, and asked him to tell Meyer Halpern to draw up the papers.

Wystan, of course, had conditions. Eddie was now, in 1946, fifty-four, and Wystan had no wish to let Frances get the house. The condition of the mortgage that Wystan agreed to hold was that the house be put in both Eddie's name and Chester's, in joint tenancy. Meyer Halpern, who was also enjoying the martinis, the calf's-foot jelly, and the caviar that Sunday with his secretary, the beautiful Marie Joyce with the Bette Davis eyes, was to draw up the papers on Monday. There was a general celebration. Chester was happy that eventually he would have his own house, and Wystan felt a warm glow of achievement. Eddie and Frances would have their house for weekends.

When the time came for signing the papers for the house, Wystan, Chester, and Meyer were again invited to sit among the hollyhocks by the cove and sip martinis. Meyer, an old friend of the family, who had not built up his multimillion-dollar law practice without skill, had only Eddie's interest at heart, for he was being paid nothing for his labors except perhaps gourmet dinners and Eddie's eternal gratitude. Meyer thus covertly inserted a clause that would have given Eddie the house *sans* Chester as soon as the mortgage was paid. ("After all, Eddie, you're paying for it.")

Wystan and Chester, sitting among the hollyhocks, read the entire agreement with all its divagations, its legal wherefores and whithers. This care paid off, since they discovered the clause that Meyer had slipped in and thought would go unnoticed. Wystan refused to sign the mortgage agreement until it was changed to his liking. Back in New York, Meyer put things right, and Wystan signed. Every month Wystan received Eddie's check for interest and amortization of the mortgage on the house, now safely in the names of Chester and his father. Frances was not to inherit one hollyhock.

Life, however, was never simple for the Kallmans. There was a complication Chester and Wystan became aware of not long after Wystan agreed to take the mortgage: The house on the edge of the sound was no paradise. With the approach of autumn the hollyhocks withered, and the sailboats disappeared as did the sun, leaving the inlet gray and bleak under the September clouds that threatened rain. Rain meant floods, and the pump system in the basement of the little house was not adequate to cope with the forces of nature. In fact, sometimes it refused to work at all. Although Eddie had lived there for a year, he had failed to see the seriousness of this and other problems.

The house that began with high hopes ended in disaster. It was an expense. After one hundred years, a number of repairs had to be made, and the workmen in the village found a gold mine in the New York dentist who thought pears grew on bushes.

Eddie finally sold the house to a shrewd entrepreneur for a thousand dollars less than he paid for it, and Wystan put the money away for Chester. But Chester never forgave his father for selling the house at the edge of the sound, the house with the hollyhocks and the spinning wheel and the white picket fence. When Chester returned from Europe from time to time during the fifties, not a week went by in which he, encouraged by Wystan, did not look resentfully at his father and say, "You cheated me out of my house."

Wystan's real estate ventures were destined to become unprofitable or to end in disaster. At least he recovered his money from Eddie's mortgage. "In fact," said Wystan to Eddie at the final payment, "I think you paid me fifty dollars too much." Bective Poplars in Cherry Grove was another matter. When, in 1948, Wystan was to trade the pale sands of Cherry Grove for the colorful landscape of Ischia, off the coast of Italy, either he was not paying careful attention to the letters from the tax offices that governed Fire Island, or his agent, who was expected to handle such matters, was not notifying him about them. Apparently Wystan owed a tidy sum in real estate taxes on the little shack near the sea. When the county finally threatened to sell the house for taxes, the agent jumped in with the highest bid, a sum considerably less than Wystan had originally paid for the property. Suddenly Wystan received notice that the auction had been held, the sale made, and his taxes paid. It was rumored abroad that now Wystan's agent had Bective Poplars for his own summer dwelling.

CHAPTER 10

Time to Say Goodbye

FOR THE AUDEN–KALLMAN circle, 1948 was the year when one lost one's youth. Everything changed or came to an end. Mary Valentine, now married to a handsome Bulgarian also named Valentine, was to give birth to a son, John, in August 1948. Frances and Eddie were to part that year for good, not without complications. David Protetch, our old friend from Ann Arbor, later Auden's physician, was to finish medical school and begin his internship in Kings County Hospital in Brooklyn. Billy Vinson, another Ann Arbor friend, was to end his career in the navy. I was to fall in love with Chester's father and marry him, somewhat illegally, in September 1948, since Syd contested Eddie's Mexican divorce, for which Wystan had paid.[1] Wystan had ended his affair with Rhoda, and it was in 1948 that he gave up his struggle to possess Chester. He was to re-

---

[1] I was not able to marry Eddie legally, according to the state of New York and the Catholic church, until January 30, 1975, after the death of Syd.

sign himself to his fate, which was to accept Chester on Chester's terms.

In January of 1947 Chester had reached the age of twenty-six—almost the year when his father expected him to abandon his homosexuality and his wild life, find a nice girl, and settle down. However, by this time Eddie knew that his son would not change. Eddie's last hope had been Mary Valentine, but that hope had been lost even before her marriage. He urged Chester to find at least a job, if not a career, so that he would not depend on Wystan for support. Chester's job at the Bureau of Censorship had ended with the end of World War II.

When Chester was in Brooklyn College, Wystan had promised him that he would support him until he was thirty if Chester promised not to publish until that time.[1] He thought early publication had been a mistake in his own case. "Nothing fails like success," Wystan used to say. By 1947, though the age of thirty was still a few years away, Chester had neither prospects for a job nor the inclination to find one. However, one of his friends, William McGuire, was working at the United Nations when it was still at Lake Success, and suggested that Chester apply for a vacancy he knew of there. Chester was finally given a job in the Public Opinion Survey section of the Department of Public Information, where he read and clipped news stories about the United Nations.

"I recall," said McGuire, "that Chester was extremely well liked by most of his colleagues . . . nearly all of them women. They often lunched together, and the girls invited Chester to their parties."[2] In return, Chester invited some of them to his parties on Twenty-seventh Street. They "must have been titillated, if not shocked," said McGuire, "by the evening's events," for there was a grand fight at one of them. "I recall that John Britton [an elderly coworker who came with his wife] comforted, in fatherly fashion, one of the girls who was weeping during the fight . . . and I believe this touching scene occurred in the bathroom, and that a U.N. security guard had passed out in the bathtub. Wystan, who was present, looked on philosophically."

Chester had jolly times at the U.N., as he had in the Bureau of Censorship. He enjoyed being with people, even his bosses, of whom he made riotous fun to McGuire. Besides, the U.N. had one advantage

[1] The author's conversation with Walter James Miller and Samuel Exler, Chester's classmates at Brooklyn College, July 30, 1982.

[2] This and subsequent quotes from a letter to the author from William McGuire, October 31, 1981.

over Censorship: a cafeteria. "After a few months in the executive office," said McGuire, "I became an editor/writer for the *Weekly Bul-
letin,* and my office was on the same corridor as that of the Public
Opinion Survey. Chester and I often had lunch together in the staff
cafeteria. I recall that he would case the menu earlier in the morning
and get into a state of almost slavering eagerness when there was something he liked especially, like a steamship roast of beef." Unfortunately, Chester's enthusiasm for the job was not so intense as his
enthusiasm for the cafeteria, and the department of personnel was beginning to suspect he was irresponsible. As McGuire put it, "His attendance was a trifle irregular. Sometimes, riding out to Long Island
on the subway, his wandering eye would be attracted [to a man], and
he'd get off the train to follow up an opportunity." He was absent
when the spirit moved him; he was late when not absent. He was discharged from his job not long after he was hired, and he returned to
the old ways of depending on Auden and borrowing from his father
and his friends. While he would promise to look for another job, he
would put the event off from day to day.

If 1948 was to be a year of changes, the greatest change would take
place in Chester. He seemed to become resigned to a world in which
he did not belong, and he seemed to realize suddenly that he was ill-
equipped to manage either himself or his life. He did not want to
have to borrow money or depend on Auden, yet he was incapable of
the self-discipline required for employment or for the career of a
writer. At twenty-seven, the brilliant, beautiful boy was still brilliant
and beautiful—but not a boy. He seemed less loving somehow and less
generous than before, more given to petulance and periods of moodi-
ness and depression. He would not hold a job but neither would he
write except in fits and starts. He suddenly realized that it was not
easier for him to be a great poet, even if he had talent, than to be
steadily employed at a prosaic job from nine to five. The same sturdi-
ness was required. He wasted away his days, sometimes doing cross-
word puzzles, sometimes cooking and entertaining friends with his
brilliant conversation and ready wit.

In the fall of 1947 Wystan found something he believed would
catch Chester's imagination and enable him to make use of his talents: He found Igor Stravinsky. Stravinsky asked Auden to write the
libretto for an opera he planned to compose, and he invited him to
California to prepare the scenario. Immediately Wystan saw an opportunity for Chester in a medium for which the younger man was admirably suited. He also saw an opportunity for himself to work closely

with Chester and thus not only supervise some of his time but also enable him to earn some money.

The selection of Chester as a collaborator did not win the ready assent of the composer. Indeed, Stravinsky had not even been consulted when Wystan notified him that "Mr. Kallman, a better librettist than I am"[1] would be his collaborator in writing the libretto for *The Rake's Progress*. According to Robert Craft, Stravinsky's biographer and assistant, "The composer was greatly disturbed, both because he had not been consulted and because it was Auden alone whom he wanted."[2] However, Wystan was able to persuade Stravinsky upon a second meeting in Washington, D.C., where the composer was conducting, that "Mr. Kallman's talents have not been more widely recognized only because of his friendship with me."[3]

The force of Auden's personality and his formidable reputation as a poet won out over the composer's objections, and from the spring of 1948 until the première of the opera in Venice on the evening of September 11, 1951, Chester and Wystan were involved with *The Rake's Progress*. They began planning and writing immediately. The libretto was finished by February 9, 1948.

With the prospect of money coming in from the opera, Wystan decided to take Chester away from New York for a while. Chester had always said he wanted to travel. "I have always wanted to see Prague," he used to say dreamily. Thus, in early April of 1948 he and Wystan sailed to Europe for one last fling, Wystan promising to pay his travel expenses. In return, Chester promised to find a job when the trip was over. Their departure occasioned a great celebration, and everyone, drunk with champagne, wished them bon voyage. Chester was manic with joy. Wystan, sullen from moment to moment, awaited grumpily the signal for all visitors to leave the ship and for the celebrations to come to an end. He was looking forward to being rid of all of Chester's pals and relatives—David Protetch, Rhoda, Eddie, Malcolm, Mary, me—and having him safe at sea.

Sea, however, presented its own problems, since the ship was filled with English sailors. Wystan was offered a prophetic vision of the years ahead.

First they visited England. Chester's letters to me during the first days there show enthusiasm for the country: "England is of a lovely

[1] Robert Craft: "The Poet and the Rake," *W. H. Auden: A Tribute*, ed. Stephen Spender (New York: Macmillan, 1975), p. 149.
[2] Ibid.
[3] Ibid., pp. 149–50.

[*sic*]." But as time went by, his ardor cooled. Wystan took him to the Lake Country to visit Dr. Auden, but Wystan's father, hoping to have his son to himself for a while and not wanting to be reminded daily of his sexual preferences, resented the American guest and made an unflattering remark, which Chester overheard. Chester did not get on well with the English in general; when he returned he mentioned their snobbishness and poked fun of their ways, so different from his own. Later, he was to make fun as well of the French, whom he did not like either, and of the Swiss, who were too meticulous for his taste. On a trip to Germany, he was reminded continuously of the Nazi Sturm Abteilung. When he came back home, he disliked New York.

If Chester and Wystan did not visit Prague that year, they did get to see Austria; but it was with Italy and the Italians that they fell in love. One day while visiting Naples they took a ferry over to Ischia to visit some friends staying there for the summer. It was here that they decided to remain. They stayed at the Pensione Nettuno in Forio d'Ischia, not well known at the time, and sufficiently out of the way of the tourist crowd to please Wystan, who wanted some solitude for his work and disliked the tourists. At the end of the summer he rented a house in Forio at Via Santa Lucia 22.

The decision by Wystan to stay on Ischia had nothing to do with the beautiful scenery. It had to do with the number of Italian lira one could get for the American dollar in 1948 and with the beauty of the Italian boys, most of whom cast covetous eyes on any dollar, proffered by whomever, after the hard days of World War II. You could have a leisurely dinner of the most delectable fresh fish, vegetables, and fruit for almost nothing. You could have wine from the Italian vineyards as you gazed on Mount Epomeo or the sea, and it would cost you only a few cents. You could have flowers from the garden tended by some Giovanni or Giocondo for sixpence a month, and you could look upon Giovanni's handsome sons for nothing as long as you just looked. After the tensions of New York, it was a leisurely life watching the warm sun cast shadows on the buildings and the rugged stones of the streets where a donkey would lean against a shaded wall. Ischia was entirely satisfactory to Chester and Wystan.

The Italians, a sophisticated people from an ancient culture, viewed homosexuality rather with a wink of the eye than with alarm and gave Wystan and Chester little trouble. Often the town mechanic had a young son of eighteen or nineteen who was willing to oblige for a price. The truth was that Wystan and Chester both fell in love with the Italians, not just the beautiful young boys but also the fishermen, the shopkeepers, the woman who cleaned their rooms, the old ladies in black who attended daily Mass at the village church, the nuns, the parish priest (the *parroco*), and even Saint Restituta herself, the patron saint of the isle, who always answered Wystan's prayers. Chester and Wystan entered wholeheartedly into the life of the town, joining in costume the various festivals of the church, particularly *carnevale* and the feast day of Saint Restituta, Wystan attending Mass every Sunday, blond and big and northern among the congregation of dark-skinned Latins—Wystan awkwardly kneeling and rising and kneeling and rising again according to the ancient rite of the Latin Mass he loved so well.

But the golden Italian summer of 1948 came to an end. Wystan had to be in New York by autumn to fulfill a teaching obligation at the New School in New York. Chester was to look for a job in New York, as he had promised, in order to support himself while he continued with his writing and the libretto for *The Rake's Progress*. Wystan left Ischia first, Chester finding some excuse to stay on for what he promised was a short time after returning from a trip to Paris, where he was to meet his old friends from New York, Ray Schultz and Bill Armstrong.[1] Both Wystan and Chester would return the next year.

In September 1948, with a letter written from the *Queen Elizabeth,* Wystan began a series of letters to Chester in Italy. This correspondence, from 1948 through 1952, interrupted only by Chester's infrequent sojourns to New York or Wystan's summers on Ischia, conveys the tone of the Auden–Kallman relationship more than any other source. The letters also give an insight into Auden's impressions of life and of people, for in the letters to Chester these observations are given unself-consciously to someone with whom Auden was intimate. One glimpses through them the conversations Wystan and Chester must have had when they were alone together. With Chester, Auden did not need to strike an attitude. He could say what he could not say in public or even to his literary friends or those in the world of art or the academy. He did not have to be polite; he did not have to watch his words. With Chester he was most truly himself.

These letters are not so much love letters as letters of love and concern written to an old and beloved friend and companion, whose absence left a void in Auden's life. They invariably begin "Dearest Chester." Affectionate phrases appear throughout. The closing is generally "All my love and prayers," or "All my love, Darling." Wystan

[1] Not their real names.

had become dependent on Chester, and he had reached that point at which he was willing to endure Chester's infidelity, his petulance, his periodic black depressions, his financial irresponsibility, his often unwise choice of friends, his impulse toward self-destruction—all this as long as Chester remained at his side.

"Here I am again in mid-ocean," Auden wrote in September 1948 from the *Queen Elizabeth* on his way back to New York, "but without you, it isn't the same. I really miss you dreadfully. The cabin is lonely and vast. . . . I keep wondering how you are getting on in Paris. Do write soon and tell me."[1] He signs the letter, "Your tiresome, jealous, but devoted pal." After he arrived in New York, he wrote (October 1, 1948), "I had an awful attack of the willies when I got back and felt the impact of New York again, without you. . . . Love and kisses." He kept asking Chester, not always the best of correspondents, to write: "Will write again the moment I have a letter from you." When the letter from Chester finally arrived, Auden wrote (November 1, 1948) "My heart gave such a delighted thump this morning when after many mornings of disappointment it at last got what it had been waiting for." He ends with: "All my love and kisses and do be nice and go on writing me, as I really feel very lost without you, even if a little less tormented." On his birthday, February 21, 1949, Auden wrote that Chester was "the one comrade my non-sexual life cannot do without." Always in the letters there was present the concern "I was worried and cross at not having heard from you" (December 27, 1949). "I was worried by the silence" (October 1, 1948).

But life with Chester was never smooth. First came the usual financial problems. Auden tried valiantly to encourage Chester to be responsible about money. Already Chester had put off the promised return to New York where he was to look for a job. During his trip to Paris at the end of the summer, he had run out of funds and borrowed a sum of money, which he did not return, from one of Wystan's acquaintances, much to Wystan's embarrassment when he discovered the debt. On November 22, 1948, Wystan wrote, ". . . I don't like to think of you getting a reputation for 'loans.' "

At first Wystan put forth a valiant effort to nudge Chester into seeking financial independence: "How, darling, are you going to live if you go off to Forio now I don't quite understand. . . ." (November

---

[1] The author is indebted for these letters of W. H. Auden to Chester Kallman, 1948–1952, first to Dr. Edward Mendelson, who discovered them; then to Dr. Edward Kallman for permission to publish from them.

1, 1948). "I certainly do regard the money I left for you as a loan as your advance [on the libretto for *The Rake's Progress*] to be repaid immediately. . . . Will you let me know *at once* how much you spent or took with you? If it is less than $675 (625 + 50 travelling expenses which are my responsibility) I will send you the balance by return mail. I can't extend the loan, because I see no immediate possibility of its being paid back" (December 2, 1948).

Apparently Chester was offended by the letter, for on December 13, 1948, Wystan wrote, "I'm sorry, darling, if I hurt you about our financial relations. It's not your intentions I mistrust, but your estimation of the future. . . . Just because you *know* I couldn't or wouldn't let you be stranded in Europe penniless, you mustn't put me in the position of being morally *compelled* to support you."

If in the early days of 1948 Wystan was trying to be strict with Chester about money, as time went by he gave up the attempt. While Chester was receiving some money from his share of the libretto, his funds were continually being supplemented by Wystan, who with most of his letters enclosed checks for living expenses as well as for repairs on the house and wages of the servants, Giocondo and Gisella. In addition, Wystan continued to send packages of food from New York. "Glad the ham at last arrived," he wrote in December 1949, "which should be followed soon by the package intended for Thanksgiving since it contains canned pumpkin which I sincerely hope will be all consumed before I arrive."

Wystan was not the only one sending Chester food and money from New York. Although Chester's letters to Wystan have all been lost, a few of his letters to me still remain. They either thank me for packages received, show concern for packages and checks not received, or ask for more money or more food. On March 1, 1949, he wrote from Italy:

> Here, myself, I've been well enough, even if a bit, on occasion, depressed. But even that doesn't last long, and only comes and goes in spells; usually when the first of the month comes and the storekeeper gives me that payment-due look. Here it takes the form of unusual deference, but it's basically the same look. Still and all, February ended well. *Commentary* accepted a poem, which will be published in March or April—and, of all things, *Mademoiselle* took another poem, which will be published, I assume, when there is some space left over between the glove and perfume ads. Anyway, between the two of them, I may be able to pay the butcher.

Chester was receiving money from his father, too, for on October 5, 1948, he wrote:

> When I got back here both your letter and the bank draft were waiting . . . both money and letter cheered me out of seasonal distemper. . . . As for financial help, naturally I can use it. Passage back I have, but have no intention of using for quite a while, perhaps another year. . . . Italy and living in the country suit me. . . . I should feel more heartened if, in addition to all this, editors were not so reluctant to publish and pay for my poems. . . . Perhaps the renting of the house in Sea Cliff will contribute a bit to stability. And it's stability of all descriptions that I need most.

Yet he would not return to the States and find a regular job, which would have given him the stability he craved. In his letter to me of December 31, 1949, he wrote:

> Thanks, and thanks again for the enclosure. A check. As for the foodstuffs that I need. To tell the truth, there isn't anything that I need, but there are lots of things that it is impossible to get here and which it is very nice to have. And chief among them are the following: cans of bacon, chili powder, maple syrup, dried coconut, Major Gray's Chutney . . . soy sauce, bean sprouts, kidney beans, dried legumes like split peas and black-eyed peas, canned soups like tomato and mushroom and spinach and anything that looks interesting, dried celery, spices like chervil, tarragon, dillseed, mustard powder, etc.

Chester in Italy was following his old patterns in many ways, including whatever it was—carelessness, taking up with the wrong people—that caused him continually to lose money. He wrote to me after he had met old American friends in Rome (January 17, 1950):

> In such a madness did I rush off to the train that I dropped my last ten thousand lira (about twenty dollars) out of my pocket. Leave in haste, be miserable at leisure. . . . All I know is that things disappear between here and Rome. . . . On the other hand, though I should be the last one to vouch for Italian honesty, I don't think that my money was picked out of my pocket. I was in such a flying rush that no one could have gotten to me long enough or close enough to reach into what was, after all, an inner pocket. No, I'm afraid it was my own fault.

Chester's irresponsibility with money was not confined to the loose change in his own pocket. When on December 13, 1949, Wystan sent him a sum of money, "Enclosed is thirty dollars—twenty for the poor via il parroco and ten towards a Christmas dinner," one could have predicted that something was bound to go wrong with the amount intended for the parish priest, who, Wystan hoped, "will now greet us when we pass in the street." Surely enough, the money disappeared, for Wystan wrote Chester on February 8, 1950:

> Your mother[1] may have her head in the clouds but her daughter, my dear, is too naive to be out alone in this wicked world. How you—and still more Giocondo—*could* have entrusted twenty whole dollars to that old man instead of taking it to the Parroco passes my comprehension. And if you did, how could you not be suspicious when the Parroco didn't come to thank you? (You may remember I asked in a letter for his reactions.) After all, that quantity of cash doesn't come his way every year.

Apparently Chester, instead of giving the alms to the parish priest in person, entrusted the money to someone else who pocketed it. One hopes that Chester was not lying, that he did not keep the money himself.

In spite of his continuing requests for packages and checks, and despite his propensity for losing money, Chester was enjoying life in Italy. In a March 1, 1950, letter to me, he described his part in the pre-Lenten festival before Ash Wednesday:

> Mardi Gras was pretty giddy here this time, with almost all the kiddies in drag. I wasn't going to oblige the natives this year with another glimpse of my incomparable loveliness in violet voile; and so, determined to resist the blandishments of the two mad sisters who run the café, I came downtown the afternoon of carnevale with a two-day beard and my best Warner Brothers scowl. But some friends arrived from Rome with false eyelashes and my goose, if that is the expression, was cooked. Up we went and, a half an hour later, out we came. My friend Bob F. had a shoulder length blond wig made of hemp, Milanov eyes, a natty little hat that chiefly featured a chin-caressing red feather, and a crepy black gown with lots of gathered do[2] and pleats. He looked like a

---

[1] Auden was fond of referring to himself as "mother" or "your mother," a not uncommon camp expression.

[2] Complicated ruffles.

Madame at an Opening Night. Our joint cavalier wore a rubber
Frankenstein mask which, if a bit static, was certainly effective. As
for me, well—beard and all—I can't describe it. Anyway, fotos were
taken, and, if you care to have one when they're developed, I'll
risk the lusts of any possible censors and send you one. Anyway,
the effect of the three of us on the aborigines was electrifying: they
threw confetti; we threw kisses. Everyone had a wonderful time.

He had at this time, in true Latin fashion, become enamored of
the Roman Catholic saints, taking the same intimate, though irreverent, manner with them as the Italians themselves. He went on:

I hardly know how to explain why I selected St. Antonio as my
particular Saint. Maybe because the first Italian friends I made
were all called Antonio; maybe because I always seem to lose
things and he has proved a great help after a brief supplication;
maybe because Wystan has found a great ally in one of the local
Saints (St. Restituta, who likes human sacrifices and is generally
quite formidable and now obviously has it in for me—) and I
wanted a good strong manly Saint to oppose her if need be. Anyway, there it is; though I sometimes think that I may switch my
loyalty to a stronger character if I can discover one. Maybe the
B.V.M.[1] herself; I'm sure she can't bear Restituta, whom she obviously refers to as "a nice girl." As for Restituta's attitude towards
her, *well!* There's a mosaic in a Neapolitan Church showing the
Virgin enthroned with St. John on one side and Santa Restituta
on the other; and, judging by the look on Restituta's face, she can
see no reason at all why she isn't on the throne herself. As you can
see, she's a determined lady.

Chester was determined, too—at least about not coming back to
New York in 1948, as he had promised, so he put off the trip as long as
he could until it was almost impossible to get traveling space. Wystan,
who had expected him as early as late autumn, wrote him in December, "I have been assuming that when . . . you went to Italy, you
were planning to return on December 29th." Chester again delayed.
Then he expected to be in New York by February 7, 1949, much to
Wystan's joy: ". . . it will be so lovely to see you again" (January 18,
1949). Then came another letter and another disappointment. "You
do keep a girl on edge," Wystan wrote on January 24, 1949, "with
your changes of plans. Was so looking forward to seeing you." In the

[1] Blessed Virgin Mary.

meantime, Chester was entertaining his friends from the States who never ceased to arrive at his doorstep on Ischia to spend an afternoon, a few weeks, or even a few months. There were old friends from Brooklyn College traveling in Europe after the war, and old buddies from Ann Arbor and New York.

Two of these, Ray Schultz and Bill Armstrong, whom Chester had known in New York, were his guests in Italy that year and they were to cause Chester on Ischia and Wystan in New York some apprehensiveness. The story of Bill Armstrong is an example, among many, not only of Auden's forbearance and compassion but also of his willingness from time to time to put up with especially difficult people, impatient as he could be with others. Auden was attracted to, or at least sympathetic toward, people whose spirits had been blunted by the harsh realities of a brutal life. Like Thomas Hardy, one of his early exemplars, Wystan believed that life often battered the most worthy and rewarded the undeserving, and he would take to heart a tragic story.

Armstrong, allegedly an illegitimate son of a Finnish-American housemaid, was a likely candidate for Wystan's sympathy. A tall, handsome Scandinavian, he had been the victim of his own romantic illusions. An ardent Bolshevik, he had fought during his teens in Spain, where he did demolition work for the Loyalists, and had come back to a cold-water flat in Greenwich Village to write poems and articles for the Communist publication *The New Masses*.

During World War II, the U.S. Army, having learned about his experiences in Spain, gave him a job as an army instructor in guerrilla warfare. One day, while he was teaching a lesson in demolition tactics, the hand grenade he was using in the demonstration blew up in his right hand. From that day, before the age of twenty-five, he was physically impaired for life. Sometimes I thought him psychologically impaired as well, not only because of the loss of his right hand but also because of his obsession about his illegitimacy, about which he ranted and raved, though no one cared one way or the other, and for which he spent a great deal of energy blaming the capitalist system. Nevertheless, he was indeed a tragic, romantic figure with, however, a strong streak of violence. He once for no apparent reason struck me and flung me across the room at one of Chester's parties.[1] Chester had met him along with Ray Schultz, also a writer, some time during the war,

[1] I am five feet six inches tall and weighed 107 pounds at the time, so one can get an idea of his physical strength.

and he even took Mary and me to visit Bill during the spring of 1944 in his flat in a tenement at 10 Downing Street in the Village, an address we all found amusing.

Sometime in 1948 Bill and Ray followed Chester and Wystan to Forio and presented themselves as guests. Both were living on a small income, Bill on a pension from the army and Ray on an inheritance, and, since both thought of themselves as writers, neither expected or wanted employment, hoping that in a friendly climate they could devote themselves to their art. They decided to settle down in Ischia, where living was cheap, at least in comparison with living in New York. Chester, always sociable, happily agreed to put them up for a time, and Wystan was not reluctant to have them stay on to take care of the house while Chester (as he hoped) would be in New York for the winter looking for work.

Trouble was quick to follow. The pension Bill was expecting from the army did not arrive, nor did the check he was expecting as payment for some poems and articles in *The New Masses*. Further, his mother had died. His money was running out, and Ray's stipend was not enough to support them both. In addition, the buffets life had dealt him and which had endeared him to Wystan were leading him toward an escape into alcohol, his fondness for which was increasing daily. When he was drunk—and he was drunk much of the time—he was an enraged bull. All his resentments surfaced. He threw Wystan's crockery against the walls of the little house at Via Santa Lucia 22, and he smashed the furniture. He started political arguments that ended in barroom brawls. He staggered down the streets of Ischia, an outraged Nordic giant, pushing from his pathway all the terrified Latins, who called him Beega Edna and scurried for cover whenever they heard him. From time to time he threatened to murder first Ray and then his host, Chester, and he came close to doing so.[1] When he was sober, he was repentant and lovable again, promising to repay all debts promptly, if only he might have enough money to buy one bottle of *vino grande*. Somehow he always managed to get the money, and then everything started all over again.

Life with Chester's latest houseguests was becoming more difficult by the minute. Finally Chester and Ray were locking themselves into a bedroom in order to escape Armstrong's drunken seizures. The experience had a chilling effect on Chester, who disliked scenes and

---

[1] Accounts told to the author by Chester Kallman.

feared violence. Some months later, on September 1, 1949, he wrote
to his father:

> Glad to hear that you saw [Ray], but you shouldn't really question
> him too closely about Bill. Take my word for it, we passed an ex-
> tremely bad and frightening time on his account and for both of
> us . . . the subject is still too sensitive to be freely and easily
> discussed . . . any reference to those past events is likely to cause
> strain and tremors of emotions. Even, at times, fear.

As was usual in an emergency, Chester ranted and complained, but
he was powerless to do anything. Finally he wrote to Wystan, describing the plight of himself and Ray as well as the financial difficulty of
Armstrong, who could not leave even if he wanted to do so. Wystan's
response was at first sympathetic, for he felt sorry for Bill. Thus it was
that Wystan spent his autumn afternoons contacting anyone of influence he knew in New York and Washington in order to find out what
had happened to Bill's army check. On October 1, 1948, he wrote to
Chester: "Mixed news for Bill and [Ray]. The State Department
won't help. I made inquiries here and was advised that it would be
a mistake to bother Washington, because that would have the opposite
effect, i.e., instead of not helping they might actively enter on the
other side." Apparently someone in Washington was disenchanted by
Armstrong's bold Communist stand. Wystan suggested that he write
to the Veterans' Administration instead.

Wystan also visited the business offices of *The New Masses* in order
to find out why Bill's check had not arrived from there, and he wrote
on January 18, 1949: ". . . tell Bill, if he hasn't heard from Bolshy
Bella[1] already, that the trouble about his check bank account was that
a joint account is closed on the death of one of the principals (they
called me to know whether the transferred 200 was really for him
alone) and can only be re-opened when they have a copy of the death
certificate." Armstrong had had a joint account with his mother, and
complications started at her death. Wystan goes on: "Tell him that
the first time I called Miss D——— she was very friendly, but since
then has been extremely *chilly*. I can only conclude that she made inquiries and found out I was a fascist hyena."

Despite the light tone in the early letters, Auden became impatient
with Chester's houseguests as time went on, and he wrote to Chester
on February 13, 1949:

[1] Auden's camp name for an editor of *The New Masses*.

What do Bill and [Ray] respectively intend to do? . . . About Bill,
it is a little embarrassing for me. I can't ask him to leave when his
money arrives. (I enclose a letter to him on the subject.) But *entre
nous* I should prefer it. (Incidentally, dear, it sounds as if there
wasn't a piece of crockery left in the house.) I must just dump this
jolly little diplomatic job in your already over-filled lap.

A few weeks later, he wrote (March 15, 1949) concerning Bill: "Are
you *sure* that he has written to the V.A.? Did either of you see the letter and see it posted? If not, make him write another one and post it
yourselves." Eventually, of course, in order to solve the problem,
Wystan sent money, five hundred dollars to Bill and some to Ray. In
return, he asked that Bill leave and that Chester and Ray remain to
look after the house, since both Chester and Ray, unable by this time
to live in the same house with Bill, were preparing for flight. Bill,
who now had money, was not as generous with his friends as they had
been with him. Chester had to write Wystan for additional money, a
sum of thirty dollars, to pay the gardener.

By this time Wystan was angry. In a letter dated "Wystan's day"—
his birthday, February 21—he drew a picture of a hand pointing out,
with the caption "BILL MUST GO" in large printing. On February
24, 1949, he wrote Chester two letters. In the first: "It would have appeared to my picayune mind that Bill owes me enough by now to pay
for the landscaping. . . . As I said before, I don't want to [have the
house] left either alone with Bill, or completely alone, and would
much appreciate it if either you or [Ray] or both would stay on." In
the second letter of the same date he is furious: "I'm a little drunk
and in a paranoiac mood for which you must make allowances, but
thinking over things, I'm beginning to boil. I do *not* see why I should
suffer because of other people's troubles. I want you or [Ray], or,
better still, both, to stay. If you will say you want to stay, but cannot
if Bill does, I shall order him to leave."

Bill, who eventually received his pension and had Wystan's five
hundred dollars as well, finally left Ischia, moving to various Italian
cities and eventually back to New York, complaining along the way to
all who would listen about W. H. Auden, who had ordered him out
of Forio, and about Chester Kallman, who had conspired against him
and had alienated his friend Ray. He was in no haste to return the
money that Wystan had lent him, for some months later (November
22, 1949), Wystan wrote to Chester: "Am beginning to get letters from

Big Edna again which are a little mad again so be careful. Not a word I may say about the five hundred dollars." Armstrong, who reserved for himself the right to decide how his friends should spend their money, felt himself entirely justified in not returning promptly or not returning at all the sums he had borrowed. "After all," he would say, "Wystan can afford it." If Wystan had at first seen Bill Armstrong as a modern Clym Yeobright,[1] the vision had by now faded.

Armstrong died of cancer a few years later. He was still bitter about Wystan when Eddie and I visited him for the last time in New York's Trafalgar Hospital. When he was buried, his coffin was draped romantically in an American flag and on it was placed a single American beauty rose. Faithfully sobbing beside it was the young widow who had adored Armstrong for many years and was one of the few present to bury him. She apparently never knew about his sexual preferences and drinking bouts.

Bill Armstrong was not the only one who was to account for Wystan's statement: "I must say, I am not very lucky with my creditors (still out $300 from Bill)." He had had the problem with Eddie and the house in Sea Cliff, and he mentioned to Chester some old friends who also owed him money. He wrote on January 29, 1950:

> O yes, a little brush with [X] and [Y], who accused me to [Z] of being too occupied with careerist parties to see them, at which [Z] replied that perhaps I was cross at their ignoring of their debts to me and at their treatment of you. I had dinner with them soon after; the subject of one debt (the smaller one) was brought up but nothing else.

Wystan, who was generous by nature, and who considered himself to have "a lucky life," was glad to help others less fortunate than himself. Often others took advantage of him financially. Wystan, rich in so many ways one could not count, could somehow, in their eyes, always "afford it."

Not long after the conclusion of the Armstrong affair, Chester had two other houseguests, this time friends of Wystan's. The letters Auden wrote concerning them show another facet of his nature, along with the surprising naiveté he continued to display concerning Chester's ability to handle practical matters responsibly. Auden had a great respect for older people, and, since the guests to whom he had offered

[1] The hero of Thomas Hardy's *Return of the Native*.

his home were over sixty, he began coaching Chester concerning how to provide for their comfort some weeks before the date of their arrival.

Wolfgang Köhler, a prominent psychologist whom Wystan had met at Swarthmore, planned a trip to Italy with his wife, Lily, in early 1950. Wystan suggested that they use his house in Ischia, for which they would pay an agreed sum, instead of incurring the expense of a hotel. Wystan wrote to Chester on November 6, 1949:

> When the Kohlers come, [they] are going to pay all the rent [as well as] all Gio and Gis's [wages],[1] they will give you the money, and it is for you. (They don't know this.) They are my p. g.'s,[2] and you have the trouble of looking after them. The only difference is that I shall deduct 10,000 lira (as Giocondo and Gisella's wages) from the monthly $70. I'm afraid that when they do come (beginning of Feb.) Bu[3] and any other of your guests will have to leave as they want peace and quiet. The Food Bill for the K's should of course be 2/3 of the total.

These new guests were about as different from Schultz and Armstrong as frost from fire, and it was well that the previous guests had moved out before the next were to arrive. Wrote Wystan on December 27, 1949:

> Impress . . . on Giocondo that they are not only grand but elderly and need more precise looking after (e.g., beds, and I think breakfast coffee) than we younger set need. I think I told you before that Lily K. is very nice but Wolfgang is a great man with quite a lot of neuroses—i.e. death is a subject which must never be mentioned and even age is risky.

On January 29:

> The Kohlers sailed last Friday. They go to Genoa where they plan to hire a car and drive down. I told them—I hope you don't mind—that if they would send you a telegram in time you would fix a night's accommodations for them in Naples, meet them there and bring them over. With them comes another battery for the radio. Remember to instruct Giocondo in his slightly stricter duties: e.g.,

---

[1] The wages of Giocondo and Gisella, the servants.
[2] Paying guests.
[3] Bu was one of Chester's boyfriends who was living with him at the time.

he must always have the toilet buckets[1] full of water and have breakfast coffee ready for them at whatever hour they want it. They were quite mad with joy at the prospect of Ischia. I hope the cold isn't going to upset them. If there are any new things like another brazier or anything needed for the house, buy it and let me know the cost. They should arrive about the 11th or 12th Feb.

On February 8, 1950: "It is only in February that you have to pay half of Giocondo's wages owing to the K's not arriving till so late. You must charge them the % of the rent by their date of arrival. In March they pay all of Giocondo. Meanwhile, I enclose $10 as a contribution towards carnevale expenses. Please, my angel, don't get *too exalté* and shock the K's out of their wits."

Dr. Wolfgang Köhler may have been a director of a research station on Tenerife in the Canary Islands; he may have been, before the Nazi ascendency, director of the Psychology Institute in Berlin; he may have been one of the founders of the school of Gestalt psychology; he may have been the author of distinguished scientific tomes, one, *Gestalt Psychology,* the other, *The Mentality of Apes;* he may have been a professor at Swarthmore; but to Chester he was an unwelcome middle-aged guest who interfered with his life, particularly his life at *carnevale.* Worse, he did not even contribute to Chester's financial welfare. "Wystan cut twenty off my stipend this month," Chester wrote to me on March 1, 1950, "on the theory that the guests in the house (Wolfgang Kohler and his wife) were paying the overhead! They're not; so I'm almost back where I started." The Köhlers were, of course, an inhibiting factor, since Chester's boyfriend was expected to leave, or at least keep out of the way. But the crowning disappointment was that for some reason or another they either forgot to bring, or they lost, the battery for the radio-phonograph, and Chester was addicted to music. On March 21, 1950, Wystan wrote from New York in response to what must have been a nervous letter from Chester: "Alas, I can't bring a battery myself by air; one was sent off today, but goodness knows how long we shall be without music. Drat the K's." They were already proving themselves less than Olympian.

One cannot be sure how mad with joy the Köhlers were once they set foot on the island. What may have appeared to them a romantic prospect might have seemed less so when they were faced with reality, including the primitive plumbing and Chester's—and Giocondo's—

---

[1] The toilets did not flush automatically; the buckets first had to be filled with water.

indifferent housekeeping. Whether anyone, particularly anyone middle-aged, heterosexual, unbeautiful, and not paying his fair share,
could cause Chester to be less *exalté* at *carnevale* is also doubtful.
What the Köhlers really thought of *le ménage* Auden–Kallman must
have been interesting, particularly their reaction to Chester's friend
with the long hemp wig, fake eyelashes, and natty hat with the scarlet
feather caressing the chin. At any rate, they did not stay their full
term. One suspects that Chester did not get on famously with Lily and
was a bit catty in his letters to Wystan about her, for on March 7,
1950, Wystan wrote: "Your accounts of L. don't surprise me, as that
is everyone's experience. Try, if you can, to take it as a joke. Hope,
however, you like W. who is a great and good man." When he returned to New York, Chester spent at least one afternoon regaling his
father and me with stories about the Köhlers and their many outrages,
allegedly economic, committed against himself.

The real mystery in the Köhler affair is Wystan. How he could have
invited this very conventional, heterosexual couple, whom he obviously respected greatly, to share a house, particularly a house on
Ischia—where the plumbing was crude and the electricity almost nonexistent—managed by Chester, of all people, staggers the imagination.
Was he still naive enough to believe nothing would go wrong? Did he
not, after almost ten years' close association with Chester, know him
better than to expect things to run smoothly? Apparently no disappointment of his hopes was great enough to cause Wystan to lose faith
in Chester's ability to be responsible—Chester, who usually forgot to
renew his passport, always lost money, and generally missed his trains.

If Bu, Chester's current boyfriend, had left when the Köhlers arrived, he came back soon enough after they had gone, for he was a
guest at Via Santa Lucia 22 later on in the spring, much to Wystan's
annoyance, for Wystan was planning to return to the island that April
to spend the summer. In his letter to Chester of February 8, 1950, he
wrote: "Since I shall catch that early train from Rome and get through
in the day, I would like to be met at the dock in Forio." On February
17: "As to our place of reunion, 1. I like to be met at what I think of
as Home Sweet Home by whom I think of as my family. 2. I don't
want the joy of seeing you again shadowed by that Big-City-Gleam in
your eye. 3. Maybe I want a day or two's fun which your presence always makes so very *faute de mieux*."[1] On March 7:

[1] This statement is confusing. However, I interpret it to mean that Chester's
presence when Wystan was with another lover made the other lover seem *faute de
mieux*—i.e., second-best to Chester himself.

1. You've *got* to do something about Bu. I'm not camping when I
say it will completely ruin my time if he's there. Somebody one
dislikes one can be rude to and get rid of but a) I don't, but I
rather respect him and find him amusing and b) for some reason
which I don't understand but which is, I'm afraid, more than a
little connected with me, you seem to like him. I must say, knowing how I feel about having him around—it's an agony of embarrassment—I do think you might have discouraged him from returning. You've had his company for the whole winter and isn't
that enough? Please, Please, Please do something. It really means
a very great deal to me.

Unfortunately, there are no letters extant from Chester to Wystan
during this period, or, indeed, during any period. One can only guess
what he wrote by reading Wystan's responses. Many of Chester's letters to his father and to me were also lost over the years, but Chester
seldom wrote to us about his problems with Wystan, for Eddie was
not a sympathetic listener, usually taking Wystan's part. Apparently,
however, Bu vanished from the scene, for Wystan arrived on the dock
at Naples in the spring of 1950, and Chester was there to greet him.
Wystan was wearing a wide-brimmed straw hat with wisps of what
appeared to be straw emerging from under the brim. "Take that hat
off. You look ridiculous," were Chester's first words of greeting. "What
on earth have you done to your hair?" he cried as he looked closer.

"Dorothy bleached it at my going-away party. I rather like it."

"You're crazier than she is. Do something about it immediately.
You can't seriously expect to walk around here without a hat. And
you surely can't expect me to be seen with you and that hat. Or that
hair." Chester, who was against make-up of any kind and any kind of
artificial hair coloring, finally had his way, and Wystan's head was
promptly shaved. His hair grew back during the summer to the mousy
shade of blond that it had become with the passing of the years. When
Chester returned to New York in the fall of 1950, he scolded me
roundly for bleaching Wystan's hair, angrier than I had ever seen him.

"He was so unhappy," I explained, "about the fact that his hair
was growing dark—looking into the mirror and being so sad and all
about his lost youth—that all I did was make it blond again."

"Yes. The way you did Rhoda's."

"Yes. He was very happy with it until you came along to spoil
everything."

"You're mad. Pure mad. Always have been. Why does everybody

have to be a platinum blond like you—like Mildred in *Of Human Bondage*." Yet Chester was inordinately proud of his own natural blond hair and later tried every preparation for the scalp, hoping to keep himself from becoming bald.

As for Wystan, he did not mind one bit having his head shaved. He settled down happily in Ischia for the summer of 1950, set up his daily time schedule, went upon occasion to the baths, talked to the cats, studied Italian, listened to music with the new battery, and drank his morning coffee as he gazed absently upon Mount Epomeo and composed his poetry. Chester was with him now, and he was at home again, for it was not yet the time to say goodbye.

CHAPTER 11

I'll Never Forget You

DURING 1948, WHEN Auden was alone in New York, it was Billy Vinson, now living in Chester's apartment at 129 East Twenty-seventh Street, and Billy's friends whose company he preferred to any in the city. Auden was drawn to the apartment on Twenty-seventh Street, even going there when Billy was out in order to listen to music on Chester's old phonograph. Although he kept his own apartment, now at 7 Cornelia Street, and frequently visited other friends uptown, he was closest to Billy's circle. His letters to Chester are filled with bits of gossip about Billy's friends and news of cheerful holidays spent in the apartment where Wystan had often stayed with Chester in the early forties. If Auden had been sympathetic to Bill Armstrong because he perceived him to be an innocent and worthy victim buffeted by the caprices of circumstance, he was even more sympathetic to Billy V., whose hour of tragedy had been unexpected, swift, and irreversible.

J. William Vinson, usually referred to by his friends as Billy V.

or, later, as Willy-Mae (or Willie-Mae), was slim, blue eyed, and smooth featured, with the soft, aristocratic manners of the South. The nonchalant languor of his gestures masked a sharp scientific mind. He had been a graduate student at the University of Michigan, where he had met Chester in 1943, receiving his master's degree in public health. In the same year he joined the navy as a lieutenant junior grade and saw action in the war. He remained in the navy, rose to the rank of first lieutenant, and was in 1947 well on his way to becoming a commander when disaster struck.

Billy V. had been stationed in Washington, D.C., after the war, and there he had met a widow, a society figure influential in Washington circles of power. She promptly fell in love with him and decided he was to be her next husband. She was puzzled, however, that this soft-spoken southern boy, with his good manners and romantic ways on the dance floor, should be so elusive in the boudoir. Then she discovered why. Billy V. was writing love letters to Lieutenant Horace Stepole[1] and sharing the boudoir in the lieutenant's Bethesda apartment on Saturday nights after the dancing was over.

In the spring of 1948, Billy V. and Stepole were allegedly summoned to appear at navy headquarters and forced to listen to tape recordings of their private conversations. Both were allegedly dishonorably discharged from the navy that summer. Billy's father, who was promptly notified of his son's trangressions, was outraged and spiteful. He disowned his son, at least according to Billy, leaving him penniless and disgraced to face the world. Billy hastened to New York to hide in Chester's apartment.

It was at this point that Billy went to meet Auden at the docking pier of the *Queen Elizabeth*. Wystan went home to 7 Cornelia Street, but not without expressing his concern to Billy V., and from then on at every opportunity he included Billy in social invitations and went to visit often at 129 East Twenty-seventh. He helped Billy both psychologically and financially.

Despite the dishonorable discharge, Billy V. was working before October. He found a well-paying job, and if he had borrowed money from Eddie in the summer and from Wystan in the autumn, he had paid them both back by Christmas. In fact, Billy V. was eventually to rise like the phoenix from the ashes. A year or so after his discharge from the navy, he was sent by his company to Harvard University,

[1] Not his real name.

where he was to earn a Ph.D. in microbiology and eventually become a professor there in that field. But in 1948, Billy V. was still suffering the anguish of disgrace. He found solace in the little group of friends in New York, the star and inspiration of which was Wystan. It was at Billy V.'s place that Auden was to meet that winter a person who would for some time to come assuage his own feelings of loneliness.

Auden's letters to Chester were full of gossip, not only about Billy V. and his circle but also about bits of local news as well as news of the music and art worlds, particularly the concerts he had been attending. He did not mention to Chester, at least at first, the new acquaintance he was meeting at Billy's and with whom he was attending the concerts and operas. On October 1, 1948, he wrote:

> The immediate news is that Willie-Mae has got herself a wonderful research job with a biotics firm at $100 a week.[1] She and N——— met the boat. Then she went off to N. Carolina for a holiday and returns tomorrow. The [Valentines][2] had the key, so I went over twice to listen to music. On the first night I played the Chopin Concerto, the *Siegfried* finale, etc. The second, straight through *Don Pasquale*. David [Protetch] was in town and came over one morning. What an old neurotic he is: he spent half the time saying how terribly piss-elegant Miss V. [Billy] is.

On November 1, 1948: "Have heard very little new music except *Orpheus* which I loved. Have bought the Fauré piano quartet—heavenly—*Danses Concertantes*—and have the Berlioz *Requiem* on order. Everyone keeps asking after you, so it's nice to give them news. Billy V. is fine and really perked up by her new job." On December 2:

> Went on Tuesday to the Met for *L'Elisir d'Amore* with Sayão, Tagliavini (not good but with a mad, efficient claque) and Valdengo, a magnificent baritone. Felt very miserable not having you with me. Yesterday to hear Nathan Milstein (excellent) play the fiddle, pieces of Nabokov's. Have also heard records of *Mavra* which has its American premiere Dec. 29. A very odd work with a passage like *Tristan*. New records in our collection. Fauré quartet, *Danses Concertantes,* last half of *Elektra,* Mozart Piano Quartet in

---

[1] This was a very high salary in 1948, before the days of inflation. The average salary at that time ranged from twenty-five to thirty-five dollars a week.

[2] Mary Valentine and her husband, who were living temporarily in Eddie's old apartment at the rear of the building.

G Minor, and the Berlioz *Requiem*. . . . Heard TSE[1] lecture on
Poe. Rather thin. St. John Perse sent me a lovely edition of *Vents*
inscribed: *"Au Wystan Auden qui j'ai rencontré, tête nue, sous les
grandes neiges de Washington, 1947."* Have to broadcast this evening about All Hallows Eve. . . . Stephen [Spender] wrote and
published in *Partisan* a piece of his autobiography all about me,
inaccurate and making me out a madly unpleasant eccentric. Am
really very cross with him.

On January 18, 1949, Wystan wrote: "Heard a wonderful performance of *Figaro* with Sayão, Steber, Tajo, Busch; an equally wonderful *Barbiere,* with Valdengo, who is a great singer; and a horrendous
Walküre. Max Lorenz as Siegmund was inaudible. The Cowbell's[2]
gown was pure Westchester,[3] and Stiedry,[4] my dear, doesn't know his
baton from his bum."

If on receiving the letters in Italy Chester noticed they were in a
more cheerful tone than he might have expected, and if he attributed
Wystan's lightness of heart to the influence of Twenty-seventh Street,
he would not have been mistaken. Wystan was having a good time. He
felt at home with Billy V. and enjoyed meeting the members of his
group. Wystan, who looked forward to holidays with all the excitement of a ten year old, always liked to be invited to someone's home
for a sit-down dinner (he did not like buffets) with roast pig or goose
and plum pudding for Christmas and suckling pig for New Year's.
Billy V. shared this enthusiasm for holidays, and he always invited
Wystan to the apartment to celebrate whatever festive occasion was
coming up, including Wystan's birthday. On December 30, 1948,
Wystan wrote to Chester:

> We had a little Christmas Eve with Willy-Mae which was quite
> nice except that both he and I were almost in tears at your not
> being there. We had duck (a little tough) and for the party mulled
> claret which was quite a success. Dorothy was a bit emotional as
> usual but kept within bounds. Present were Billy, me, Dorothy,

[1] T. S. Eliot was lecturing in the United States at this time.

[2] The Cowbell was a name Chester gave Helen Traubel, a famous Wagnerian
soprano of the 1940s and 1950s whose singing he could not abide.

[3] This was a term coined by Wystan and Chester referring to a style of over-
dressing—all frills and furbelows—they associated with the buxom suburban ma-
trons of Westchester County, New York.

[4] Fritz Stiedry, the conductor.

Rhoda, Nigel Dennis,[1] Johnny H. (a tea-cup friend of B.'s), and [Keith Callaghan],[2] my *en titre* (*O Beatrice mia, Quanto mi costi.*[3])

It was this letter and Keith Callaghan to whom Chester would later take exception.

The autumn of 1948 was to end Wystan's flirtation with heterosexuality and the conventional life that had begun after his months of army service in Germany. After Billy V.'s disaster, Wystan became more partisan than ever in his homosexuality and seemed to retreat into a circle more self-protective and clannish than ever, each member fearing in his own future a plight like the one that befell Willy-Mae. Having nothing to fear for himself, as he had always been able to be open about his sexual preference, Wystan nevertheless took up anew the moral fight he had begun years ago at Oxford.

The group on Twenty-seventh Street, a more or less closed homosexual enclave by this time (they even excluded Mary and me), had another advantage, that of being an inner-circle occult group, having a secret-society aspect that always appealed to the adolescent still alive in Auden's psyche. Though his return to a strict Anglicism had caused him, at least on the surface, to reject occultism except as an interest, he still enjoyed the social trappings of groups like Yeats's Order of the Golden Dawn, for they were cozy and exclusive, and they offered him protection against an inimical world. Billy V.'s experience had reminded Wystan how tenuous was the luck in his own "lucky life."

As time went on, however, things began to change. In late 1949 Billy V. decided to move to a better apartment, leaving 129 East Twenty-seventh to another tenant, a Dutch Martell,[4] who had taken refuge there upon his return from a trip to Europe, where he had met Wystan. Dutch, however, did not arrive alone. He arrived with a friend, one Charles Henry,[5] whom he had met in Paris, and in his letters Wystan ever after referred to Martell and Henry as the Mat-

[1] Nigel Dennis, the English novelist, author of *Sea Change* and other works.

[2] Not his real name.

[3] "Oh my Beatrice, how much you cost me." Auden was splitting his references here. "O patria mia, quanto mi costi" is sung by Aïda to her father, Amonasro, in Act III of Verdi's *Aïda,* in one of the great "mai più" arias. Here Auden is substituting Beatrice, from Dante, for Patria. *Aïda* was one of Chester and Wystan's favorite operas, and they played it continually.

[4] Not his real name.

[5] Ibid.

tress Girls, probably one of those code names invented by Chester. The Christmas of 1948 had been one of the last happy holiday times that Wystan was to spend in the old apartment. Once Billy moved and Dutch and Charles took over, things were not the same. Apparently Charles suspected that there had been something between Dutch and Wystan, and he was jealous. At any rate, Wystan wrote to Chester on December 27, 1949, the next Christmastide: "The Mattress Girls have repainted the apartment a light brown and there are abstract pictures and sculptures. If I sound catty, it is because I was terribly hurt that there was no Christmas dinner at 129 E. 27 this year; we were only invited to come in at 9:00 p.m. Willie-Mae very sweetly cooked a dinner at her place, but we felt that a tradition [was] broken. Cock-robin Charlie is evidently determined that [Dutch] shall have no past." Then on February 17, 1950: "Am giving my birthday party at the Mayers'[1] this year, no suggestion having emanated from 129 that I might have it where I am used to having it. Have invited the Mat-tress Girls, but with not too much warmth in my heart, I must admit." March 7, 1950: "Went last Thursday to dinner at the Mattress Girls (the fourth visit this winter—two of them after dinner only). Charlie fell asleep after dinner in protest."

Eventually the apartment was abandoned as Chester's friends moved elsewhere when they became prosperous, and what was left of Chester's belongings was stored with friends or simply broken and dis-carded, or lost. Chester himself had abandoned his claims on the apart-ment by this time because of Wystan's descriptions of its renovation by Billy V. and then the Mattress Girls. He who did not mind the cracked walls and dirty windows of the past would not return to an apartment cleaned and painted turd-brown, as he called it, and with abstract paintings on the walls. It was time to say goodbye to 129 East Twenty-seventh Street.

Because of Wystan's close association with Billy V. and the group that gathered on Twenty-seventh Street in 1948, it was natural that, if he were to look for a lover at all, Wystan would find one there, if not in Billy V.—and there is no evidence that his relationship with Billy V. was at any time erotic—then in someone else. In seeking a lover Wys-tan did not view himself as being unfaithful to Chester. He knew that Chester was not faithful, and he knew that Chester did not love

---

[1] Elizabeth Mayer and her husband, William, a psychiatrist who had escaped the Nazis. Auden had met the Mayers through Benjamin Britten and Peter Pears. Mrs. Mayer, seventy years old in 1950, was said to resemble Auden's mother in appearance and manner.

him erotically. Chester would fall in love romantically from time to time, usually with a boy who was primarily heterosexual, but usually these affairs would end unhappily, and Chester would go out, the Big-City Gleam in his eye, to search for a stranger with whom to spend the night. Wystan was emotionally dependent on the conviction that no one but himself could satisfy Chester's need for both a protector and an intellectual companion. Sex was something else, and Wystan realized that if he could not have Chester, he needed some other erotic element in his life. Not long after he returned from Ischia in the autumn of 1948, he met Keith Callaghan.

Keith Callaghan arrived in New York City to attend the Juilliard School of Music, to which he had won a scholarship, in the autumn of 1944. Four years later he met W. H. Auden. While in his junior year at Juilliard, he was introduced to some graduate students from Columbia University, English majors who knew some friends of Chester Kallman. It was not long before he was going to the apartment at 129 East Twenty-seventh Street to visit Billy V. and his circle. One evening in the late summer of 1948, Auden was one of the guests for dinner. The homosexual set was not unknown to Callaghan, for he had, despite his innocent choirboy manner, been seduced at the age of fifteen by a male English teacher from his high school in Dallas. By the end of the evening, Auden had invited Keith to come for dinner the next week to Cornelia Street alone.

The dinner invitation to Cornelia Street was successful. By the winter of 1948 Keith was Auden's steady boyfriend. They were seen together at restaurants, at concerts, and at the opera. Wystan seems to have found in Keith a close and satisfying sexual relationship, for the affair lasted five years, from 1948 to 1953. During this time Callaghan, whose fondness for wine and alcohol increased to the point of interfering with his classes, was asked to withdraw from Juilliard. Keith found a teacher of violin outside of the conservatory, one of the most celebrated in the world, in fact; and before long he had the advantage of private lessons, paid for partly by Wystan.

However, Callaghan was proud and had a distaste for the idea of being supported. He was glad to enjoy the luxuries that he could not afford and Auden could supply, such as operas, good restaurants, and books, but he always worked for a living and expected to continue to do so. Wystan knew how Keith felt, and they used to enjoy fantasies together of Keith supporting Wystan in his old age, both living in a garret.

During the years from 1948 to 1953, Wystan, when away in Europe for part of the year, corresponded regularly with Callaghan, and in 1982, Keith had at least two dozen letters and postcards, of which I saw a few. They were charming, full of good humor, high spirits, and news of the poet's various activities during the early 1950s, from lecturing in India to rehearsals of *The Rake's Progress* in Italy. When Auden returned every fall to take up his residence in New York, he notified Keith to meet him, or to find him a room in the George Washington Hotel until the apartment he had sublet for the summer would be vacant. Often there was in the letters an affectionate "wish you were here" or some endearment such as "darling" or "carissima." There were charming anecdotes about his animals in Italy, his dog, Mosé, who was delighted to see him upon his return, and his cat, Leonora, who slept with him, ". . . I find she has fleas which prefer me."

Most of the letters I saw have a lighthearted schoolboy quality, the same tone that one finds in his letters to Chester. On August 16, 1949, Auden spoke about his attachment to an old book: "My reading has been odd—I suddenly got a mania for reading *The Hill* (a school story about Harrow, the sub-title of which is 'A Romance of Friendship') over and over and over again till I now know it almost by heart." On April 10, 1951, after returning to Ischia from India, he wrote: "Arrived on Sunday night more dead than alive after one of the most exhausting fortnights I have ever spent. There is no hell like Public Life, banquets, speeches, etc. In addition to which, Bombay, my dear, has PROHIBITION so that one had to lead this life sober."

Despite the affection and esteem in which he held the young man, and despite the sexual experience which had obviously been satisfactory, Auden never suggested their living together or made any serious arrangements for Keith to go to Europe. Auden was still living with Chester in Forio, and now they were beginning to collaborate on various operatic librettos, the first important one being *The Rake's Progress* with Stravinsky. The pattern of Wystan's life had now been set. For better or for worse, it was Chester and Europe in the spring and summer and New York in the fall and winter to earn a living and to live by himself.

He continued to see Callaghan frequently and, for a short time, Rhoda, but no one except Chester ever lived with him on a permanent basis. Indeed, Wystan did not attempt to hide his relationship with Chester from Callaghan, who remembered that, "Gradually, at some point, he told me about Chester and how it had been, that they were not going to bed together and had not for some time," said Calla-

ghan.[1] "I know I was extremely nervous or anxious about meeting
Chester when he came back from Europe in 1949, because I didn't
know how he'd like me or I'd like him. Chester and I seemed to get
along very well right off, to everyone's relief."

Whatever Callaghan believed about his getting "along very well
right off" with Chester, Chester clearly had objections to Keith's relationship with Wystan, for in a letter dated "Wystan's Day," Auden's
birthday, February 21, 1949, Auden responded to what must have
been an angry letter from Chester:

> Your lecture ill-received. I've never noticed, *darling,* any re-
> luctance on your part to confine experiences, operatic, intellectual,
> etc., to me. (If you've never gone with a lover to *Tristan,* it wasn't
> because of me, but because Miss Butch preferred jazz. *Entre nous,*
> I would have minded that less than the great *gang* of chaps [?]
> that always were at the Met.) If I'm anxious for you to approve of
> Keith it's not because you are the Beatrice for whom I cherish a
> grotesque passion, but because you are the one comrade my non-
> sexual life cannot do without. Expressions like "bowing out" and
> "disappear" are twists of the knife which, as you know only too
> well, you beast, hurt. Still I adore you and I suppose you must de-
> serve it.

Chester must have written again from Forio, this time objecting to
Keith's having been invited for Christmas at Billy V.'s. Wystan's letter
of March 15, 1949, attempts to be reassuring:

> I know you won't believe it but there was honestly no malice,
> conscious or unconscious, in his being at 27th Street on Christmas
> Eve. He was Billy's friend (not in that sense) long before I met
> him, which was through Billy. Do you think I should have re-
> fused to go to Billy's for Christmas or that I should have gone but
> refused to take him with me?
> As to our relationship, I'm sure that you have a pretty good idea
> of how it is. I am Poppa to him; he, unfortunately, cannot be Big
> Brother to me, only Young Brother. . . . I can talk to him and
> educate him—he cannot educate me. I'm not being catty about
> him, because you would realize at once if you met him, how decent
> he is. Once again, darling, what do you expect of me? One night
> stands with trade? I have neither the taste, the talent, nor the time.

[1] This and subsequent quotes from Keith Callaghan from his conversation with
the author and Mary Valentine, April 4, 1982.

A chaste fidelity to the Divine Miss K?[1] Miss God, I know, says
that, but I haven't the strength, and I don't think you, sweetie,
have the authority to contradict me. If it is wrong, at least I don't
behave badly to him as I do to you. Enough. We're a funny pair,
you and I.

When Chester returned to New York for a few months later in
1949, he was still antagonistic to the idea of Callaghan and sat pouting
with Mary and me in his father's former apartment on Twenty-
seventh Street while Wystan was with Keith in the front studio. As
time went by, however, and Chester became better acquainted with
the young man, his attitude changed. In fact, he paid Keith the compliment of giving him one of the comical code names he was fond of
using for everyone at the time: Winona Bell. Why Winona? It was my
hometown in Minnesota. What was the logic? There was none, of
course.

The letter of Wystan's Day surely reveals the state of the poet's true
affections and the spiritual permanence of the Auden–Kallman relationship. The marriage that took place in 1939 was a marriage in the
truest sense.

Keith Callaghan's memories of Wystan during these five years reveal
the personality traits of the poet as he grew into middle age as well as
some of his qualities as a lover, and they also provide some insight
into the details of Auden's daily life. Callaghan observed that Wystan

> . . . seemed to have a great deal of structure to his life and strong
> feelings about what was appropriate and what was inappropriate—
> some of which I couldn't quite see, you know, when he'd be at
> Town Hall reciting his poems and blowing his nose into his hand.
> I didn't know whether that was appropriate, but then. . . . Things
> like punctuality or having a routine for doing his own work were
> very important. Things like reliability. I don't think he ever stood
> me up or was late for an appointment.

According to Callaghan, Wystan had not entirely given up dab-
bling in magic when he left Ann Arbor. "I remember," said Callaghan, "in Wystan's apartment on Cornelia Street he had some scrap-
books. There was one picture of Chester which had been taken when
he was nude and it was cut into little bits and pasted on the page in
scraps. It was dismembered, actually, and then glued to the page."

[1] I.e., Chester.

Those conversant with magic practices are familiar with the ritual of dismembering a portrait in order to achieve a dominion of will over the original. Perhaps Wystan, in extremis, could not imagine any other way of achieving power over Chester, since Chester would not yield to him sexually. Some of Chester's friends believed the whole magic idea a camp. Others held that Wystan, who was in fact superstitious, secretly believed in the efficacy of these rites and used them more often and more seriously than was commonly thought.

Wystan had a theory that the homosexual act was an act of high magic, but only in the philosophical sense,[1] because it dealt with symbols and correspondences. One was acting out either the mother–son relationship (oral) or the man–woman relationship (anal). Therefore, according to him, you had to know what a given homosexual did in bed if you wanted to understand him or his work. Thus it was that he always insisted on knowing, in the case of a homosexual artist or even of a friend, the artist's or the friend's sexual preference. According to him, the heterosexual act was essentially different because it was less symbolic. One was not "acting out" in the same way. Wystan's sexual preferences were oral.

In describing Auden as a lover, Keith remembered that, although "he was not affectionate in the sense that he wanted one to cuddle with him for hours, he was a kind man and cared about your feelings." When asked whether sex in and of itself was important to Auden, Callaghan answered, "I would say so, yes. I don't think he was so compulsive as many people are. I think he had enough to do during the day so he didn't feel driven. I know he wasn't faithful, but then neither was I, and he never made any pretense of being. I think we both knew that the other would be hurt if we took up with anyone else on a permanent basis."

Many people expressed theories about why Chester, who slept with a great many people, refused to sleep with Wystan, who loved him. Keith's theory was that "Chester had much more sexual imagination and need for more variety and maybe more role playing. With Wystan, it was just about one half-hour of mutual oral sex, taking turns. I don't think Wystan was interested in anal sex." It did not strike Keith as strange that Chester refused to oblige Wystan. "Maybe Chester realized that he would have had to be faithful. It would have been an impossible situation to have to be faithful to Wystan in that rela-

---

[1] An attempt to achieve by symbolic means what could not be obtained by practical ones.

tionship and he decided it would be better just not to have anything
to do with him sexually."

Wystan apparently kept a few racy pictures about the house. While
visiting Auden, Keith remembered:

> I was at Cornelia Street one afternoon and Wystan said he was
> expecting a relative of one of the ladies who was his neighbor in
> Ischia. A middle-aged, nondescript type of woman in black came
> by with a little girl about seven years old. The little girl went look-
> ing into the bottom of the bookcases to amuse herself and imme-
> diately pulled out a photograph of the [Paul] Cadmus painting of
> Lust, a nude woman with a condom over her head. "What's this,
> grandma?" asked the little girl of her Italian Catholic grand-
> mother. Wystan screamed, "Put that back! Put that back!" He
> grabbed the photograph from under the eyes of his bewildered visi-
> tors and shoved it into a drawer out of sight.

One evening in 1949 Keith had dinner with Wystan, Rhoda, and
Nigel Dennis, and later Wystan suggested that it might be amusing
for Callaghan to have an affair with Rhoda. Apparently he was not
jealous when his lovers slept with women, for in 1953, when Keith
fell in love with a Hungarian countess, "Wystan was interested and
highly amused," according to Callaghan, "and would ask me all about
her." The poet found it diverting to think of a countess with a long
distinguished name selling clothes at Bergdorf-Goodman and having
a brother who was an automobile mechanic, and he did not resent her
presence in the life of his lover.

Although Wystan may have found Callaghan's affair with the countess "vastly amusing," he did not find at all amusing Keith's affair nine
months later. Ironically, Keith had suddenly fallen in love with
Charles Henry, one of the Mattress Girls, the very one who had interfered with Wystan's visits to Twenty-seventh Street back in 1948.
Callaghan, honest if not faithful, confessed all. Wystan was shaken,
and, according to Callaghan, "He cried and was very upset." He had
never minded Keith's fugitive encounters with sailors, and he had not
taken seriously the love affair with the countess, but he had been in-
tolerant of a serious homosexual relationship, one that hinted at
friendship and romance and excluded himself.

"Probably my desire for independence," Keith was to remark years
later, "and Wystan's perhaps subconscious feeling about that may have
had as much as anything else to do with the termination of our affair."

The affair with Keith Callaghan underlines the tragedy in Auden's life; namely, that nobody ever loved him the way he wanted to be loved. At some point his lovers would leave him for someone else, as Keith did in 1953 and as Chester did in 1941. There would always be tears at parting, a sexual renunciation, and a farewell scene. But Wystan would always remain friends with the erstwhile lover. Once when discussing the morality of acquitting a murderer for committing the *Crime Passionnel,* he said, "Of course, the only sensible thing is for one to shoot the unfaithful lover, not the rival. But one is not always rational, my dear."

Other members of the Auden–Kallman circle of the late forties and early fifties who were to play a significant role in the lives of Wystan and Chester were David Protetch, Alan Ansen, and Anne de la Vergne Weiss and her husband, Irving. Protetch was to become Auden's personal physician; Ansen, first as Auden's secretary, then as his friend, was to follow Chester and Wystan to Europe and was eventually to be near each at the hour of death. The Weisses were to supply Wystan and Chester not only with a close and happy friendship but also with the experience of sharing the life of a family with children.

After Billy V. had left for Harvard, Wystan began to see more of David Protetch, of whom he had once been grumpily jealous. The young man who was to become the physician of Auden and Stravinsky had danced all night with Mary and me, his old college chums, while he was still a lieutenant junior grade in the navy on leave during the war. Chester, David, Mary, and I waltzed in Yorkville to Viennese bands and did the lindy, the jitterbug, and even at one point the tango as we gulped down Riesling in the Cafe Geiger or beer at the Bauhaus and the Switzerland. We danced in Times Square on V-J Day, hysterical with the other New Yorkers at the prospect of peace, and kissing everybody. We ate spaghetti and meatballs in small Village restaurants and ajem pilaf in the Orient and the Balkan. We gobbled down hot dogs at Nathan's in Coney Island and lay on the sands of Jones Beach as I sketched the rocks, Chester, and everyone else. If Billy V. was on leave at the same time, he would join us, and Chester would cook dinner at our apartment; and Mary and I would make lemon meringue or apple pie with rum. Once we all went to Washington together to see the galleries and to visit Willy-Mae.

David Protetch, tall, dark, slim faced, and graceful, glittered when he walked, like Edwin Arlington Robinson's Richard Cory. He bore a striking resemblance to Czar Nicholas I, to whom he claimed to be

related illegitimately through a Jewish matriarch, telling the sad story
of his family's tragic exile to Igor Stravinsky one afternoon years later
in Paris, at least according to Wystan. Dave was born in Ohio, where
his father was a prosperous businessman. He met Chester in Ann
Arbor during his senior year, and they had been good friends ever
since. When David obtained a temporary job in a cancer research laboratory on Welfare Island while awaiting entrance into medical school,
he moved into 129 East Twenty-seventh Street. Forthwith, he determined to reform Chester.

He hung cozy chintz curtains of pink, beige, and green on the
grimy windows, which he had attempted unsuccessfully to wash, and
he laid a matching chintz bedspread over the dusty flannel blanket on
the daybed in the living room. He swept the rug, scrubbed the floors
and the linoleum, and carried the garbage regularly down to the trash
can near the door at the entrance. When Wystan returned later on in
the summer, also to stay temporarily at Chester's, he decided that
David Protetch was mad.

Once when David reached down to empty the garbage, a mouse
jumped out. "Yipe, a mouse," he bellowed.

"It's not a mouse," said Chester protectively. "It's only a cock-
roach."

David would remark daily to all who would listen—to Chester's
father in the back apartment, to Mary, to me, to Billy V. when he was
in town—"Chester has to learn to be more neat. More careful. The
place is a hotbed of bacteria. Do you know," he would confide, lower-
ing his voice, "I think Wystan and Chester are feeding that mouse!"
He was right, of course—they were, and Wystan did it partly to be
humane to the mouse and partly to outrage David. David would sweep
and scrub, grumbling all the while, and Wystan would remark whenever he was alone with Chester, Mary, and me, "I really do think
David has gone mad, my dear." Chester baptized David "Polly," for
polyclinic.

In a few months David left for medical school in his home state,
much to Wystan's relief, and, homesick for New York, he would write
long, sad letters to Mary and me. He returned to New York in 1949,
with his medical degree and a red Cadillac convertible, in order to
intern in Kings County Hospital and to take his state boards. All the
young nurses at Kings County and all his fellow interns' sisters had
made up their minds to marry him. Now and then he would make the
mistake of taking one or another to Chester's parties, and they would
sit there stricken, regarding the scene before them, their dreams of a

house in the suburbs, a family, and a husband who was a doctor turning swiftly to dust.

It was when David returned to New York from medical school that he began to visit Wystan on Cornelia Street. They would talk about the opera and the latest musical recordings; they would gossip about their friends. Gradually, when David went into private practice in internal medicine, Wystan became his patient. Some say that David enabled Wystan to continue leading "the chemical life," supplying him with enough Benzedrine (huge amber bottles of it) to get through the spring and the summer in Europe, where drugs were scarce. Wystan once said that David also allowed him to experiment with other drugs, such as LSD, but that these drugs had had no effect upon him. One hopes that David really gave him only a harmless injection of vitamins.

Though I could not deny David's considerable charm, skill, and generosity, I noticed, as time went by, his stretches of melancholy and ill humor, alternating with fits of heightened activity of a tyrannical nature. He was to rule those of us who were his patients with an iron hand as firm as that of the first Nicholas Romanov. The truth was that his erratic behavior had behind it a medical history: He was a diabetic. His disease had been diagnosed in the navy shortly before the end of the war, after he had seen action in the Pacific. From then on he injected himself daily with doses of insulin. If he deviated from his prescribed diet, he would go into a diabetic coma. He did so once on Eddie's dental chair, and Eddie and I fed him bread and jelly sandwiches until he recovered.

Auden, in his poem to David Protetch, "The Art of Healing," mentions one reason he chose him as his doctor. The poet's father, also a physician, had warned him against: "the sadist, the nod-crafty, / and the fee-conscious,"[1] and Wystan believed that Dr. Protetch was a doctor of whom his father would have approved. However, the real affection Wystan felt for David was based upon his perception of David as a victim, as he had perceived Bill Armstrong, Billy V., and a number of others:

> *yourself a victim*
> *of medical engineers*
> *and their arrogance*
> *when they atom-bombed*

[1] This and forthcoming poetry references from Auden, "The Art of Healing," in *Collected Poems*, pp. 627–28.

>   *your sick pituitary*
>   *and over-killed it.*

When his eyes began to be affected, David went for treatment to a hospital in California where a new procedure was supposed to have been developed for treating diabetes. His health was worse after he returned.

David's illness endeared him to the poet who would not have wanted a hale and hearty doctor with a charming bedside manner, or one who told him comfortable lies:

>   *Was it your very*
>   *predicament that made me*
>   *sure I could trust you,*
>   *if I were dying,*
>   *to say so, not insult me*
>   *with soothing fictions?*

Wystan could not resist his penchant for applying psychology to medicine. At one time he referred to diabetes as "the sweets of sin." In the poem he gives at least a symptom:

>   *Must diabetics*
>   *all content with a nisus*
>   *to self-destruction?*
>   *One day you told me*
>   *'It's only bad temper*
>   *that keeps me going.'*

The boy that had danced all night in Yorkville died in May 1969, after having been married only a year to one of his patients. Auden, his favorite patient, was to live only four years longer than he.

>   *But neither anger*
>   *nor lust are omnipotent,*
>   *nor should we even*
>   *want our friends to be*
>   *superhuman. Dear David,*
>   *dead one, rest in peace,*

having been what all
doctors should be, but few are,
and, even when most
difficult, condign
of our biassed affection
and objective praise.

In the autumn of 1946, Alan Ansen, a recent graduate of Harvard University, with one of the highest averages that university had seen in many years, became the friend of W. H. Auden. Said Ansen thirty-seven years later:

> I attended Wystan's lectures on Shakespeare at the New School for Social Research, beginning in October 1946. I enrolled for the additional seminar he gave on Saturday afternoons (the lectures were on Wednesday evenings), I helped him carry records home after a small riot he caused by playing Verdi's *Falstaff* in lieu of lecturing on *The Merry Wives of Windsor,* which he described as a very boring play.
>
> It was good education, but he rather rubbed it in by spending the time absorbed in the libretto rather than providing the scintillating commentary of which he would have been perfectly capable. I wrote a paper for him on *The Sea and the Mirror*,[1] and after he read it, he said, "You've seen the figure in my carpet." He introduced me to Chester in January of 1947. I succeeded Rhoda Jaffe as his secretary either late in 1947, or some time in 1948. It was certainly before his first visit to Ischia.[2]

It was partly because of the paper Alan wrote on *The Sea and the Mirror,* which Wystan told Chester was the most brilliant he had ever read, that Alan eventually joined the group on East Twenty-seventh Street. He was embraced, if not always wholeheartedly by all of Chester's friends,[3] at least wholeheartedly by Chester's family, who adored him, for he was a weekly visitor at Eddie's. Alan would come to New York on Saturday evenings from his home on Long Island, where,

[1] Auden's series of poems that serves as a commentary on Shakespeare's *The Tempest.*

[2] Letter to the author from Alan Ansen, February 13, 1983.

[3] In the late forties, a snowstorm, said Alan in his letter to the author of February 13, 1983, "trapped me in Chester's flat, much to the annoyance of Billy V."

since the death of both parents in 1948, he was living with his guardian, an elegant maiden aunt who wore white kid gloves and hats. First he would appear at Eddie's new place in the London Terrace for drinks and dinner. Then he would go out to celebrate Saturday night with his friends, and, bedraggled but happy, return to Eddie's for Sunday supper. "I decided to come back," he would say each week, "because I am just in the mood for a quiet, soap opera kind of Sunday afternoon *en famille*. I am also ravenously hungry. What's to eat?" and he would turn his face shyly to the side, giggle, and walk into the living room. Whereupon Eddie or I would serve him a drink, a stinger or the usual dry martini, and he would sit down to brains vinaigrette, braised kidneys, and a fowl served with white wine before he left to catch the 10:58 back to his aunt, who by this time was nervously making telephone calls.

When you thought of Alan, you immediately thought of his laugh. He would bend his head coyly to the side, focus his brown eyes demurely upon the rug, giggle, and at the same time pat his forehead with his thick-fingered right hand. Then, if really amused, he would roar with full-throated ease, raising his face heavenward, all the while continuing to pat his forehead, the more energetically as he enjoyed the joke. Chester had already baptized him Allegra from the third stanza of "The Children's Hour."[1]

Although he came from a well-to-do family, he was more than economical. As he himself put it, he did not want ever to work. He wished to spend his time as a gentleman and a scholar—and a poet— and that takes money. He had an inherited income, and he had to make it last. Therefore, he never spent a penny unwisely. He took to the habit of wearing secondhand clothes, mostly those worn by his father before him, and once appeared on a beach with Chester's brother Malcolm and Malcolm's fiancée in a bathing suit of a generation past, so moth-eaten that one could hardly discern the suit. When he voted, he voted for the man who was best for real estate.

During the week on Long Island, where he was beginning to cause his aunt-guardian much concern, he systematically studied his literature, kept up with his ancient Greek, and wrote his poetry from prime to sext (he was now following W. H. Auden's *horae canonicae*), and from sext to nones he listened to soap operas. He could discuss every plot of every soap on the radio. In the evening he would read himself

[1] "Grave Alice, and laughing Allegra, / And Edith with golden hair"—Henry Wadsworth Longfellow.

to sleep from his vast library, at least two shelves of which were devoted to detective stories. Like Wystan, he liked detective stories, but they had to follow prescribed rules, one of which was that they provided their readers with sufficient evidence to solve the problems themselves. He always carried at least two of these paperbacks in his pocket when in New York, and if you rode with him on the train or on the subway, he would take one out, hand it to you, say, "Here, read, but give it back," and immerse himself in the other book forthwith. He was also an authority on W. H. Auden and stated his intention at that early date of being Boswell to Wystan's Johnson, until, that is, he discovered that W. H. Auden did not want a biographer or a biography. He could quote poem after poem—Wystan's as well as those of others—as the spirit moved him, and he could quote them letter perfect.

One day in 1947, Alan discovered that one of his favorite professors from Harvard, one Francis Peabody Magoun, was visiting New York, and he decided the professor should meet Wystan. Thus he invited both distinguished men to be his guests for dinner at the Chambord. The threesome, Wystan and Alan in their secondhand clothes, and Francis Peabody Magoun in his navy wool broadcloth, settled cozily in at the elegant round table decked with white linen and old silver, as waiters glided over the greige velvet carpet to obey every command.

Alan and his guests ordered the first and then the second round of predinner double martinis. Alan was drinking something called a zombie, attracted by the name. They ordered French champagne with the dinner, and, afterward, French brandy. Alan had another zombie, attracted by the taste. Wystan and Magoun were by this time conversing at fevered pitch, unconscious for the moment of their young host, who was eyeing the expensive bottle of French champagne, still half full and sitting in its bucket to his right. "Why waste all that good champagne?" he asked himself.

When the waiter eventually brought the check, Wystan and the professor, glancing about in panic, could not see their host. Alan had vanished. The chair in which he had sat was cold and empty, though it seemed he had been there a moment before. Neither was he in the men's room. Alan was gone from the face of the earth. Having returned to the table, Wystan suddenly felt something soft against his foot. Apparently the professor did, too, for both raised the white linen tablecloth at the same time and looked under the table. There was Alan, prone upon the greige velvet carpet at the feet of his idols, the glittering world around them pretending not to notice. Alan had to be carried out as W. H. Auden and Francis Peabody Magoun settled the check and the tips.

Alan Ansen remained in the Auden–Kallman circle until both Chester and Wystan were no more. In the early fifties, after the sudden death of his aunt-guardian, Alan moved to Europe, settling in the country that gave the most generous exchange rate for the American dollar. At first he lived in Italy and could be seen in a red suit on the canals of Venice or at Peggy Guggenheim's. His friends looked him up in Harry's Bar near St. Mark's Square. Later on he moved to Athens and was influential in Chester's taking up winter residence in Greece from 1963. Each year Alan would be invited to spend a month with Chester and Wystan in Kirchstetten, where Wystan was to buy a house in 1958.

Alan was to travel to Jerusalem with Wystan and Chester in 1970, where Chester began his last poem, "The Dome of the Rock"; where he and Alan prayed in Hebrew at the Wailing Wall; where all three were invited to lunch by the mayor. Chester called Ansen to Vienna in September 1973 when Auden died. He was living in Athens in January 1975, at the time of Chester's death. He was to call himself, during the last years of Chester's life—over which he was to act as permissive but solicitous guardian—"The keeper of the keeper of the flame."

Auden was always fascinated with the concept of marriage, of whatever kind, and with what makes a marriage succeed. Perhaps Auden was interested in marriage only because he wanted to understand how to make his own succeed with Chester, for he believed himself still married. At any rate, at various times he made friends with young heterosexual couples who had children and whose marriages appeared happy. As he had befriended the Stevenses and the Rettgers back in Ann Arbor, he was to befriend Irving and Anne Weiss *en famille* eight years later in Italy.

When Chester and Wystan returned to New York from time to time in the middle 1950s, I used to see this young couple, the wife often pregnant, accompanied by young children at Chester and Wystan's parties at St. Mark's Place. Although I knew little about their personal life, they impressed me as having an ideal marriage. I was sure they had married for love, but I was equally sure they had married to have a family. They clearly wanted children. They seemed to regard the raising of children as a joy as well as a responsibility, but they were also interested in the things of the mind and cultural pursuits. They said that they were writers, he a poet, and I was told that he taught English at various colleges when he returned with his family to New York.

I knew about Wystan's interest in the Stevenses and the Rettgers, of course, but I was not used to seeing such symbols of conventional domesticity as the Weisses among the denizens of the Auden–Kallman ménage in New York. What struck me was the seeming intimacy of this relationship *à quatre* between the heterosexual and the homosexual couples. I took an interest in the Weisses and asked Chester how he happened to meet them and become friendly. Apparently he had known Irving Weiss before he lived in Ischia and had met him again by accident some years later overseas.

In December 1949, when Chester was transacting business in the American Express office in Rome, he ran into his old classmate from Brooklyn College and the University of Michigan, Irving Weiss. Weiss was in Rome with his fiancée, Anne, a lively American girl. Chester took them to a bar for an aperitif and felt an immediate rapport with Irving's girl. Thus began the close friendship with the couple. Anne and Irving were married a week later. After they returned from an Austrian language school in the fall, a friend suggested they settle in Ischia, for Anne was now pregnant, and Ischia appeared a good place to bring up children. In November they rented a house on Forio, where they were to live until 1954, when they returned to the States.

During the course of the next four years, Chester and Wystan saw a great deal of the Weisses. Since his Ann Arbor days, Wystan had been developing theories about children, childbearing, and the place of children in society, and he was especially interested in observing a woman who was carrying a child or had just given birth. He regarded childbirth as a woman's highest function and believed a special benediction to be attached to her presence. Anne Weiss was to provide him with abundant opportunity for benefaction, since she gave birth to four children during the next seven years.

Anne first met Wystan when a friend brought him to visit her after she had returned from a maternity hospital with her first child. Having made a polite fuss over the baby, he said the baby looked like an Anglican bishop. The observation may have been one of Wystan's set conversation pieces, for he said to Mary and me one day: "All babies look like either Queen Victoria or Winston Churchill."

If at first Wystan's interest in Anne was clinical, as time went on he was attracted to her as a person. He liked the couple and accepted them as family. While Wystan was usually polite, sometimes frigidly so, he did not encourage close friendship, so his ready acceptance of the Weisses was a singular compliment. Anne, Irving, Wystan, and Chester used to go out together in the evening and were seen in the various cafés on Ischia and at various cultural events in Naples. When Wystan was in his cross moods, Anne apparently could charm him out of them.

Traditional in many ways and a lover of the home, Wystan was interested in the concept of children as the source of the ongoing life of the family and the continuation of the species. He would certainly have chosen the family life for himself had he been heterosexual. Even as it was, he spoke on various occasions about fathering a child. At one point he even asked a young American woman whom he had met on Ischia to marry him and suggested that they call their first son Chester. Needless to say, his offer was not enthusiastically accepted.[1]

Apparently Wystan discussed his theories on marriage and the family with Irving Weiss. Wystan believed in the findings of modern psychology and psychoanalysis and his reading of Freud and Groddeck had intensified his interest in the child and childhood, since, according to his mentors, so many human problems began there. Although never sentimental about childhood, he believed it to be a link between one's present and former selves, the link between one self and one's ancestors. By losing touch with one's childhood, chronologically as well as psychologically, one lost one's identity.

At any rate, Wystan's interest in the child as a link to the past and as a vessel through which to achieve the continuation of a tradition led him to expound his ideas on childbirth. When Anne became pregnant again, Wystan made his pronouncements as if from on high and voiced his theories with all the authority of one who had fathered a number of children himself. One of these assertions was that every father should witness the birth of his own children. Thus when the Weisses' second child was born, the delivery was at home, and the midwife handed Irving his second daughter with the umbilical cord still uncut. The young couple respected Wystan's age and wisdom, if not all his theories, and had decided to take him at his word.

Wystan's theory about the father's seeing the birth of his child apparently was successful, at least for the Weisses, for the experience was a memorable one. By the time they returned to the United States, they were committed to having their babies at home. Their third daughter was born in their New York apartment. At this time Chester or other

---

[1] Auden also proposed later to Hannah Arendt, the political scientist and philosopher.

old friends of Anne's from her Columbia days came over each night to cook dinner and keep Anne and Irving company. David Protetch, the family doctor, refused to have anything to do with a home birth, however, for he thought it excessively primitive; thus another doctor had to be found. It was, however, a comforting and heartwarming experience for Anne.

If the Weisses followed Wystan's advice about the birth of babies, they did not follow his advice about food. Wystan did not approve of the rage for health foods or organically grown vegetables, believing such theories to represent a false primitivism. Neither did he object, as did the Weisses, to eating synthetic food. He was perfectly satisfied with Coffee-Mate, a synthetic cream, and chided Anne for not supplying it for his coffee when she did not have real cream. She was horrified.

For Anne, the time in Italy with Wystan and Chester was the happiest in her life. "Those were the golden days," she once said to me. "Chester had a gift for laughter. So did Wystan much of the time. Conversation with them was always wonderful. I've never met anyone like them since."

Wystan, with his grumpy moods and arctic silences, could be difficult socially, but apparently Anne, with a temperament similar to that of Chester, could beguile him. According to her husband, Anne's relationship with Chester was close, too. Although he and Chester had enjoyed each other's company ever since college days, Irving believed Chester and Anne's intimacy was closer. They had the same quick-witted responses and were always amusing themselves hilariously.

When the Weisses returned to the States and were living in New York, as, later, when they moved to a house in Brooklyn, Chester and Wystan were frequent visitors when in town. They saw each other regularly at each other's houses for dinner, especially on Thanksgiving and Christmas Eve. From time to time, when the Weisses would visit St. Mark's Place, where Wystan and Chester moved in 1953, they took the children. Said Irving Weiss:

> We'd put the girls to sleep in Greenwich Village in Wystan's bed, and we'd leave late in the evening. Someone looking on from outside would have wondered what was going on, I suppose, because Anne was pregnant and here we'd come in with these two little girls, and all of a sudden the place would fill up with young men. Though most of the guests except us were homosexual, they enjoyed sharing our family life and loved having a pregnant woman

and two children with whom to spend a holiday. There was never any lack of decorum or any misbehavior at any of these gatherings.[1]

With the Weisses in or near New York, Wystan again had children and a real family to enjoy. He could test his child-raising theories on them, give them advice, and, best of all, he could celebrate Thanksgiving, Christmas, and his birthday with them. He no longer had to rely on a make-believe family on Twenty-seventh Street. He even became a godfather again. On January 5, 1957, the Weisses' last baby, a boy, was born, and Wystan had another godson besides Wystan Auden Stevens.[2] At this time the couple was in Pennsylvania, so Chester called long distance, saying: "Couldn't you at least have waited for two days? Hugh could have been born on my birthday!"[3]

Both Chester and Wystan were fond of the children, even avuncular, but Chester could join in the fun directly. Wystan was more formal, behaving like the English schoolmaster he was. The children enjoyed being with Wystan and Chester, who did not pay much attention to them, but included them with occasional looks and smiles into the conversation, and it was often above their heads. The Weisses sent the children to bed after dinner before serious adult conversation began, for, like Wystan, they believed children should know they are children. One evening, however, one of the daughters was found sitting behind the living room door in her nightdress. She had slipped quietly out of bed to listen to the conversation, by this time wickedly racy, in the living room, much to the delight of Wystan, who, despite his strict theories, could often play the child himself in a way that was exasperating.

The Weiss children had a real affection for the moody Wystan and took delight in his schoolmaster poses and various eccentricities. According to reports, at least once every dinner one of the children would drop a napkin to the floor as an excuse to peer under the table to see whether Wystan had taken his shoes off yet. When he had done so, one child would nudge the others. Yet, Wystan would invariably talk about forbidden subjects so that Chester as well as Irving and Anne would switch to Italian, trying desperately to make Wystan switch,

[1] The author's conversation with Irving Weiss, February 11, 1983.

[2] It will be recalled that Auden's first godson was Wystan Auden Stevens, born in 1943 in Ann Arbor. Philip Spender, Stephen Spender's nephew, was another godson.

[3] The author's conversation with Anne Weiss, February 11, 1983.

too. Unlike Chester and the Weisses, however, Wystan, though he could read French, Italian, and German fluently, not to mention Latin and ancient Greek, never learned to speak these foreign tongues without effort.

Chester, who had been in Italy most of the time when the Weisses were there, had known the two older girls as infants and was developing an avuncular style that blended with his sharp sense of the comic. He enjoyed in the Weisses' home a domestic security that did not stifle his self-expression. At such times he had no need to shock but was charming and witty.

At one point Chester decided to teach the older girls to cook. They were fond of sweets, much to the dismay of their parents, and Chester on several occasions brought Duncan Hines mixes. They would make together a cake or doughnuts, which the girls called chesternuts, and had a hilarious, if somewhat greasy, baking spree. Now and then the parents would look in at Chester alone with the girls. Apparently he was having a great time, happy to be able to assume the role of teacher one moment and child among children the next. Wystan, however, the English schoolmaster, never unbent to the degree Chester did and was usually quite stiff.

From conversations with Anne and Irving, I obtained a vivid picture of Wystan and Chester together on Ischia. They were essentially happy with each other and well suited. Their minds were true in the sense of architecture or carpentry: comfortable, of the exact angle, adjustment, and fit. Their relationship was in that sense a marriage. Irving said that they

> had the same sort of camaraderie when they were alone with each other as we all had when we were together. I saw that upon the few occasions that I came upon them when they did not expect me. When one of them approved or did not approve of something in the literary taste of the other, the objection would come out or the approval, but the range of reference was so intimate and yet so apt and so far reaching, that it was not surprising that they had remained together for so long.
>
> What may have started as a sexual relationship matured. Intellectually and artistically, they complemented each other. Anybody who looked at the collaborative efforts of Chester and Wystan on the operas would, unless familiar with Chester, have no idea how much Auden relied upon his friend's taste and judgment. . . . Wystan depended upon Chester's sense of taste and Chester's

knowledge of music, particularly the opera. Although Wystan gave the impression that at the age zero he was born with an impeccable musical sense, it was Chester who had given him this taste.

When you saw them together, you saw that Chester had just as much self-assurance as did Wystan, and that Chester frequently directed, or at least influenced, Wystan's taste. Because they were both intellectually powerful, each in his own right, they could talk to each other and have a lasting relationship. Chester was the only one in the world who could have had such a relationship with Wystan. One felt between them an instant electrical connection, particularly when they were talking about literature or music.[1]

When Wystan and Chester's translation of *The Magic Flute* was presented on NBC-TV in 1956, the published libretto was dedicated to Anne and Irving Weiss. In July 1963, Wystan wrote two poems about the four children, dedicating the poems to their parents: "Down There," about cellars, and "Up There," about attics. Perhaps the use of two areas of a home was appropriate in writing about the Weisses, for their home, wherever it was, had been a symbol to Wystan of the civilized family, a bulwark of the heart and of the mind against a savage time.

[1] The author's conversation with Irving Weiss, February 11, 1983.

CHAPTER 12

Words and
Music

THE INCIDENTS OF Auden's life—his difficulties with Chester; his various love affairs, their complications and disappointments; his employment here and there; his lectures; his prizes; his social activities—all these were on the surface only. His one abiding constant, next to which all other considerations were as fugitive reflections on the water, was his writing. His writing defined him, his personality and his character. The advice he gave to Chester in his letter of January 1950 he had learned at his mother's knee: "Treachery, unrequited love, bereavement, toothache, bad food, poverty, etc. must count for nothing the moment one picks up one's notebook." Life must have an inviolate center. For his mother that center had been her religion. For Wystan it was his poetry.

By conforming to a rigid time schedule, Auden was exerting his control over time as surely as did those ancient Benedictine monks in the Cluniac and Cistercian monasteries of France—Saint Guilhem-le-Désert, Paray-le-Monial, Anzy-le-Duc, Fontevrault, Vézelay—who,

living by the canonical hours, were asserting their will over time in
order to live in eternity. Each division of time—matins to compline—
was allotted its ordered activity, and thus the Lord's work was gradually done in the world, each period as much a prayer as any other,
from weeding the vegetable garden and feeding the cows and horses
to assisting at Holy Mass.

Most of the time Auden lived a monastic time schedule from lauds
to compline.[1] Usually he arose before six and preferred to retire by
nine or ten. He worked at his writing from prime through sext. He
claimed to become depressed around the hour of three in the afternoon, a fact which he attributed to something in his psyche that recognized nones, or the hour of three, as the hour of the death of Christ.
No wonder that he was to publish in 1951 a book of poems called
Nones.

Auden did the most important task first, his writing, early in the
morning, usually working until noon. During the summer months, as
in Ischia, his schedule would vary somewhat: He would arise later,
perhaps, and retire later. But generally he held to the hours. To the
end of his life he would permit nothing to interfere, even refusing to
answer the telephone until after noon. Like a boy in boarding school,
he took delight in writing out his time schedules. Every time he
moved to another location—Ischia, Kirchstetten, New York, Oxford—
there is usually a letter to someone describing in detail his new schedule for the day. The new one varied little from the old. There was
always the early rising, work until noon, and free time in the afternoons and evening. His letters to Keith Callaghan gave two such
schedules. He sent the second, dated June 2, 1949, having forgotten
he had already sent the first. It went as follows:

> 7:00 get up and make the coffee. 8:00 AM call Chester and sit
> drinking coffee on the balcony, I facing Mt. Epomeo, Chester fac-
> ing the sea. 9:00 AM start working. 12:00 Noon go down to the
> piazza and have a Cinzanino. 12:30 back to help prepare lunch
> and lay the table in the garden. 1:15–2:15 lunch with usually some
> music from the radio. 2:15–4:00 sunbathe at the beach. 4–4:30
> coffee. 4:30–6:30 work. 6:30 help getting dinner ready. 7:20 martini

[1] CANONICAL HOURS

Matins	12 midnight to	Sext	12 noon
	5:00 A.M.	Nones	3 P.M. (hour of the
Lauds	5 A.M.		death of Christ)
Prime	6 A.M.	Vespers	6 P.M.
Terce	9 A.M.	Compline	9 P.M.

time. 7:40–8:40 dinner. 8:40–10:00 Drink coffee, a double Strega
and some wine in Maria's Cafe. 10 home to bed. On Saturday afternoons instead of sunbathing, a hot bath up the road; on Sunday
mornings a breakfast with eggs at 9:30. If I get tired of working
there is always some plant in the garden to be watered, etc.

Auden simply sat down at his desk, and if the Muse—he referred
to her often—would not come, he kept working until she did. He addressed himself without fanfare to the task at hand, and he could
write anywhere: in the subway, at a café table, on a train, in an air-
plane, at a counter in a coffeehouse. However, he did mention once,
when looking for a new apartment in 1945, that he hoped he would
not have to take a studio, because he preferred sleeping in a room
other than the one in which he did his work. He finally had to settle
for the studio at 7 Cornelia, which he never liked. When at St. Mark's
Place later on, he wrote in the parlor on a long pine *bureau plât,*
made for him by a carpenter in the Village. When he collaborated
with Chester Kallman, he sometimes worked in the afternoon or in
the evening, but that was in addition to his morning stint, a kind of
play time, a companionable occupation that he shared with the person
whom he loved. Usually, however, they worked separately, Chester at
night.

Auden was by nature solitary; few people ever knew him well. He
kept hidden from the world the ultimate secret of his nature and thus
tended to inspire awe even in his most intimate friends—all, that is,
except Chester. "He was a monster," said one friend of long standing, "although a lovable one." More often, the awe he inspired caused
his admirers to refer to him as the Master, but the title was partly a
tease used by Chester.[1]

At least one way of glimpsing the personality of a man is to read
the random remarks and observations contained in his letters. Auden's
letters to Chester allow as intimate a glimpse as we can hope to
achieve. In them he removed the mask he usually wore in public. In
Auden's letters to Chester and to Keith Callaghan during the late
forties and early fifties, there are references to the events of every day,
to the current musical scene, to his animals, to literature, to people.
He even gossiped a bit and discussed the cost of coffee and the local

[1] The tease was based on Henry James's being referred to as the Master by
writers (as the result of the James story "The Lesson of the Master," about a great
novelist). Wystan was always enraged at being called this, and Chester seemed to
enjoy using it as a joke.

elections. He talked as well about money. He was both wildly generous and stringently economical, depending upon his mood and the
day. In all these references the man comes through.

Chester and Wystan were fond of animals, especially cats, and they
always talked to them—on the street, in the houses of their friends,
anywhere. In talking to cats, Chester would greet them with "Prrrow,"
in the most gentle of voices, and Wystan would lunge at them, saying,
"Come, Puss, come, Puss," and the graceful creature would rush away
in terror. Chester and Wystan always had a number of cats, taking
great care with their names. In Forio there were Lucina, the Duchess,
Nero, and Dorabella, to name a few, and a dog, Mosé, which Wystan
had found shivering in a swamp. In New York there was the calico
cat, Cenerentola (Cinderella), named for the opera. Wystan and Chester eventually would have their cats neutered, but they would often
take in a pregnant stray, such as Lucina or the Duchess, for whose
kittens they would have to find homes: "Alex was over for dinner the
other day," Wystan wrote from Ischia on June 16, 1952, "and took
back with him for the family Giuseppe, Lucina's only son. Tekla gets
Restituta and Margherita gets Maria."

Chester and Wystan would refer often to their cats in conversation:
"Lucina is such a snob, my dear. She won't even talk to Nero"; "Nero
simply adores eels and ate one alive for breakfast"; "the Duchess was
spiteful that day in Rome. She scratched me horribly when I took her
out of her favorite box." It was only after some time that a newcomer
to the conversation was able to discern that Wystan and Chester were
talking about cats. In Wystan's letters it is not unusual to find lines
such as, "I do hope our beloved Dorabella has survived the surgeon's
irreverent knife" (October 6, 1948). "My love to Nero and the Duchess" (September 20, 1950). "I trust that the Duchess has returned from
Rome. How did she like it?" (October 25, 1950). "This morning N.
and I left Forio. Giocondo came running after us to say that Lucina
has kittens; how many and what colors I don't know" (May 16, 1951).
In a letter to Chester in New York from Ischia (May 3, 1951), Wystan
sent the following envoi:

> *Saluti a Pete*[1]
> *Prrrrou a Cenerentola*
> *et a te*
> *tanti baci e belle cose.*

[1] Peter Komadina (not his real name), a mutual friend who was sharing the
apartment in New York.

Wystan had few illusions about human nature. He did not regard mankind sentimentally, and he did not see mankind as the center of any cosmos; he saw him, rather, in the spirit of Saint Francis, and with detached compassion, as part of a Divine Order under God. He despised humbug and pretense; he often observed his fellows with a clinical eye that would not have pleased them had they known. Just after returning to Ischia, Wystan wrote to a friend comments on the people he met in India while attending a conference of the Congress for Cultural Freedom (April 10, 1951):

> As for my colleagues, [A] is a booming old bore. [B] all right on genetics, but, like so many American Scientists, will want to take literary flights and talk of HUMANITY REACHING TO THE VERY STARS THEMSELVES. [C], intelligent, but not quite intelligent enough, [D] excellent at telling funny stories and with a good heart, but still boring on nineteenth century liberalism. [E], a bird brain, and [F], sociologist, a birder. Which leaves De Rougemont and myself as the Bright Boys. I opened my speech by saying, "If you want to know why this conference had to be held, the answer lies in the following question: 'Why are all of us in this room bored to death and wishing we could go home?' " Nobody laughed. Calcutta was better, but I still had to be social. . . .

From the *Queen Elizabeth,* he wrote Chester about his fellow passengers (September 1948):

> My companions are a president of some minor college in Virginia, one of those prissy Americans with a featureless face, no lips and rimless glasses, and a refugee who lives in England, but I have seen very little of them; both, thank God, are on the first sitting. Our table consists of a Miss G. (Canadian), her niece (Spotty), who is at teachers' training college in Chicago, Mr. D., a Belgian in the old clothes business who reads Hebrew books, me, and a very nice (though not pretty) young man, called P., who was at Groton and now works for World Federation. The waiter, alas, is quite plain. One or two pretty pieces aboard, but so far I haven't got to know any. The clocks are put back at midnight, so one is terribly hungry by breakfast time.

To Chester he wrote from Mount Holyoke on January 6, 1950:

> Came up here yesterday for a week's visit with two lectures and a lot of student teas. The first lecture was last night and the most

severe I have ever given—a cross between Whitehead and Heidegger—but my Dickens–Firbank one will be gentler. Have just had Prof. Dodds for a week which meant letting him have the apartment and sleeping over at Rhoda's. Rather inconvenient, but he's such a dear. . . . La Truman C[apote] had a triumph at the YMHA. The first lecturer ever to have to have a police escort to get him out.

On February 8, 1950:

Went yesterday to Yale for a literary society dinner at which I intensely expected to flirt with the young gents, especially since I heard they had had Gore Vidal down to teach them how to write. Well, what happened? I was seated between Mr. and Mrs. Cleanth Brooks. Henry York, alias Henry Green, is staying at the Gotham Hotel under the name of H. V. Young. He and wife are coming to dinner on Thursday. He's ever so nice.

In his letters to Chester, Auden shared his reactions to books he had been reading, many recently published, and his evaluation of them. On November 1, 1948:

Have been reading Robert Graves' grammar of poetic myth, *The White Goddess,* quite dotty but full of fascinating material. One of his lines is that you can recognize the true poet from the physical description he gives of The Muse (alias The Triple Goddess, alias Laura Riding, etc.). According to Gertie Graves,[1] . . . you would fit the archtype exactly.

October 25, 1950, from Mount Holyoke, where he was a visiting lecturer in autumn, 1950:

I do hope you haven't fallen into your dumps again. Talking of which, I have been reading the life of Edward Thomas [the poet and critic], who suffered from them dreadfully and perpetually. In one letter he speaks of an anxiety state thus: "having heard one report, one keeps listening for the second barrel." There is a photo of him at 22—wow! Am reviewing Boswell's *London Journal* for *The New Yorker.* According to himself, he was very large.[2]

[1] Auden often used alliterative camp names to please Chester, who made them up, though Auden did not usually speak this way in conversation.

[2] Auden was referring to Boswell's private parts. He also mentioned the fact in conversation about this time.

I'm really enjoying it here despite . . . no one to let one's hair down with.

Knowing how much Chester loved music, Auden shared with him the performances he had been attending in New York, most of them with Keith Callaghan, whose presence he was at first slow to mention. He wrote about recent acquisitions of records and about his reaction to the performance of *The Age of Anxiety,* a ballet choreographed by Jerome Robbins to music by Leonard Bernstein, named for Auden's book published on July 11, 1947. Auden's chief recreation during the months in New York from 1948 to 1952 seems to have been music in one form or another.

December 30, 1948:

> Went to the Yiddish Y yesterday to hear a concert performance of *Mavra* which I thought a lovely work, all about a huzzah in drag. Tonight to *Rape of Lucrece,* the performance of which I hear is awful.

February 17, 1950:

> O yes, my *dear,* you should see the ballet *Age of Anxiety* to a rehearsal of which I went. (It comes on soon, I believe.) [Jerome] Robbins far outdoes all the lezzie[1] Modern Dance in horror. Have read the first 200 galleys of [Jacques] Barzun's book on Berlioz. Quite good, but O so donnish.

March 7, 1950:

> The week before last was *Age of Anxiety* week with the Bernstein symphony and the Robbins ballet, both . . . well received, especially the latter. I've just put my agent on to them both as I think I'm entitled to a percentage. Went last night to see two heavenly new Balanchines, *Bourrée Fantasque* (Chabrier) and *Pas de Deux Romantique* (Weber Clarinet Concerto) and a Freddy Ashton–Cecil Beaton–Bengy,[2] *Illuminations*—bits all right, but the singer was hell.

Every now and then Auden would include in his letters to Chester a joke he had found amusing. These jokes often had a puerile quality,

[1] Wystan's camp term for "lesbian." Ironically, Chester and Wystan were, of all things, prejudiced against lesbians.

[2] Benjamin Britten, the composer.

reminiscent of days in boarding school. On July 5, 1952, he wrote: "Am much enjoying re-reading [Corvo's] *The Desire and Pursuit of the Whole;* I love silly jokes like the Anglican clergyman who sings *My Pew*[1] at a tea party, and ends telephone conversations with 'ah river dertchy.' " In another letter (November 22, 1949): "Have another funny story about two immensely rich old ladies called Wetmore who live in Newport. During the war one of them had to take a bus for the first time in her life. When the conductor came round with the ticket machine, she looked up, smiled graciously, and said, 'No, thank you so much, but I have my private charities.' "

Another joke that Auden loved was one he once told Chester's father: "There was a man sitting opposite me in the tramway, and he was reading a newspaper upside down.

" 'Don't you find it difficult reading that way?' I asked.

"The man answered: 'Extremely so.' "

The letters contain numerous references to various aspects of everyday life, some vexing, some pleasant, some comical. On September 20, 1950, upon arriving back in New York from Ischia, he wrote to Chester: "I got into the George Washington [Hotel] last Saturday more dead than alive at 2:30 p.m. We had nine hours in Brussels which was quite fun for me, for I was able to look nostalgically round the old place." October 31, 1950: "This is just a hurried note before I run off to donate blood and then give a class. . . . The last few days I have been in a manic phase, writing limericks incessantly. . . ." February 13, 1949: "One interesting piece of news. The pet tortoise of the late Princesse Eugenie which ran away from her when she went to the opening of the Suez Canal and the debut of *Aïda* in 1869 died last week in Cairo zoo." January 6, 1950: "Don't forget you have to renew your passport in February. Please let me know if and when any of the other packages arrive. I think I'm going to send a lot of Borden's powdered coffee in advance, as I do really prefer American coffee for breakfast." September 20, 1950: "Sen. McCarthy's secretary was picked up by the police for guess what."

From the beginning Auden thought of Chester as a gifted poet. Though this opinion was not always shared, there is no doubt that Auden took Chester Kallman's writing seriously and made every effort to see that the poems were polished and fit for publication. Further, Wystan himself sent Chester's poems off to editors whom he knew and

[1] A pun on a phrase in an aria from Verdi's *Aïda* (Act III. O Patria mia) in which "mai più" (no longer) is stressed.

who were likely to publish poems Auden had recommended. In his letters to Chester in 1948 and 1949 particularly, he set about giving detailed evaluations as well as suggestions for improvement of the poems Chester had sent him for criticism. The examples of Auden's criticisms are of academic interest only, since no specific purpose of instruction other than the most general could be served unless one were to see the original drafts, now lost forever. The criticisms do show, however, the time and care Auden took, writing as he did in detail by hand, indicating often even the smallest mistake in punctuation.[1] The completed poems "Elegy" and "Sunday Evening" appear in their corrected form in *Storm on Castelfranco* (Grove Press, New York, 1956), with a dedication to James Schuyler, one of Chester's old friends of the forties. Chester was to publish two other books of poetry: *Absent and Present,* in 1957 (Wesleyan University Press, Middletown, Connecticut), which he dedicated to Auden: and *The Sense of Occasion,* in 1971 (Braziller, New York), which he dedicated to his father and me.

In 1948 Chester was still at work on the long poem called "Elegy," which he wrote in memory of his mother. The inspiration for the poem came one summer afternoon when he was listening to Chopin's First Piano Concerto in E Minor (opus 11) with Mary and me on Twenty-seventh Street. We all agreed that the music was elegiac, and Chester began writing even as the music was playing. He was also attracted on the same afternoon to a painting by Giorgione[2] called "Tempesta," which shows a woman in the foreground nursing a baby. In the background, around which thunderclouds are gathering, is a tower that is possibly Castelfranco. Chester was still working on the poem during the autumn of 1948, and Auden, in his letter of November 1, 1948, said: "I am most impressed by the 'Elegy' so far. Much less turgid than you used to be without getting loose. My only criticisms are minor, mostly punctuation. . . . Anyway, I found the whole piece moving indeed so far. . . ." He took time for a page and a half of corrections in punctuation, and on December 13 he wrote again, mentioning he had reread the poem a number of times and still retained his first impression: "The 'Elegy' is quite magnificent; for God's sake, don't get frightened."

Apparently Chester had included with "Elegy" and "Sunday Eve-

---

[1] Auden admitted to being weak in punctuation, but his mistakes tended to be a matter of carelessness rather than insufficient knowledge. When he took time to think about punctuation, he could get it right.

[2] Giorgione was a sixteenth-century Venetian painter.

ning" another poem, a pornographic one, called "The Fly," for Wystan responded on December 13, 1948, with: "Deciding that there ought to be one [a pornographic poem] in the Auden Corpus, I am writing a purely pornographic poem, *The Platonic Blow*. You should do one on the other Major Act. Covici would print them together privately on rubber paper for dirty old millionaires at immense profit to us both. (Illustrations by Cadmus?)"

Most likely Chester made the necessary corrections in the other poems, for on March 15, 1949, Auden wrote: "I think the new stanza much better and will try to get the whole typed and sent off, though you ask a lot of a girl in my present whirl. I did show the poems to Geoffrey,[1] who liked them very much, particularly Part II of 'Elegy.' His chief criticism, and I think it just, is that too often you end lines in unimportant words, so that the rhyme pattern or even the line length itself seems artificial in the bad sense."

In spite of the time Auden took away from his own work to correct Chester's manuscript, to make suggestions, even to send the poems off to publishers, Chester apparently was not taking the suggestions with a glad and grateful heart. As early as November 8, 1949, one of Auden's letters gives evidence of some resentment, even paranoia, on Chester's part: "Your letter received this morning. I hope you don't think that I like having to alter your work—it's annoying enough when it's one's own—or that I try to spoil it. I wish, too, that there was something *I* could do about *They*, but, as you know, there isn't. You must often wish that you had never set eyes on me, but I hope not all the time. . . ." Auden's attitude here, almost apologetic for his own successes, must strike one as at least remarkable. It was in a later letter to Chester (January 6, 1950) that he gave him the classic advice that is seldom taken, advice about forgetting all personal problems once you open your notebook. Chester, who saw himself as a victim in other areas of life, saw himself also as a victim of Wystan's fame: "They think I can't do it on my own," he used to say.

During the months that followed Auden's first visit to Stravinsky in the fall of 1947, he and Chester were working on the libretto for *The Rake's Progress* as well as writing their own poems. Auden, always prolific, partly as the result of his monastic hours, was to publish his *Collected Shorter Poems, 1930–1944* on March 9, 1948, and *The Enchafed Flood,* a book of lectures, on March 17, 1950; and in February

---

[1] Unidentified; possibly Auden's friend Geoffrey Grigson, poet and editor.

1951, he was to publish *Nones*. Chester's *Storm on Castelfranco* did not come out until 1956.

Auden and Stravinsky had drafted the outline for the libretto of *The Rake's Progress* in September 1947, during Auden's trip to California. Auden completed Act I by January 16, 1948. He and Chester worked on Act II, which they completed by January 28, and they sent Act III to the composer on February 9, 1948. By September 11, 1951, the score was finished and the opera was ready for its première in Venice after a rehearsal period in Milan.

One of the major themes of the opera is the fidelity of true love. Stravinsky was inspired by a series of six Hogarth[1] engravings called "The Rake's Progress" that he had seen in the Art Institute of Chicago. The engravings tell the story of a wastrel who dissipates his inheritance by gambling; breaks the heart of his true love, whom he has seduced and impregnated; marries a rich old one-eyed woman; wastes his second fortune; and ends in a madhouse, his first love still true to him. Although Wystan and Chester made some minor alterations in plot and character, introducing the devil in the person of Shadow and substituting Baba, the bearded lady, whom Tom marries in an *acte gratuit,* for the rich old one-eyed woman, the plot follows generally the theme of the six engravings. The opera was conducted by Igor Stravinsky at the première and directed by Carl Ebert.

In Auden's letters to Chester from 1948 to 1952, and also in some to Keith Callaghan, one finds references to the writing of *The Rake's Progress,* including suggestions concerning the various aspects of staging and production, to which Chester made a number of contributions. Stravinsky, the most charming of men, was, nevertheless, easy to imitate, with his heavy accent and Russian ways, so the librettists, always ready to laugh when they were alone together, were not above some affectionate fun-making at the composer's expense. They baptized him Il Maestro, and they called him Uncle Igor, Stravigor, or Stravvy. On October 1, 1948, Wystan wrote to Chester: "The first act of Olive[2] is finished, I also hear, and someone reports that the music is wonderful. The Maestro only says, 'Eet vill be vary eesy to leesten to.' "

---

[1] William Hogarth (1697–1764) was an English painter, engraver, and satirist, as well as an art theorist. He achieved success with six morality pictures entitled "The Harlot's Progress," whereupon he did a similar series, "The Rake's Progress."

[2] The camp name Olive refers to Olive Opera; namely, *The Rake's Progress.*

February 24, 1949: "There is a new plan about *The Rake*. To have the preview in Central City, Colorado, in the summer of 1950. A nuisance for us, but there might be the consolation that Stravinsky has agreed that you and I shall direct the staging, for which we shall get paid. Singers so far wanted by him are:

Anne	Sayao or Steber
Baba	Elmo
Shadow	Valdengo if his English is good enough.

None of us can think of a tenor. Can you? (Bjoerling is too Scandinavian and fubsy.)"[1]

February 21, 1949:

> Your letter . . . and the wire all arrived beautifully this morning. Bless you all. Luckily, too, just in time before I went off to the Ambassador Hotel to go through Act II [of *The Rake*]. All your suggestions were conveyed and enthusiastically received; I wish you had been there to get the credit. I'm afraid you'll have to swallow my couplet for the Cabaletta:
>
> > Time cannot alter
> > My loving heart
> > My ever-loving heart.
>
> I was faced with fitting it into the music and it was the only thing I could think up that would fit. The performance was from the piano score with the maestro at the piano, Bob Craft, Balanchine, self, etc., screaming parts. Craft (a very intelligent young conductor) is at my request writing out an analysis of Act I to send you.[2]

March 15, 1949: "Have not passed on your suggestion about the silence[3] for the following reason. The Prelude to the Act is to be a

[1] Stravinsky did not get the singers he originally wanted. The original cast was:

Tom Rakewell	Robert Rounseville
Anne Trulove	Elisabeth Schwarzkopf
Nick Shadow	Otakar Kraus
Baba the Turk	Jennie Tourel

[2] Kallman was responsible for the writing of half of the second act: the first part of Act II, Scene 1, and all of Act II, Scene 2.

[3] The silence was to represent the yawn with which Tom Rakewell succumbs to the temptation of the devil in the person of Shadow. Chester thought a silence not dramatic enough for the audience to understand its significance.

musical hunt (i.e. the hunt of nature and R.'s[1] chase for Baba). There will be no natural noises like scraping of chairs or even street cries."
November 22, 1949:

> Last night I had to put on tails and recite at Carnegie Hall in the midst of a Stravinsky programme. *Pulcinella* (better than I thought though too long) and *Persephone* which is very remarkable. Some of the Princeton choir who took part were very fetching. It conflicted with opening night at the Met. *Rosenkavalier* with Steber, Stevens, Berger, List, conducted by Fritz Reiner (who is to do *The Rake*). I saw the final scene on the television screen while having a nightcap with Lincoln [Kirstein] and Fidelma [his wife]. My *dear,* you can't imagine what it's like—the make-up makes everyone look like a Welsh documentary film about coal-miners, and Octavian close up with Sophie looked like Dracula—it was too obscene.
>
> Tried to get tickets for tomorrow to see *Manon Lescaut* with Bjoerling and Valdengo, but nothing better than balcony was to be had, so shall wait.

December 27, 1949: "Uncle Igor, by the way, arrives in February with Act II. Act I is very soon going to the printers, and Elizabeth Mayer[2] is being commissioned to do the German translation. I have a ticklish diplomatic job to make the Maestro see that it is in his long-term interests not to conduct the premiere at Edinburgh and then hand it over to a second-rate conductor, but to let Fritz Reiner do it from the start."

March 7, 1950: "Went through the libretto of Act III with Stravigor the other day. No changes wanted yet. The only thing I had to add was the exact figures for the bidding in the Auctioneer's song. Balanchine's description of the music which he is overwhelmed by is 'Don Giovanni reflected in a Coney Island Mirror.'"

September 20, 1950: "I just saw Lincoln this afternoon and it seems that the premiere will probably be Central City, Colorado, in June or July. England in '51 seems out, as Benjy [Britten] has the floor. The other piece of news apropos is that Ralph Hawkes dropped dead last week. Who'll run the business [Boosey and Hawkes][3] no one seems to know yet."

[1] R. is Tom Rakewell.

[2] Elizabeth Mayer, a friend of Auden to whom he dedicated *New Year Letter* (1941).

[3] Boosey and Hawkes, music publishers.

May 16, 1951, to Chester from Repton, England, where Auden was visiting his father: "Saw Stein and Co. at the London office of Boosey and Hawkes who told me they have been sending you the proofs of *The Rake* to correct. They lent me the sketches for Act III. The bits I was able to puzzle out such as the Baba-Anne-Auctioner trio and the Baba-Anne-Tom duet seemed lovely.

"In Italy everything is in an inconceivable mess. . . ."

Apparently there was a tiff between Stravinsky and another member of the group and a controversy over who was to do the sets. Finally, after bursts of artistic temperament, delays, and spats, all was settled, and the première was to be given not in the wilds of Colorado after all but in Italy on September 11, 1951, in Venice. The rehearsals, however, were to be held in Milan.

Stravinsky was not sorry to have Chester as one of the collaborators. According to Robert Craft, a conductor himself, and Stravinsky's right-hand man, "Kallman was not only easier to understand than Auden, but the younger man could also bring out the older man's sometimes dormant affability—as well as subdue his tempers, which the poet usually proclaimed with 'I'm very cross today.' "[1]

Chester was never happier. He had written half of the second act and was responsible for a great deal of work on the other acts. He was in his glory, particularly after the libretto had been completed and he could work at rehearsals with the musicians, call Stravinsky "Stravvy," visit international cities, and entertain socially. When visiting his father in New York in 1954, he was bristling with opera gossip, and he would amuse his friends and relatives with imitations of the composer as well as of the opera singers.

First had been the rehearsals in Milan. Said Craft:

> The outstanding event during the sojourn in Milan was a dinner that the librettists gave for the Stravinskys. After it they all attended a performance of Giordano's *Fedora*,[2] which was very disappointing in comparison to Chester Kallman's hilarious preview of it. At such times Auden relinquished the stage, except to contribute scraps of background information or to alert the Stravinskys to imminent high-points. He was proud and happy. But, then, Wystan Auden's devotion to Chester Kallman was the most important fact of the poet's personal life, as well as the real subject of the libretto (the fidelity of true love); it transcends the confes-

[1] Craft, "The Poet and the Rake," *Auden: A Tribute,* p. 151.
[2] An opera (1898) by Umberto Giordano (1867–1948).

sion of Auden's most popular lyric. More touching still, when Chester Kallman was unable to attend the second performance of the opera in Venice, Wystan Auden quietly left the theater before the end, not wishing to risk having to bow alone and to receive credit due to his friend.

Kallman was indispensable to Auden in at least one considerable area of his work: the older poet could never have written librettos without his younger colleague. What is more, in everything that Auden wrote, he relied on Kallman's critical judgment. No less important, Chester Kallman, though hardly an adherent of bourgeoise behavior himself, succeeded in imposing some of his Brooklyn common sense on his partner.[1] Kallman was also the domesticator—if only to a degree—for he was so mild a tamer that the animal was never entirely housebroken. Finally, and appearances often to the contrary, the two poets took care of each other. Kallman always knew, despite Auden's protective friends, that no matter how lost his colleague might seem to be, he was actually capable of finding his way home, of handling his business affairs, and of attending to his physical needs.[2]

Another advantage of having Chester along was Chester's fluency in Italian. He spoke well, understood the many dialects of the country, and was seldom taken for a foreigner. Wystan, despite his Italian lessons, his conscientious New York Italian teacher, and all the homework of which he complained in his letters, was never able to speak the language freely. But Chester would sit at the corner cafés drinking Strega or at the coffeehouses drinking espresso and exchange jokes and gossip with the patrons and the waiters as if he had lived there all his life. He was even able to imitate, in his actor's way, the typical Latin grimaces and gestures. After six months' residence, Chester, who never took a lesson, spoke Italian like an Italian.

In the letters that Auden wrote to Callaghan during this time there are many references to Stravinsky and *The Rake*. "There seems to be quite a serious possibility," Auden wrote on July 29, 1951, "that Chester and I may actually direct *The Rake*. I'm petrified with terror and it will mean going for rehearsals in ten days to Milan which has the worst climate in Italy, but it will mean a little cash and should provide a fund of anecdotes." On August 21:

[1] Chester and Wystan tended to be outrageous in different ways, and often one modified the behavior of the other.

[2] Craft, "The Poet and the Rake," *Auden: A Tribute*, pp. 153–54.

Il Maestro arrived last week, thinking he had pneumonia. Two bars are missing from the score and cannot be found. The singers are all engaged, but rehearsals haven't started yet and the curtain goes up on September 11. Tenor: Rounseville; Baritone: Otakar Kraus; Contralto: Tourel; Soprano: Schwarzkopf. Chester and I go to Milan next Monday. Ebert, alas, is directing, but we are to advise in return for our expenses which are going to be *very* heavy. Seats for the premiere are being sold on the black market at 180 dollars. Sept 3 we move on to Venice. On the 8th there is to be a Ball given by a Mexican millionaire to end all Balls. We have not yet been invited, but it is rumoured that we will. The Windsors are to be there and the Aga Khan and food will be specially flown in from Paris. The Drut[1] will be green with envy, not only over that but also because we have been seeing Burt Lancaster who is quite preposterously vain. Warner Bros. are making a film here, mostly with English actors who all seem to be Old Etonians.

The [Italian] Press is excelling itself at misprints; the opera is either *The Rackes Progress* or *The Harlot's Progress,* I am V. A. Anden and Chester is Mr. Calmer.

When he was in Germany in 1938, Stravigor was arrested in a restaurant as a Jew: Schoenberg wrote a whole satirical cantata about him and Papa Bach. I lead a life of unparallelled chastity.

September 9, 1951:

Today there are no rehearsals as the chorus are rehearsing the Verdi *Requiem,* and I have a second to myself for the first time for nearly a fortnight. The stories about the production would fill a large book and I shall wait till I get back to tell you them.

The music is quite terrific—one lovely tune after another. Schwarzkopf and Tourel and Grenault . . . first rate. Kraus . . . OK and Rounseville has a nice voice (but is no musician).

In the same letter he mentioned that Il Maestro was very deaf. "One rehearsal Tourel missed her cue and he went on for sixty bars without realizing that she wasn't singing. Ebert who was hired over our screams to direct is not only the worst sort of Kraut, vain and insolent beyond belief, but also totally incompetent. If we get through the performance without disaster it will be a miracle. But it really *is* a masterpiece."

In 1954 Chester and Wystan arrived in New York for the première of *The Rake's Progress* in the United States. Eddie and I sat grandly

---

[1] A nickname for one of Chester and Wystan's friends.

in a box off stage left, and during the intermission all Eddie's women patients and all his cousins and second cousins rushed up to him saying, "It's all because of you, Eddie." Chester stood coolly by, smiling and sipping a martini from the old Metropolitan Opera bar as he made appropriate remarks to all the friends and relatives that had assembled, and Wystan lost himself as soon as possible in the crowd. At the end of the performance Chester and Wystan took their bow along with the brightly costumed singers on the stage of the beloved Old Met, and all the diamond horseshoe applauded. For Chester it was a dream come true. As for Eddie, he had furtively turned off his hearing aid halfway through the performance, and now looked up at me, saying: "Is it *finally* over?" Eddie did not care for Stravinsky's music.

After *The Rake's Progress* Chester and Wystan collaborated on a number of operas, some translations and some original. The original operas were: *Elegy for Young Lovers* (1961) and *The Bassarids* (1966), both with music by Hans Werner Henze. Although neither Wystan nor Chester believed that operas should be given in any language other than the one in which they were written, they were willing to compromise for a price. "As long as operas are going to be translated into English anyway," they said, "we might as well do it." Thus they translated Mozart's *Don Giovanni* and *The Magic Flute,* as well as Brecht's *The Rise and Fall of the City of Mahagonny* and *The Seven Deadly Sins.*

Neither original work was popular at the time it was given; in fact, the audience was said to walk out from *Elegy for Young Lovers* during its première in England. Friends of the librettists insisted that the fault lay in Henze's music. Of the translations only *The Magic Flute* won popular acclaim. It was presented over NBC television in April 1960. *Mahagonny,* considered by some the finest translation extant of the work, was never produced.

Chester did some translations without Wystan: *The Coronation of Poppea* by Monteverdi; *Anna Bolena* by Donizetti; *Falstaff* by Verdi; *Bluebeard's Castle* by Bela Bartók. *The Tuscan Players,* with music by Carlos Chávez, was an original libretto.

When Chester was in New York he used to tell a story about the first rehearsal of Mozart's *The Magic Flute.* The singers, most of them European and true lovers of music, objected violently to having to sing in English an opera that was written in German. They criticized every word, interrupted every phrase, and were generally so sullen that the rehearsal could not continue. Finally Chester asked to speak to them. "I know why you are all annoyed with our translation," he said. "You are right to be annoyed, because you are true musicians. Wystan and I agree with you. Every opera should be sung in the language in which it was written. We don't approve of translations either. But people now want to hear the opera in English. We have to do this translation whether we want to or not. I can't change that. Let's not make it more difficult than it is already." After that, the rehearsal went on without difficulty and without temperament.

CHAPTER 13

"That Big-City Gleam in Your Eyes"

BY THE TIME *The Rake's Progress* was produced in New York, Chester had already met Peter Komadina, who was to share Wystan and Chester's dwellings in New York, first the loft on Seventh Avenue near Twenty-third Street, and then the apartment on 77 St. Mark's Place. He was the only outsider ever to live for any length of time with Wystan and Chester. The amazing fact was that the day he left the Auden apartment for a job in Greenland, almost a decade later, Chester and Wystan both were just as fond of him as they had been the day he had entered their lives.

Peter Komadina arrived in New York in the summer of 1950, a few weeks after his graduation from the University of Chicago. He wandered down to the San Remo, a bar and restaurant on the northwest corner of Bleecker Street at MacDougal, not far from the Provincetown Players. It was popular among artists and intellectuals at the time, and sooner or later he was sure to meet some of Chester's friends. Pete met Chester through David Protetch, now practicing medicine uptown. Chester and Pete became friends, and Chester immediately baptized him the Shiksa.[1] The name remained with him throughout his life.

Since Pete had no permanent residence in New York and was, as he said, drifting, he moved into Chester's temporary apartment. It was a small ground-floor apartment on East Seventy-eighth Street, with a living room, a bedroom, a kitchen, a bath, and a back door leading into an unweeded garden. What furniture there was had been gathered from what the Hawaiian veterans and their children had not broken before they vanished from Eddie's house in Sea Cliff without paying the last month's rent. Eddie had had it moved, at some expense, to Yorkville, so that in case Chester finally found a job, he would at least have a bed, some chairs, a table, a couch, and a chest of drawers. Wystan was away, and Chester was as usual out of money; but Pete had a job, so at the beginning of the month they could usually gather the rent. As Pete recalled years later:

> I used to sleep on the couch. There was never anything physical between Chester or Wystan and me, not even once. We were really good friends. When I first moved in with Chester, I had a night job at the Friars' Club, where there was also a restaurant, so I used to bring home this big bag of seeded rolls and some leftovers. Half the time that's all he had to eat. Chester was working at something or other—I think a book of poems or revisions of some libretto. Things were grim, but eventually Wystan would send a check. Chester never thought of finding a job.[2]

After the première of *The Rake's Progress* in Venice, Chester and Wystan returned to New York, where Wystan sublet a cavernous cold-water loft on Seventh Avenue near Twenty-third Street, not far from Eddie's place in the London Terrace. Wystan also liked Pete, so Pete moved into the loft and agreed to pay twenty-five dollars a month rent. In return for the reasonable rent, Pete was to care for the loft and occupy it when Wystan was away from New York. The loft had the same general atmosphere as Chester's place on Twenty-seventh Street except it was larger. The flea-market furniture, which came with the sublet and for which Wystan was paying a tidy sum, consisted of a number of round, ultramodern dark blue canvas chairs that you avoided sitting on because they tended to tip you over; three or

---

[1] Yiddish for a gentile woman.
[2] The author's conversation with Peter Komadina, October 18, 1982.

four dusty studio couches; and two or three glass-topped coffee tables laden with jelly jars used both as wine glasses and ashtrays.

To this apartment came a number of prominent guests: Igor and Mrs. Stravinsky, Robert Craft, Christopher Isherwood, and Lincoln Kirstein, among others. After serving gin martinis in the jelly jars, Wystan would regale his guests with stories of the visiting mouse for whom Chester and he left out food each day; and the guests, glancing about them uncomfortably, would sit down to dinner to a table set with dishes showing evidence of the last meal.

The next year, when Wystan and Chester were in Europe, Pete lived in the loft with David Protetch. By this time, Pete had met Chester's father, so he and David joined Chester's other friends at the dinner parties Eddie liked to give from time to time. When Chester and Wystan were not in town, their friends were invited anyway, for Eddie enjoyed intelligent young people, particularly the friends of his son.

In 1953 the prime tenants of the Seventh Avenue loft returned, so Wystan had to look for a new dwelling place for his surrogate family. He learned from one of Eddie's patients, a young artist called Larry Rivers, that there was a vacancy on the second floor of the building in which Rivers was living with his mother-in-law and two sons. The building was on St. Mark's Place, the easterly extension of Eighth Street, between First and Second Avenues, and a block from Tompkins Square Park. Number 77 was on the north side of the street near the corner of First Avenue. Two battered lions, remnants of happier times, greeted you on either side of the stoop as you entered through an old-fashioned double-doorway paned in frosted glass. The apartment on the second floor suited Wystan, who tended, since his days in Berlin, to live in blue-collar neighborhoods that had seen better days. Not only was the apartment large enough, but it was also located near St. Mark's Church in-the-Bowery, the ancient landmark Episcopal church where Wystan attended services every Sunday.

The area around St. Mark's Place had an appealing history. In the middle of the nineteenth century it had been called "Doctors' Row" and was lined with rows of townhouses and apartment buildings in which the prominent medical men of the day had their offices and sometimes their homes. It had been part of an aristocratic section of Old New York that spread from Washington Square eastward to the Sag Harbor Home on University Place; to Wanamaker's on Broadway; to Astor Place on Fourth Avenue; to St. Mark's Place; to Tomp-

kins Square Park near the river. Grace Church on East Tenth Street
and Broadway and St. Mark's Church in-the-Bowery served the religious needs of the community. Wystan was fond of telling his guests
that 77 St. Mark's Place had also been the location of a press supporting Trotsky during his sojourn in New York after the revolution in
Russia.

The area began slowly to deteriorate as its inhabitants moved elsewhere shortly after the Civil War. When Eddie Kallman was a boy
playing ball in Washington Mews, the deterioration had already pro-
gressed. By 1953, when Wystan moved in, the area was inhabited by
working people—emigrants from Poland and the Ukraine—but sections
along Fourth Avenue were already beginning to feel the impact of
the Drug Culture, with its attendant crime, and the incursion of the
hippies that was to take place in the sixties. Yet if one looked closely,
one could see in the basic architectural grace of the buildings—now
defamed by signs, ill repair, and tasteless renovation—in the marble
fireplaces and parquet floors; in the ornamentation of ancient molding
on the walls and ceilings; in the sturdy construction of the doors; in
the sure aesthetics of the windows; in the generous proportions of the
rooms, the remnants of the old days.

Wystan now had an apartment large enough to give his own Christmas dinners and birthday parties, and he was to keep it as his permanent residence in New York until the year before his death. He even
employed a heavy, middle-aged black woman from the Caribbean
called Esther to clean the apartment once or twice a week. His con-
cessions to middle-class living did not go further than to employ
Esther, however, for no apartment in which he lived ever strayed too
far in tone from 129 East Twenty-seventh Street. All had the dank
smell of drains, stale scrub water, and ancient dust. All had steps that
creaked as you climbed them from the dismal entryway. All had an
unsteady banister and walls in need of paint. All were redolent of the
tenement.

The newly acquired apartment was an old-fashioned railroad flat,
popular at the turn of the century. It spread from the front parlor,
facing south on St. Mark's Place, to the back sunroom, facing north to
East Ninth Street. To the right of the parlor as you faced the street
was a door leading into Wystan's bedroom, a spartan room with a
large window, a bed, a bookcase, an end table, a chest of drawers, and
a door leading out into the hall. Extending north from the parlor was
a good-sized alcove shut off on either side by French doors with glass
panes. It had bookshelves lining the walls and a large library table,

which served also as a dining table. The room was used as both a study
and a dining room.

Extending northward from the study toward the back of the apartment was a room about the size of the parlor. It was called the music
room, because all along the eastern wall was the musical equipment:
the phonograph, the speakers, and the innumerable records that made
up the Auden–Kallman record collection. This room was also the social room where Chester's friends gathered and Wystan went, too,
when he finished his work. In it was a sagging couch, the One Comfortable Chair, a number of other chairs, a canopied seating contrap-
tion called "Chester's Folly," and a door leading out into the hall.
Against the north wall was a sunroom with two large bay windows
that looked out toward East Ninth Street. Extending to the left of the
music room and the sunroom as you faced north was a narrow hallway, to the left of which was an old-fashioned bathroom with a pull-
chain toilet and a discolored bathtub and sink, all as ancient as the
building itself. At the end of the hallway was a large kitchen with a
window to the right, and, on the left, a door leading out into the hall.
The official entryway was through the music room. All other outside
doors were kept locked.

Although the flat was more commodious than any Wystan had had
in New York, comprising at least 2,500 square feet, its atmosphere,
as the atmosphere of the building itself, was like that of all his previous apartments. There was the same clutter and the same dust, despite Esther's efforts, and the same kind of anonymous makeshift
furniture, either newly made by a local carpenter, or bought secondhand from a Lower East Side flea market or the Salvation Army. Always some mechanical difficulty put a blight upon the day. Seldom
did all the antiquated fixtures work at the same time or did any fix-
ture work as it should. Either the drains were clogged or the toilet
would not flush; either a window would not open or an electric socket
had gone dead. The floors, beautiful in themselves, had not been
scraped for generations, and the high ceilings and the walls were in
need of paint and plaster.

In fact, one wondered when one visited the flat just how much
cleaning Esther did. There were times when one was convinced that
it was not Wystan but Esther, who, true to her Biblical namesake,
reigned over the household and made her own rules. She had obviously intimidated Wystan during the first days of her ascendancy. The
only member of the household she could not intimidate, though indeed she tried, was Wystan's cat.

Wystan's first act of husbandry when he moved into St. Mark's Place was to have the back sunroom made into two alcove bedrooms, one for Pete and one for Chester. His second was to have a large desk made for himself, a long, flat wood surface mounted on two saw-horses, that extended in the parlor from the bedroom door along almost the full length of the west wall of the room. Books and papers were piled at one end of the desk, a typewriter sat on the other, and Wystan wrote his poetry and prepared his lectures and other publications on a large space in between, sitting at first on a kitchen stool and later on the grandfather's chair that someone had given him.

His third act of husbandry was to acquire a calico cat. If Esther was the reigning queen of the household, Cenerentola, the calico cat, was the crown princess, reserving the One Comfortable Chair for herself (if Esther did not push her off), unless the table was set in the study for a sit-down dinner and guests. At times like this Cenerentola preferred to sit in the middle of the table for her evening meditations, trailing her tail over the olives, the hors d'oeuvres, the bread sticks, and the butter.

The flat was divided into two dominions psychologically as well as physically. The parlor and front bedroom were Wystan's for his writing. The library–dining room was neutral territory. The music room and all the other rooms were Chester's. These divisions of the flat were at no time more evident than at the parties. There were a number of annual parties. There was Wystan's birthday party, usually given on February 21 but sometimes on Washington's Birthday, for which engraved invitations were sent out ending with "carriages at one." There were other birthdays such as Chester's on January 7; there were parties to celebrate occasions, such as the performance of *The Magic Flute* and *The Seven Deadly Sins,* and a party with the Stravinskys and Robert Craft to celebrate *The Rake's Progress.* There were, of course, the holidays dear to Wystan's heart—Christmas and New Year's. Chester's friends and most of the younger crowd would gather in the music room, where drinks were served and sometimes food, though one or two special guests had usually been invited to a dinner beforehand.

Wystan's birthday parties were the most elaborate. The guest of honor, usually some dignified eminence from the literary world, still somewhat aghast at the neighborhood and the entranceway he had just passed through, particularly in view of the elegant invitation he had received, was ushered into the parlor and made to sit on the grandfather's chair. He was expected to talk to the other elite chosen for the occasion and for whom Wystan was on his best behavior. These he gathered into the parlor as into a temple—men in stiff dark suits and women in flowered silk dresses from the universities and the publishing houses—for fear they might be shocked by Chester's friends in the music room. The guest of honor would be someone like Robert Graves, Edmund Wilson, or the Sitwells. There were, of course, always the elite regulars invited to make small talk in the parlor with the famous person. There was the poet Marianne Moore, white haired and amiable, in a navy suit and a hat, looking the perfect librarian. There was the black-eyed and arresting Elizabeth Mayer. There was the distinguished Lincoln Kirstein, *soigné* in black, who could not be restricted to the parlor, but who circulated among all the guests as did Anne and Irving Weiss and Chester's father.

At one party Robert Graves, who had made no secret of his dislike for Wystan, who was not at all to his taste, now appeared to be reconciled with him but ill at ease,[1] and sat in the grandfather's chair off to the side near the fireplace, viewing with alarm as in a siege all who entered into the parlor. At another party, Sir Osbert and Dame Edith Sitwell, in a peacock green turban, talked in the parlor of astrology, Sir Osbert squeezing the arm of the unbelieving Eddie and asking, "What sign were you born under?" Cenerentola, mad with glee, was swinging all the while from the plum-colored velvet curtain, which miraculously held up that night. The Sitwells watched her antics with delight. Finally Dame Edith said, "It must be such fun to be a cat. I always say that in the next life, I should like to come back as a cat." Later on Dame Edith went home with my new "mink" coat. When I was about to leave, I discovered that my coat was missing, so Wystan, spying Dame Edith's mink under everyone else's cloth coat on the bed, winked and said, "Here, take this one. It's fur. They're all the same anyway." The next day Wystan called Dame Edith to inform her that she had taken the wrong coat. "Oh, dear," she said. "I didn't see any other one there, so I just took the first mink I saw." What Dame Edith did not realize was that the coat she had taken was a pure fake.

Igor Stravinsky always appeared at Wystan's birthdays with his wife when the couple was in New York. They celebrated Chester's birthday together, too, for Mrs. Stravinsky was born on the same day. Stravinsky, the most agreeable of men—friendly, talkative, courtly—seemed

---

[1] A peace had been negotiated between Graves and Auden in 1958 with Chester and Irving Weiss acting as intermediaries.

to enjoy everyone he met and joined readily into the conversation, not only of the parlor but also of the music room. Most of the eminent who were invited to Wystan's gatherings were much more affable and less forbidding than Wystan himself, who inspired more awe, even in his old friends, than did anyone else. When one met Christopher Isherwood for the first time, one was struck by his charm and social grace. He, like Stravinsky, was easy to meet. Wystan, on the other hand, could be extremely difficult, particularly when he was in one of his I'm-very-cross-today moods, and, sitting among a pleasant gathering, he could bring down thunderclouds on the room.

Of course, there were always the regulars of the music room: David Protetch, Pete Komadina, and Chester's old circle of the forties who were still present. Alan Ansen was by this time in Europe, but Anne and Irving Weiss, recently returned from Ischia, were always there with their little girls, now sleeping in Wystan's bed. There were also strange faces from Wystan's various circles in New York. Since he seldom introduced one group to the other, each traveled in its separate sphere, forming its own cliques even at the parties.

Guests would walk back and forth from the music room to the parlor, enjoying the society in both realms as they drank their champagne—French for the parlor, New York for the music room—poured into numberless glass jelly jars from numberless bottles that had been chilled under ice in the dirty bathtub. Intimates and relatives would gather in Chester's kitchen with Chester's father and Lincoln Kirstein, exchanging jokes and ribald stories and drinking champagne from the inevitable jelly jars.

Wystan had found an apartment that suited him. It allowed the privacy he needed for his work, but it provided enough room for his parties, his holidays, and his surrogate family. He occupied it from 1953 to 1972, the year before he died. If Wystan's surrogate family in the persons of Pete Komadina and Chester giggled and gossiped over after-dinner coffee, and if Wystan, in his I'm-very-cross-today-mood, complained that they carried on like shopgirls, he enjoyed having them about, nevertheless. Wystan, essentially a homebody, required a surrogate family despite his solitary nature. He needed people for whom to provide.

Pete, who looked for his sexual partners elsewhere, presented no complications. There was no sexual jealousy; there were no erratic outbursts. Pete was steady and affable. He was temperate in his drinking; he always had a job; he always looked well; he had impeccable manners—he was conscious of what suited the occasion. To Wystan,

Pete, who could be mad as a hatter himself at times, represented the bedrock of reliability, at least compared with Chester, and seemed to have a calming, sustaining influence on the household that had become his permanent dwelling place.

In spite of its problems, most of which could have been solved with the services of a house painter, an electrician, a plumber, and a good cleaning agency at less cost than Wystan, who had a good income, allowed himself for foolishness, the apartment suited its tenants admirably. It was large enough. Wystan could have his privacy when he wanted it by merely closing the French doors off the parlor. Chester and Pete could play records, entertain their friends, and gossip and giggle without restraint. In addition, Chester finally had a large kitchen in which to cook his gourmet meals. In 1953 Wystan was forty-six; Chester, thirty-two; Pete, still in his early twenties—the possible ages of brothers in a large family. By this time, Chester had baptized Wystan "Miss Master."

For over six years Pete paid his twenty-five dollars a month for rent. He kept house and cared for Cenerentola when Wystan and Chester were in Europe. When they were in New York, he shared their daily life, contributing his share to the meals, the grand sum of $1.25 for dinner, according to Wystan's bookkeeping. After work, he spent his free time with Chester, who had now found Pete to replace Mary and me. They went to the opera and the ballet with free tickets from Lincoln Kirstein. They went to matinees of Broadway plays with free tickets from someone else. Afterward, they would visit the bars—sleazy bars on Eighth Avenue; gay bars in the Village. Often they went to dinner at Chester's father's place and brought along their friends.

If any two people had "that big-city gleam" in their eyes, it was Chester and Pete at large in New York. Years later, Komadina was to speak of the old days as if they had been the day before yesterday— giggling at the events that took place then; at the people; at Wystan; at Chester and his remarks, often with a shaggy dog quality; at all the private jokes and private words, some of which found their way into Wystan's poems; at happenings in local bars; laughing even at himself.

Said Pete:

> One of the Chester remarks that I always remember was Chester's favorite "famous-last-words-before-death" remark: "I've never done this before." Another of my favorites has always been one that took place when Wystan was on a panel for the Mid-Century Book Club back in the early fifties. Wystan was saying that he and

Jacques Barzun were fishing for a name for a monthly magazine they planned to publish. As we were all sitting there trying to think of a title, Chester suddenly suggested: "Period: A Monthly." Another of Chester's remarks was one that concerned a play on the names of a brother and sister whose surname was Boule, the French word for ball. They were friends of David Protetch and had invited him to go to the circus. However, that particular night Chester wanted David to go with him to the ballet. "Oh, cancel it and come to the ballet," said Chester. "You're with the Boules all the time. What's going on?"

"They have already bought tickets," replied David, ignoring the question. "Besides, I promised them."

"What's the matter, can't the balls go anywhere without the *shwantz*[1] in between?" retorted Chester.[2]

Often when Pete and Chester went to the City Center to see an opera or a ballet, they would stop after the performance to cruise the midtown bars, particularly the rough ones, for which Chester had a fondness. One of these excursions led them to what they referred to as "the penultimate ugly dwarf story." Remembered Pete:

> We had a running gag that whenever we would see two people together, one gorgeous and one awful, either Chester or I would say, one to the other: "Well, you're not going to like the one *you're* going to get." One night as we left the old City Center, we walked across to an Eighth Avenue bar, an odd place where boxers hung out. Sitting at the bar among the bottles and the faded photographs of boxers was probably the most handsome man in the world with, believe it or not, this dwarf who was not just a dwarf, but the penultimate ugly dwarf. We walked out after having a beer, sauntered down to this other bar on Forty-first Street, and sat in a booth toward the rear of the bar. Across from us in another booth suddenly appeared this same couple, the handsome man and the penultimate ugly dwarf. That was the point at which I said, "You're not going to like the one *you're* going to get." Chester went into howls of laughter, and neither one of us could stop laughing from then on every time we thought of the situation. At times like this, Wystan would grunt and say that we were behaving like silly shopgirls.

[1] Yiddish slang for the male sex organ.
[2] This and subsequent quotes from Peter Komadina from his conversation with the author October 18, 1982.

Wystan himself often contributed unwittingly to the store of hilarious incidents. Recalled Pete:

> I once had a guest at St. Mark's Place one night very late. Wystan had apparently got up to use the bathroom early in the morning. There was just a very dim light on, and we were sitting in the back music room through which Wystan would have to pass in order to reach the bathroom. The glass doors leading to the music room opened and all of a sudden this nude vision of Wystan appeared. He had not realized that anyone was still up, and when he saw us, he grabbed his genitals like a shy maiden and dashed back into his bedroom to put on some clothes. My guest, a merchant seaman, was as surprised as Wystan, and he said: "Who was that, Mammy Yokum?"

Chester and Pete told the story all over New York as much to the delectation of friends and relatives as to Wystan's intense embarrassment.

Pete had vivid memories of Chester and Wystan together.

> They got along fine in general. They had great intellectual affinity, but there was never any suggestion of any sexual life between them. With Wystan, everything was very structured. Everything had to be done according to a time schedule. There was, for example, always a cocktail hour at five o'clock and dinner had to be served exactly at six. During the early days at St. Mark's Place Chester and Wystan were both working on a revision of *The Rake's Progress,* but they did not work together. Wystan's way of working was early to bed, early to rise. Chester worked all night and slept until noon. There were periods when I would go out early in the evening, and when I returned early in the morning, Chester would still be working. Wystan frowned upon Chester's work habits and complained about them. Chester's main complaint about Wystan was that he did not engage in small talk in company but rather lectured, or relied upon set pieces or made-to-order questions for the occasion. Wystan's letters to me are campy and funny, but that's not the way he was in conversation.
>
> Once in a while Chester and Wystan would have a real screaming fight. Chester did all the screaming; Wystan never made scenes. He would just sit there with a wine bottle, pretending to ignore Chester. I remember once they had an argument about something or another and had apparently been brooding about it all day.

They ignored each other all during dinner. Chester and I were planning to go out that evening, but apparently while he was dressing something happened to prolong the argument. Anyway, Chester became furious and began to scream again. Wystan, now in the music room with the wine bottle, put a record on the phonograph and turned up the volume to drown out Chester's voice. When Chester was finally ready to leave, he stopped at the door, looked disdainfully at Wystan, now drunk, walked dramatically to the phonograph, and, with an exaggerated gesture, adjusted the speed control. "At least you can learn to play a record at its correct speed!" he growled. Wystan had been playing a thirty-three speed recording of Wagner's *Siegfried Idyll* at forty-five, as strange, lugubrious moans issued from the recording machine.

But Chester and Wystan could not be angry at each other for long. The next day they made it up, and things went on as usual.

Both Chester and Wystan were back and forth from Italy, sometimes together, sometimes apart, during the fifties. They traveled by steamer in those days, usually taking the Italian line. "After Chester arrived home from Europe," Pete recalled, "usually a crew member would show up at St. Mark's Place a few days later." One day Esther was cleaning in the apartment when a young Italian sailor arrived to see Chester. The sailor completely forgot Chester, however, once he set eyes on Esther, for whose middle-aged body he suddenly conceived an inordinate passion. Although he spoke no English, he began to stalk her, making amorous sounds as he followed her from one room to the other, ardor burning in his eyes. Esther, indignant, approached Chester, stamping her foot furiously: "If you don't get that little creep away from me right now, I'll go straight home and you'll pay me for the whole day and finish cleaning this place yourself!" After some persuasion, Chester was able to convince the sailor in his native tongue that the lady did not want his attentions. The sailor, certain of his charms, could not believe his ears until Chester told him that Esther would put a hex on him if he continued to court her. Esther was finally able to work in peace.

Chester and Pete found Esther's experience with the sailor extremely funny, but Wystan was cross that Chester should have allowed things to go that far. He respected Esther and always wished to show her his good will. Thus it was that at Christmas time, according to Pete, "Wystan, out of the goodness of his heart and in the spirit of

Christmas, invited Esther over for Christmas dinner." Esther arrived
as the other guests were having their first martini but in a maid's uniform, complete with cap, and started happily for the kitchen where
Chester was making the plum pudding and the suckling pig.

"Oh, no, my dear," said Wystan, already tipsy, as he awkwardly
guided Esther back into the music room. "You must be a guest today
and let us serve you." Esther was not pleased. Although she allowed
him to take off her maid's cap and sit her down with a gin martini on
the One Comfortable Chair (Cenerentola was now sitting among the
salad things on the table), one could see in her darkening eyes and
sullen mouth that all was not well. Finally the martini had its effect,
and Esther stated sulkily the message of her soul: "I want to work. I
thought I was going to be paid for today. Double time for Christmas."

Thus it was that Wystan, glimpsing the truth that comes from gin,
relented. Esther donned her cap, straightened her apron, and joined
Chester in the kitchen whence she served the suckling pig and the
plum pudding to Wystan's guests, her ascendancy once more established.

Wystan felt deeply about racial equality. For years he refused to do
readings in the deep South to segregated audiences.[1]

Although Wystan *en famille* could at times be a monster, and not
always a lovable one, he was always unfailingly courteous in ways that
counted. He was generous and polite to those who served him, and
he was a gracious and liberal host, always eager that his guests have a
good time and that they laugh. He was fond of funny stories and,
though he himself was not an accomplished storyteller, he always encouraged Chester or Eddie, expert raconteurs, to tell again and again
the ones he liked best.

In addition to funny stories, Wystan enjoyed ribald limericks and
confessed to writing them compulsively. He gave Pete Komadina a
number of them, written in his own hand, sometime during the late
fifties. Two of the less prurient follow:

I

After vainly invoking the Muse,
A poet cried, "Hell, what's the use!"
There's more inspiration

---

[1] The author's conversation with Edward Mendelson, May 21, 1982.

At Grand Central Station
I shall go there this moment and cruise.

II

A queer friend, who is peripatetic,
Writes: "Ireland, my dear, is magnetic.
The fairies and elves
Simply offer *themselves—*
Rather small, *but most sympathetic."*[1]

Every now and then while Pete was living at St. Mark's Place, Wystan would invite his old girlfriend, Rhoda Jaffe, for lunch. "They would have the most awful-looking burnt omelette that Wystan had made," recalled Pete, "and they would just sit and talk. It was purely a social occasion, and there was no suggestion of anything sexual between them. They were relaxed together, and Rhoda treated him like an old friend." In his relationship with Rhoda Jaffe, as in his relationship with Keith Callaghan and other lovers, Wystan usually sustained the friendship long after the affair was over. *Eros* having taken flight, *agape* took his place. Wystan, in fact, seemed to be more comfortable with *agape*.

As the fifties drew to a close, things began to change. Chester did not come home to New York as often as before, since his fugitive American lovers from the tough local bars often robbed the flat on St. Mark's Place just before they left in the early morning, and Wystan finally objected strongly and made Chester promise to take them somewhere else. Since tough lower-class lovers seemed less violent in Europe, Chester decided to look for them there. Pete, too, decided to begin life on his own. Although from time to time he had taken trips to Florida or worked for a while in another town, he always came back to St. Mark's Place. Now he wanted to be independent. In 1960 he applied for a government position that had opened in Greenland. He was given the job, pending security clearance, and was forced to sign up for three years, so there was no returning. So by 1960 Wystan was alone during his winters. Even Cenerentola was dead of a mysterious cat ailment.

Wystan was fond of saying that he had had a lucky life. If there is such a thing as luck, St. Mark's Place had been lucky for Wystan.

[1] The author is indebted to Peter Komadina for these limericks.

While he was living there from 1953 through 1971 he won a number of gold medals and distinguished prizes. He was elected professor of poetry by the M.A. graduates of Oxford, his old university, and he published ten books of poetry. He even appeared once on a Merv Griffin talk show and on a special television program for the BBC—worldly honors that he accepted with a certain wry good humor.

CHAPTER 14

Cockaigne

SHORTLY BEFORE THE time that Pete left for Greenland, Chester and Wystan were preparing to abandon Italy and the languid Mediterranean life. At first Chester did not talk about the trouble on Ischia. When he was in New York from time to time during the 1950s, he spoke in glowing tones of Sandro, the young Ischian waiter, handsome as the day, with his large, dark, soulful eyes. He even took an old photograph of Eddie and me so that, in true Italian fashion, he, like Sandro, could have a picture of his family on his bureau: of Eddie in an old fedora hat and me in an old beret.

"Not that one, for heaven's sake, Chester," I said.

"Why not? That's the one I want. Nice and homely," and he put the photograph into his pocket. It was clear that Chester was in love again for the first time. Wystan, determined to keep Chester at all costs, contented himself, it is said, with the fugitive attentions of his houseman.

Chester spoke at great length about Sandro's family, impoverished by the war, to whom Eddie was persuaded to send package after care package of food and sundries, gathered at the Smiley Brothers' Market in the London Terrace and sent off with great difficulty at the post office. After Eddie and I received the touching thank-you gift of three homemade doilies embroidered in red, green, and gold—the colors of the Italian flag—by the work-worn hands of Sandro's mother, Chester's father wanted to know particulars about the family whom he wished to help further, for he, like Wystan, was partial to victims. It was then that Chester divulged the secret he had been keeping for some time. He and Wystan were thinking of leaving forever the island in the sun, whose charms had begun to fade. All sorts of drunken Englishmen had begun to move in, along with an assortment of tourists from Europe and the United States. Paradise was paradise no longer.

Even from the beginning things had not been entirely satisfactory in Italy, once the glamor had begun to dim. Despite the ideal climate, the lush vegetation, the easy living, and the willing boys, incidents of unpleasantness had left their mark. As early as 1952 one of Wystan's cats had been poisoned. It had been his favorite—blue-eyed, white Lucina. He buried her on a hill under an orange tree at the foot of Epomeo and wrote her a touchingly beautiful epitaph:

In Memoriam
L. K.-A. 1950–1952

At peace under this mandarin, sleep, Lucina,
Blue-eyed Queen of white cats: for you the Ischian wave shall weep
When we who now miss you are American dust, and steep
Epomeo in peace and war augustly a grave-watch keep.[1]

The act of vicious and gratuitous cruelty to Lucina called to mind the plight of Mosé, Wystan's spaniel, who had been beaten and almost drowned by the time that Wystan and Chester rescued him in a swamp and gave him a home. Toward the middle of the decade other unpleasant events were to follow, though perhaps not so brutal.

Then there was the matter of Sandro. After a martini or two, Chester revealed that Sandro had married his childhood sweetheart after all, the girl to whom he had been formally affianced for some time, in the parish church of Forio; the ceremony having been performed by that very *parocco* to whom Wystan had sent his misdirected alms back

[1] Auden, "In Memoriam L. K.-A. 1950–1952," in *Collected Poems*, p. 435.

in 1948. Chester, who at first greeted Sandro's marriage with the same cheerful cynicism with which he greeted most of the rites of Western civilization, was not prepared for what followed. Sandro, having made the required general confession before entering upon the Sacrament of Holy Matrimony, was glad to be back in the arms of Holy Mother the Church and was not about to stumble into the old ways. From the day of his wedding, Sandro absented himself from the occasion of sin and remained home with his bride. Chester was again left with a broken heart, all his plans to lure Sandro to New York at the appropriate moment having come to nothing.

The nature of Chester's love life was best described in his poem, "Page from a Diary," probably written shortly after Sandro's marriage.

PAGE FROM A DIARY

Hope that had been a habit of the will,
Hope that could not believe
The body awake at dawn, filling no day,
Hope that could fill the empty morning
With one note, is still.

Circe and her menagerie appear,
Supple and shrill,
With even motions devouring Hope,
The gingerbread weather vane:
Once in a giddy year

It showed one storm the way and, showing, fell.
After the tossing vision,
What of the day? The morning carefully
Arranges that by throbbing noon
The hours will not tell.

The afternoon accumulates its dust;
The evening hangs
Like sluggish vultures at the grave of love;
Then, savage and small as pond life,
Familiar lust.[1]

[1] Chester Kallman, "Page from a Diary," in *Storm on Castelfranco* (New York: Grove Press, 1956), p. 45. Courtesy of Dr. Edward Kallman.

Love has given the poet hope, but as the affair goes on, hope slowly
vanishes. Like a weather vane that points to one storm and then falls
to the storm itself, hope dies by the very violence of the emotion that
engendered it. The poet takes solace, then, in lust, familiar and un-
attractive though it may be. What better picture does one find of
Chester's love life than the one he himself has given?

In the meantime Wystan was having his own troubles with Giocondo, his houseman. There were at least two versions of the story
extant at the time, one Wystan's and the other Giocondo's, and the
scandal that resulted was for a time to divide the island into two
camps worthy of a feud of the Middle Ages. The scandal was the result either of an honest mistake in the writing of a check, or of an
actual forgery. In the winter of 1955–1956, when Wystan sent to Giocondo from New York the usual salary check for sixty thousand lira,
Giocondo attempted to cash it for six hundred thousand. Whether
Wystan, in his uncertain Italian, had made out the check incorrectly
himself, or whether Giocondo had added the extra zero and forged
the writing, the bank in Ischia refused to cash the check because Wystan's balance was not large enough.

Giocondo had another story. He insisted that the extra lira had
been given him as a present for "services rendered" and unabashedly
told all his friends and relatives on the isle that the great man, mean
at heart and fearful of Chester's jealousy, now wanted to take back
the gift. Crimson with indignation, Giocondo, with only his regular
salary check (Wystan had replaced the check for six hundred thousand lira with a check for sixty thousand) and the last one at that, began to tell tales out of school. Prince Henry of Hesse, Sir William
Walton, and a number of other distinguished tourists that year were
regaled with the intimate habits of the poet and his household: of the
messes left in the kitchen; of the cigarettes in the fruit jars in the living room; of the disarray in the bedrooms, all of which the young and
innocent Giocondo had been expected to clean and set right. Not
only that, but Giocondo let all know that Wystan had expected and
received "special services" performed by Giocondo out of the goodness of his heart. When groups of tourists visited the café owned by
Giocondo's uncle, in which Giocondo himself was now tending bar,
Giocondo would first ask them whose side they were on, his or the
poet's. If they were not partisan to himself, or even if they could not
have cared less, they were invited to leave.

Other troubles were to follow. Although he was to win the Feltrinelli prize of more than thirty thousand dollars in June, the year 1957

was not happy for Wystan, for his father had died on May 3. When Wystan returned to Ischia after the funeral and wanted to buy the house at Quarto San Giovanni, Vico 4, where he and Chester had been living for some time now, the landlord, one Monte, having heard of the Feltrinelli prize money, asked a sum way beyond what the house was worth. The scandal involving Giocondo over the check and the greed of the landlord had put a pall upon life on Ischia, this on top of Wystan's feeling of loss at the death of his father.

It was time to say goodbye to the South, and Wystan recognized that time. In his poem "Good-bye to the Mezzogiorno,"[1] his poem of farewell to the isle where he had known happy days, he said he believed that a man with a northern soul could not live long in the South: "To 'go southern' we spoil in no time, we grow / Flabby, dingily lecherous, and / Forget to pay bills . . ." He also believed in the essentially differing natures of each geographical type. As for the Northman, he said, "Of a . . . / Guilt culture, we behave like our father and come / Southward into a sunburnt otherwhere / . . . no more as unwashed / Barbarians out for gold, nor as profiteers / Hot for Old Masters, but for plunder / Nevertheless—some believing *amore* / Is better down South and much cheaper / (Which is doubtful), . . . and others, like me, / In middle-age hoping to twig from / What we are not what we might be next. . . ." He concluded that this great essential difference could not be bridged: ". . . between those who mean by life a / *Bildungsroman* and those to whom living / Means to-be-visible-now, there yawns a gulf / Embraces cannot bridge."

Auden was beginning to be homesick at last for a northern clime. "How I envy you at this time up there in total darkness," he was to write to Pete in Greenland in December 1962. In the February of 1964: "How I envy you your lovely northern winter nights." By 1957 Auden had had enough of the South and the ways of the South, and by October 1958 he was to leave Ischia and to move with Chester into the home he would cherish until his death. His days in Kirchstetten, Austria, were his golden days, and if the word Cockaigne to a medieval Frenchman meant a place of peace and plenty, the house in Kirchstetten was to mean the same to Wystan. It was to be his Cockaigne.

While visiting Austria for a music festival, Wystan and Chester heard through some friends about a house that was for sale in Kirchstetten, about twenty-seven miles west of Vienna, a village on the edge

---

[1] Auden, "Good-bye to the Mezzogiorno," in *Collected Poems,* pp. 486–88.

of the Wienerwald where the ghost of the ancient Queen Agnes was
said to appear at dusk on a white horse. Wystan went to see the house
in October of 1957 through a driving rain and decided to buy it. The
simple farm cottage on its three acres of green lawn with its *teich*
(duck pond) suited Wystan perfectly. The village also suited him perfectly, and he knew it would suit Chester, because it was in a German-
speaking, wine-producing country near a metropolis, near great music
centers, and away from tourists. Both he and Chester spoke German.
Despite the time spent on Italian lessons, as has been mentioned,
Wystan never learned to speak the language with ease, and since his
days in Berlin, second to English, he was only comfortable speaking
German.

Wystan bought the house in 1958 for about twelve thousand dollars, using the money from the Feltrinelli prize, which also covered
the extensive renovation that would eventually permit the cottage to
have hot and cold running water, electrical wiring, and a modern
American kitchen, dear to Chester's heart, equipped with every electrical gadget possible in those days, even an electric espresso machine
that made Chester, so he said, "feel like Maria," the proprietress of a
café on Ischia. Until his death in 1973, Wystan would spend the spring
and summer of every year in Kirchstetten.

In the spring of 1958, while Wystan was at Oxford as poet in residence, Chester began the move from Ischia to Kirchstetten. First he
took the spaniel, Mosé, and the remaining two cats, Leonora from
Ischia and Rhadames (Cenerentola's replacement) from New York,
leaving them temporarily with the caretakers, a brother and sister of
middle age, the big, redoubtable Frau Emma and the stout, silent
Herr Josef Eiermann, Sudetenland Germans, refugees from the Communist takeover in Czechoslovakia after World War II. Frau Eiermann took care of the housecleaning, washing, dusting, and scrubbing
in true German fashion; Herr Josef took care of the garden and did
the heavy work outdoors. Both loved animals, so in addition to Wystan's dog and cats there were the Eiermanns' cats, a goat, some geese,
some ducks, and some pigs. Chester and Wystan were, of course,
charmed.

Wystan paid the Eiermanns a salary of one thousand Austrian schillings a month (approximately one hundred dollars at that time) and
said he was glad to overpay them. He was surprised one day when he
discovered that both were atheists. The Eiermanns had been a close,
religious family, but one day their beloved younger brother died in
an accident for which their human logic could find no rationale. They

stopped believing after that. Their religious training had stood them in good stead, nevertheless, for they were by habit virtuous.

Wystan's affection for the Eiermanns had as much to do with his perception of them as victims as with their eccentricities. Frau Emma was a forthright woman and held strong opinions. Like the Almighty whom she had rejected, she was not a respecter of persons. It mattered not to her what guest with a world-renowned name visited the estate of W. H. Auden. That guest received a dressing down from this tall, numinous[1] creature in a gray housedress who stood at a distance like a vision—flinging her arms about and screaming at him in Sudeten-Deutsch if he casually grabbed a fruit from a tree or picked a flower, the way she screamed at the neighborhood boys. Essentially a solitary person like her employer, she did not care for guests of any kind, particularly overnight guests, and when Chester and Wystan invited anyone for an extended visit, they thought twice. Wystan, who liked strong, straightforward characters, always showed her deference, acceded to her wishes, and pampered her eccentricities.

In return, she and her taciturn brother (who some said was not quite right) gave Wystan and Chester faithful service. Mourning her brother's death, Frau Emma herself died in November 1967, when Chester and Wystan both were away. Wystan's poem to her memory expresses his affection and allows one to glimpse her personality, which provides an added insight into Auden's life at Kirchstetten.

ELEGY

(In Memoriam Emma Eiermann,
ob. November 4th, 1967)

Liebe Frau Emma,
na, was hast Du denn gemacht?
You who always made
such conscience of our comfort,
oh, how could you go and die,

as if you didn't know
that in a permissive age
so rife with envy,
a housekeeper is harder
to replace than a lover,

---

[1] From numen, a divine or presiding spirit—one of Auden's favorite words.

And die, too, when we
were thousands of miles away,
leaving no one there
to prune and transplant before
the winter cold should set in.

Good witch that you were,
Surely you should have foreseen
the doom that your death
would spell for your cats and ours:
all had to be put away.

You came with the house,
you and your brother Josef,
Sudetendeutsche
made homeless paupers when Czechs
got their turn to be brutal:

but catastrophe
had failed to modernize you,
Child of the Old World,
in which to serve a master
was never thought ignoble.

Children of the New,
we had to learn how to live
in the older way,
well tendered and observed by
loyal but critical eyes.

From the first, I think,
you liked us, but to the last
assumed most callers
knocked with some evil intent
(now and again you were right).

When guests were coming,
there was always the worry:—
would you disallow?

Greeks, in your censure, were rogues,
all teen-agers delinquent.

Nor were you ever
one to behave your temper:
let Youth pick a fruit
or flower, out you would storm,
arms whirling, screaming abuse

in peasant German
at startled Americans
who had meant no harm,
and, after they'd gone, for days
you would treat us to the sulks.

But when in good form,
how enchanting your shy grin,
your soft cat-language:
no, no, Frau E, dear oddling,
we shall always be grateful.

After Josef died
(siblings can live in a bond
as close as wedlock),
you were all amort, your one
wish to rejoin him quickly.

You have, and we're left
with ten years to consider,
astonished at how
vivid they are to recall:
Du gute, schlaf in Ruhe.[1]

The house, as Chester and Wystan found it in 1958, was the shape of an L. Pale in color, having been originally erected of yellow stone, it was larger than it appeared from the outside. In addition to the huge kitchen, a good-sized living room, a number of bedrooms, and

[1] Auden, "Elegy," in *Collected Poems*, pp. 575–76.

one section of the L set off for the caretakers' cottage, it had an attic jutting out from the roof. One reached the attic by climbing an outside staircase protected from the weather only by the roof that extended over it. The attic was Wystan's domain, as the parlor had been at St. Mark's Place. It was here he did his writing. It consisted of a window that looked over the rolling countryside, a desk, and a couch. In another section of the attic, connected to the house with an internal staircase, was a large room in which were set pieces of Biedermeier furniture that had come with the house, but for some reason were not used in the main living room. Perhaps the relegation of the Biedermeier to the guest room in the attic had to do with Wystan's dislike of fine furniture in the homes of people who were not rich. Around the cottage stretched gardens and three acres of land that had once been tilled but now were green lawn where the dog and cats could roam at will without fear of poison or violence.

Wystan finally had a home of his own and three acres of land. To the end of his life he would view his property with a prayer of thanksgiving. When he wrote his long poem "Thanksgiving for a Habitat," he used Psalm 16:6 as a theme: *"Funes ceciderunt mihi in praeclaris; etenim hereditas mea praeclara est mihi."*[1] The property in Kirchstetten was to appear in many of his poems until the end of his life, and he became an honored member of the community that called him Herr Professor and during his life renamed the street in front of his house Audenstrasse. Every Sunday that he was in residence he would attend early Mass at the Catholic church in the village, and when he died, he would be buried in the churchyard. The little lot with the *teich* is now a park dedicated to his memory.[2]

In the summer of 1958 the basic renovations began. A water supply had to be installed as well as an electrical system for lights and heating. Now a true householder, Wystan made repairs continually. In 1964 he wrote to Pete: "I leave on February 25 for a six-week lecture tour in order to make money to build a new dining room in Austria." The money from the Feltrinelli prize had been wisely used, and Monte's greed and Giocondo's scandal had proved to Wystan the wisdom in the saying of Saint Teresa of Avila: "When the Lord closes one door, He opens another."

[1] "The lines are fallen unto me in pleasant places; yea I have a goodly heritage"—King James Version of the Bible.

[2] Dr. Edward Kallman, who inherited the Auden estate from his son, donated the lot to the Catholic church of Kirchstetten in 1981 as a memorial park. This lot was separate from, though contiguous with the house lot.

Chester was happy in his new home in spite of the inconvenience of renovation, at least according to his letter to the Weisses in May 1958:

> I heard my first live cuckoo a week ago; and on May 1 I saw a Roe-buck make for the horizon as though it were after a bargain; and two days ago it was a hare, twice the size of *Life* magazine, getting across the back lawn. Actually, it's incredibly lovely here: daffodils and cherry blossoms and feather beds. . . . The plumber and the electrician just left . . . me with an estimate for the purchase and installation of an electric pump and hot-water heaters and some more pipes to reach the yet-unordered modern kitchen: thirteen thousand schillings (zirka 520 bucks). *Gott Sapia wass der cucina* will cost. The Phone-volk said they wanted eighteen thou to bring the wires here, so it looks like we'll keep our pristine country silence for quite a while yet.

Wystan was perfectly happy to live forever without a telephone.

On July 22, 1958, another letter from Chester to the Weisses, now in New York, describes the problems of putting in a water system.

> Wystan arrived from Oxford about a month ago, rubbed his hands, and said he hadn't seen the sun once in Oxford, and then we had two weeks of rain. . . . Not that any of this meant that The Water Problem was in some wise solved. Oh, no. The Pump out front gives an eternal dry gurgle when plied, and it has to be regularly primed; the pump in the bathroom has long stopped giving any pretense of being a useful article; it just rusts with some hidden supply of water that it won't give up; and the electric pump that was to have replaced it and fill our hearts and our house with FLUID has not seen fit to come from the factory. Naturally the plumber hasn't finished putting the pipes in, too, nor can the electrician find it in himself to bring the *Starkstrom* as far as the intended berth of the pump. So now our lovely modern kitchen is all installed with the loveliest sink, the loveliest dry sink, in the world in it. Shall I mention that two water-heaters are also hovering still in the realm of the Ideal? And in about nine days, we flee South.

The cottage eventually had its hot water and a functioning kitchen, but Chester and Wystan went back to Italy until the renovation was completed, leaving Cockaigne in the capable hands of Frau Eiermann and her brother. In October 1958 the house was settled, and Chester and Wystan left Ischia for good. With the purchase of the house, the relationship between Chester and Wystan was established for life. Wystan had achieved a kind of marriage, although no sexual activity had occurred between him and Chester for years. They were, nevertheless, the closest of companions, and each had a role established in habit. Wystan was the primary breadwinner, still lecturing, writing, and teaching in the United States during the fall and winter. Chester did the cooking and took care of the house, whether in Kirchstetten or New York, for, until the early sixties, Chester would frequently come back with Wystan to St. Mark's Place.

Chester's role in Austria was to be similar to that on Ischia, but this time Wystan had given up the hope that Chester would find a job. Instead, Wystan found work for him in the collaboration on the libretti. At any rate, Chester contributed to the quality of Wystan's life, not only in intellectual companionship but also in practical matters, as he had done on Ischia and in New York. One of Chester and Wystan's woman friends who saw them on a daily basis on Ischia said that she wished people realized how Chester took care of Wystan, that Chester not only ran the household and did the shopping and cooking, but that he also entertained regularly and supervised the social calendar. She said he answered the phone, which rang all the time, and which Wystan hated to answer,[1] and that he protected Wystan when people were offensive or irritating. In her opinion their "marriage" was just as happy as most heterosexual marriages that she had seen, and it lasted longer than most. "Chester and Wystan," she said, "were still bound together even when apart."

Nothing would have made Wystan happier than to have Chester as a sexual partner, for Wystan was still in love with him and continued to be until the day of his death. The vow he had taken back in 1939 was the vow he was to keep, at least spiritually, for the remainder of his life. Although Wystan had other lovers, they were, for the most part, unromantic, convenient. He wanted Chester at his side whatever the cost. He was true to the boy for whom he had bought the golden wedding ring those many years ago. Nevertheless, Wystan, though moody, was not one to brood; though only one love formed the center of his life, he did not shut out others. He made the best of everything that came to him.

As professor of poetry at Oxford from 1956 through 1960, Wystan

---

[1] The telephone referred to here was on Ischia. Auden had no telephone in Kirchstetten.

was immensely popular, giving his required lectures after his winter
in New York, and meeting students informally in the Cadena coffeehouse at five, often inviting them back to his rooms for tea or a drink.
He even purchased an electric refrigerator for the Senior Common
Room at Christ Church so that his friends and colleagues who ate with
him there could drink cold martinis, instead of the usual room-warm
port. He also purchased a sound system for the auditorium; thus for
the first time in centuries a lecturer speaking from that dais could be
heard.

Wystan was becoming an Oxford institution. After many years in
American colleges, he had begun to appreciate his old school and its
ancient buildings. He also liked the institutional life with its regular
time schedules, its regular mealtimes, its monastic repose. Oxford represented home, and he did not realize how much he had missed it.
Wystan also liked being popular. He missed Chester, but over the past
seventeen or eighteen years he had learned to get on without Chester
much of the time. There was always Kirchstetten in the spring and
summer.

In the early summer, Wystan would rush back to his Cockaigne.
Except for Chester's forays into Vienna from time to time, he, too,
seemed content. He was finally working at something he enjoyed and
something he considered important. The days were productive. During the summer of 1959 Chester and Wystan translated Mozart's *Don
Giovanni*. They were also commissioned to write a plot for an opera
composed by Hans Werner Henze, *Elegy for Young Lovers*. In the
autumn they began a translation of Brecht's *The Rise and Fall of the
City of Mahagonny*. From time to time, Chester and Wystan would
travel to the music festivals in Salzburg, in Bayreuth, in Venice, and
Wystan would spend a few weeks of every summer at the Poetry International reading in England. He and Chester collaborated on Brecht's
The Seven Deadly Sins and were together in New York for its performance in December 1958. On January 23, 1959, Wystan won a gold
medal from the Poetry Society of America, and later on in the year
Christopher Isherwood asked Wystan and Chester to collaborate on
the book of the musical *Cabaret,* taken from Isherwood's *Goodbye to
Berlin*. For some reason they did not do it, as they did not do the
book for the musical produced later based on *Don Quixote*,[1] not seeing eye to eye with the producer concerning the character of Cer-
vantes's famous knight.

---

[1] Auden did write lyrics for *Man of La Mancha,* but they were never used.

In spite of their literary work during the summer, Chester was fond of entertaining, and he always welcomed houseguests in Kirchstetten, particularly old friends and relatives from America. In fact, if Chester knew that you were in Europe and had not made arrangements to visit him and Wystan, he would feel insulted. Both Chester and Wystan were generous hosts, always providing you with good food and drink, and if Frau Eiermann did not always approve of her employers' taste in company, most of the company signed the guestbook at their departure with pretty phrases about the good time they had had. Wystan still went into moods of arctic silences even with his own friends from school days, but he was usually less dour and Northumbrian during his time in Cockaigne than during his time in New York. Chester, who needed company, was an ideal host to all but the press, which, for some mysterious reason, he resented.

By 1960, Chester's younger brother, Malcolm, already thirty-one and looking more than ever like the Apollo Belvedere, had gained some prominence because of his meteoric rise in the world of retail merchants. By the end of the decade he was to become first the president, then the chairman of the board of a well-known New York department store. Later on he was to own a chain of retail stores in Chicago. Chester was proud of him and delighted when, in the spring of 1960, Malcolm, now called Matt, went on a buying trip to Vienna with his wife and promised to visit Kirchstetten. In 1950 he had married Joan Hanley, an Irish girl with large blue eyes and a quick wit. Chester loved his brother and adored his sister-in-law, so the three had a lively time together, particularly since Wystan was away and they had the house to themselves. They would sit on the patio in the morning sipping new wine as Chester made the espresso on the electric machine. After they had had their coffee, Chester would read to them from *The Importance of Being Earnest*. In the evening they would go into Vienna to have dinner at Sacher's or to attend an opera, after which Chester once introduced them to Leontyne Price. "Chester," they said, "was a fabulous host."

That same spring Joan and Matt went to Oxford to visit Wystan while he was still professor of poetry. Ever since Matt was a small boy of eleven and went to visit Bobby and Chester in Flatbush, he had known Wystan, who used to have "long talks" with him. Wystan took the couple first to his rooms in "a charming old cottage," then to lunch in the Senior Common Room. After lunch they all went for a walk through Oxford and sat near the Thames to talk. Suddenly it began to rain. Wystan, who never carried an umbrella, paid not the slightest attention to the weather but went right on talking as the shower fell upon their heads.

During the summer of 1963, Chester and Wystan received a surprise visit at Kirchstetten from Professor A. K. Stevens and his wife Angelyn, both of whom regarded Wystan as a charismatic figure ever since he had cured Angelyn of allergies back in Ann Arbor. Recalled Stevens in 1983:

> He was sitting there on the patio looking at the sky in some sort of reverie when I disturbed him by appearing at the gate. He was a little startled but very gracious. Later, when Angelyn and I came down from the guest room in the attic into the living room, there were Chester and Wystan, sitting in domestic bliss next to each other. We could see that there was a flow of love between them, and they looked for all the world like husband and wife. They had been working the London *Times* crossword puzzle—infernally difficult from my experience—and they enjoyed the challenge. It was a way of keeping their claws sharp, because it obliged them to roam the whole field of possibilities of words, no matter how recondite, to make them fit the crossword puzzle. Since both were poets, doing the puzzle improved their resources for the use of language.[1]

Later Wystan and Dr. Stevens had a talk about money. Said Stevens:

> He said he kept twenty thousand dollars in his bank checking account, and I, with my Dutch background, was disturbed enough to point out that the money was lying inert and should be earning interest. He responded that his health was not good and that he had to keep enough money there in case he died so that Chester would have it readily available to meet expenses for the funeral and to be able to have funds on which to live.[2]

If Wystan mentioned as early as 1963 that his health was not good, perhaps he knew, before his friends could guess, that he would not reach eighty-three, the age he usually predicted for his death.

In 1966 Chester and Wystan received a visit from Chester's father, who, at the age of seventy-four, was about to tour Europe again. In answer to Eddie's telegram from the Frankfurt airport, Chester and Wystan wired back: "Madly welcome, but come before August 1."

[1] The author's conversation with A. K. Stevens, April 8, 1983.
[2] Ibid.

On August 6, *The Bassarids,* for which Chester and Wystan had written the libretto to the music of Henze, was to be performed at Salzburg, and the librettists were expected to be there in advance.

When Eddie arrived, Chester and a dark young man, who reminded
Eddie of the students in the vocational high school where I had my
first job, met him at the Vienna airport. Chester introduced the young
man to his father as Yannis Boras. Yannis drove the car, which was
Wystan's Volkswagen, through the streets of Vienna, stopping along
the way at wine and pastry shops, while Chester pointed out to his
father various famous landmarks of the city. Then they drove toward
the Wienerwald and Kirchstetten.

"That's the Vienna Woods," said Chester, flicking his wrist to the
right.

"Where?" said Eddie. "I can't see it. You're going too fast." But
Yannis Boras understood only Greek and German, so he continued to
apply himself to the wheel.

"The woods over there to your right," said Chester. "They're like
any woods, Dad. I mean, Johann Strauss is not going to jump out with
an orchestra."

When they arrived at Kirchstetten, Wystan was at the cottage gate
to greet them, giving Eddie a peck on the cheek and taking him into
the house to show him the bathroom of which he was inordinately
proud, and showing him how to work the hot-water faucets. He then
took Eddie into a large white bedroom with a large white bed, freshly
made by Frau Eiermann (who approved of Chester's father) so that
Eddie could have a rest before dinner. Then Wystan looked at his
watch and said, "Drinks at 6:10 sharp. Don't be late." And he vanished into the recesses of the house.

At the cocktail hour, Eddie had presents for Wystan and Chester
(Yannis had disappeared), handing Chester some cartons of American
cigarettes and a box of cookies. He gave Wystan a box of Havana
panatelas and another package wrapped in gold paper with a silver
ribbon. When Wystan opened it, he cried, "Oh, goody!" Eddie had
brought him a box with packets of ingredients for a bubble bath.

Since his days on Ischia, Wystan had taken a fancy to hot tub baths,
particularly bubble baths. If you wanted to make him happy at Christmas, on his birthday, or at any other time, you would give him not a
book or a record—for these he bought for himself—but the ingredients
for a bubble bath, for which he was too shy to apply at a store. The
concept of Wystan, his face now deeply lined, reclining, huge and
amorphous in the effervescent bubbles of Chanel or Elizabeth Arden,

gave to his friends many moments of affectionate amusement. So
Eddie bought him a number of packets whenever the occasion arose.
Wystan's other friends indulged him, too, so one could often see sitting among the detritus in the bathroom at St. Mark's Place a fresh,
elaborate packet from Paris, decorated with gold and lace and labeled
pour le bain.

During Eddie's three-day visit he took walks in the Wienerwald
and went with Chester into the village of Kirchstetten to shop while
Wystan worked in the attic study. One morning the Greek boy appeared again with the Volkswagen and drove Eddie and Chester to a
busy shopping district some miles away. Eddie, a city boy at heart,
said, "This is more like it, Ches. I like this place."

"It's Vienna, Dad!" said Chester, snorting back a giggle.

"Chester took me around too fast," Eddie said later when asked
about his trip by friends in New York. "I wanted to see the Schön-
brunn Palace, but Chester said, 'All palaces look alike,' and that was
it. So we drove back to Kirchstetten, which is nothing but a hick
town, and I never did see much of Vienna. All I did most of the time
was sit in the sun and look at the trees."

When Chester and Wystan moved into the cottage, they brought
two cats, but since then they had attracted a number of others in addition to Frau Eiermann's, all of which seemed to prefer Frau Eiermann's rug. Wystan, however, took a fancy to a tiger kitten and decided she should dwell in the main house with him. While Eddie was
walking in the Wienerwald one morning, Wystan devised a plan to
lure the tiger kitten into his kitchen. First he went to the butcher's
shop and bought chunks of beef ("Large enough to feed a horse,"
said Eddie), which he cut up in a saucer and placed on the kitchen
floor. Taking one of the chunks, he went out into the garden where
the tiger kitten was now sunning herself and held the meat under her
nose. Interested, the kitten began to lick the meat and follow Wystan,
who was leading her somewhat awkwardly since he was bent over and
walking backward, the meat still at the cat's nose. Finally, after nearly
scaring her away by tipping over all the flowerpots in his path, he had
her as far as the kitchen door and then as far as the plate of meat
itself. She was still unsure, however, whether she would succumb to
bribery, but finally she began to nibble at the beef on the plate.

Just then Chester's father, bright as a bell, returned from his walk
in the Wienerwald and entered the house noisily by the kitchen door.
The tiger kitten fled, never to return.

Wystan, red with rage, threw up his arms, saying, "Why did you

have to come in just now? Can't you see what you've done? You scared
her away!"

Eddie, not fully comprehending the extent of his sin, said sardonically, "Tell her who I am," and walked into the bedroom to take a
nap and sulk. The next day, Eddie left for Rome.

Eddie, who was growing deafer by the year and was always having
difficulty with the hearing aid he did not want to wear in the first
place, was never quite sure what had happened that morning after
his trip from the Wienerwald. But forever after he was quick to tell
all who would listen that W. H. Auden had lost his temper because
of a cat. What kind of cat? "One hundred percent alley." Perhaps it
was hard for Wystan to realize just how old Eddie really was at this
time, for Eddie, smooth faced and bouncingly healthy, was, to Chester's profound annoyance, taken by a Fifty-seventh Street haberdasher
for Chester's brother just the year before. At any rate, all went well
with the tiger kitten. She settled down happily with Frau Emma Eiermann and grew into a comfortable tabby, but she never once went
near W. H. Auden and the main house.

During the late fifties and early sixties, Wystan, who in the past had
appealed to intellectual circles only, was becoming popular with the
general public. In 1962 he wrote to Pete in Greenland: "Really America is a very peculiar country. I got a letter the other day from the
U.S.S. *Lexington* saying they were collecting photos of poets and
would I please send mine to frame. I was very tempted to add my
telephone number to my signature, but thought better of it."

In the same letter to Pete in which he mentioned the U.S.S. *Lexington,* he mentioned Hughie, his Austrian lover, a young auto
mechanic who was not above a bit of thievery:

> We had a nice summer, marred only by the behavior of my
> Hughie who used my car to go burgling and got 15 months jail.
> One of the gang he was involved with—in order, no doubt, to in-
> gratiate himself with the police—told all about your mother. At
> the trial, no witnesses were called, but evidently the chief scandal
> paper in Vienna has someone in the police department in its pay,
> and the next day a long article appeared. I wasn't mentioned ac-
> tually by name, being "An American writer who lives in Vienna,"
> but every possible innuendo was made.

On February 6, 1963, he wrote: "My Viennese Hughie got nine
months [he was released early] and made a scandal for me in addition."
Yet Wystan was not angry with Hughie or outraged because of the

scandal. Chester suggested that Hughie allowed himself to get into trouble as a protest against Wystan, who treated him as an object rather than as a person. Wystan fancied the idea and claimed to have learned a lesson from Hughie's misadventures. At any rate, Wystan often performed acts of kindness for both Hughie and Hughie's wife in return for Hughie's favors. In 1965 Wystan sent Pete a poem that he had written to Hughie, describing the nature of their relationship and his gratitude for it. The poem was not published during Auden's life.

GLAD

Hugerl, for a decade now
My bed-visitor,
An unexpected blessing
In a lucky life,
For how much and how often
You have made me glad.

Glad that I know we enjoy
Mutual pleasure:
Women may cog their lovers
With a feigned passion,
But men are so constructed
We cannot deceive.

Glad our worlds of enchantment
Are so several
Neither is tempted to broach:
For I cannot tell a
Jaguar from a Bentley,
And you never read.

Glad for that while when you stole,
(You burgled me too)
And were caught and put inside:
Both learned a lesson,
But for which we well might still
Be Strich *and* Freier.[1]

[1] Auden's notes to Pete Komadina: *Strich*—hustler; *Freier*—client of same; and in last line of poem, *"es ist mir Wurscht"*—I couldn't care less (literally, "It is sausage to me," Viennese dialect).

Glad, though, we began that way,
That our life-paths crossed,
Like characters in Hardy,
At a moment when
You were in need of money
And I wanted sex.

How is it now between us?
Love? Love is far too
Tattered a word. A romance
In full fig it ain't,
Nor a naked letch either:
Let me say we fadge,

And how much I like Christa,
Who loves you but knows
Good girl, when not to be there.
I can't imagine
A kinder set-up: if mims
Mump, es ist mir Wurscht.[1]

In the meantime, the young man who had driven Eddie to Kirch-stetten from the airport in 1966 and whom Eddie later described to me as "like one of your vocational high school boys," had changed Chester's life.

Every year Alan Ansen, who had now settled permanently in Athens, made a journey to Kirchstetten to visit Chester and Wystan for a month during the summer. In 1963, Alan, regaling Chester with the joys of Greece and the willingness of the boys, persuaded him to spend the winters there. The climate was pleasant, the ruins were of interest, and the living was easy. Besides, Chester's forays in conservative Austria were beginning to make Wystan almost as nervous as Chester's forays in New York. For all the peace and beauty of Cockaigne, Chester was becoming restive, since the only place he could go to find lovers was twenty-seven miles east to Vienna.

Chester thus went to Athens for the winter of 1963, and it was there he fell in love again for the first time in his life. It was also the last time. In 1963 Yannis Boras was twenty-one, a slim, muscular Greek boy of the working class with jet black hair, romantic eyes, and a

---

[1] Auden, "Glad," in *Collected Poems,* p. 561.

sweet expression about the mouth. Chester had not lost, even at forty-two and in declining health, his magnetic personal attraction, and, according to Charles Heilemann, one of his old friends who traveled widely, Chester's homosexual friends in Greece were envious because, even at this time of life, apparently Chester could attract young boys as lovers.

Boras was, of course, a heterosexual, or Chester would not have fallen in love with him, and he had girlfriends on the side. Whatever in his nature inclined him to have an extended affair with Chester is one of the mysteries of life and of sex, but Boras was Chester's lover for five years. He went back to Austria with Chester for the summer, did odd jobs about the house, acted as chauffeur, and attended to Wystan's Volkswagen. Chester put him up in an apartment in Vienna, and from 1963 until 1968 Chester was happy. He was encouraged to believe he had finally found the love he might have for life.

In the winter of 1968 tragedy struck. According to one of Chester's Greek neighbors, Boras had been home for a visit and was driving Wystan's Volkswagen back to Vienna on the autobahn late one night with two girls. All had been drinking. For some reason Yannis, who allegedly was driving, stopped the car in the middle of the autobahn and turned off the lights. It was not long before another vehicle, a truck, approached the Volkswagen on the autobahn, and, not seeing the darkened car, crashed into it with full force. Yannis was killed instantly.

Chester never recovered. Micky Demarest, Sandro, and a hundred others died that night on the autobahn with Yannis, and, in a sense, Chester died, too. He never fell in love again. He poured out his grief in a last poem to the last love of his life:

ADDRESS TO YANNIS BORAS

March 3, 1942   *December 13, 1968*
Livadaki   *Vienna*

> *How, darling, this incontinent grief*
> *Must irk you, more*
> *Even than those outraged, mute*
> *Or pleading jealousies, though now*
> *This you are too pitiless to refute,*
> *Making me all you disapprove:*
> *Selfishly sodden, selfless, dirtier, a prodigal*

Discredit to our renewed belief in love;
And addressing the dead! You'd laugh.
Yet I can't imagine you dead
As I know you are and somehow
Hold this one indulgence you allow,
You who allowed me so much life.

1969[1]

Wystan, always at Chester's side when he needed him, tried to be of comfort. Yannis Boras's body was taken back to Livadaki to be buried, and his friends and kinsmen viewed the mangled corpse of the twenty-six year old with outrage, assigning the guilt of his death to the rich American who had led him astray. According to one of Chester's Greek neighbors, when Wystan and Chester went to visit Boras's grave in the Greek Orthodox cemetery of Livadaki, the townspeople threw stones at them through the iron grating, hurling Greek insults into the air.

Cockaigne had already begun its decline. Josef Eiermann had died some time before, followed in November 1967 by Frau Eiermann herself and all the cats who had shared her kingdom. David Protetch would die in New York in 1969, and Igor Stravinsky in 1971. Though Wystan and Chester continued to spend their summers in Kirchstetten; though Wystan's eyes would still fill with tears of gratitude as he surveyed his house and his lands; and though he would say as a prayer Psalm 16:6, the angel of death now hovered about him.

[1] Printed privately by Chester Kallman in 1969.

CHAPTER 15

Show Me the Way to Go Home

IN THE BEGINNING of the 1960s life on St. Mark's Place, too, began to decline. Wystan was lonely there. Since 1961, Chester had remained away from New York for long periods of time. The city had become more dangerous. The men that Chester brought home were beginning to steal whatever they could find of value. They had always stolen, but now they were more vicious than before. Wystan, fearing for Chester's safety, began to object to his nightly excursions; so Chester remained in Europe where fugitive loves were less savage.

In 1963, after he had met Yannis, Chester began to spend more time in Greece, and he continued to do so after Yannis's death. Chester still drank ouzo in the bars and sought the company of boys, particularly the Greek soldiers in their kiltlike short skirts. For a time he lived in a building where a Greek officer also lived. Seeing the soldiers going nightly to Chester's apartment, the officer had the landlord evict him. It was then that Chester moved into the apartment on the lower floor of the house of Dr. Basil Proimos, near Alan Ansen's place on Deemocharous. He was still staying with Wystan in Austria for the spring and summer, and their life together went on as before. Chester at forty-two seemed at times more dependent on Wystan than ever, at least financially. But at times he was sullen and resentful of this man whose fame seemed to dramatize his own sense of failure. "They think I can't do anything by myself," he continued to say.

In 1967 Wystan was sixty. He had begun to age overnight. The pale face, smooth as a boy's at forty, was at sixty gnarled and lined like that of an ancient sea captain. The Benzedrine, the gin, and the Mediterranean sun had dried him out. His health, however, was fair, though he was still taking Benzedrine—some said a Benzedrine substitute—in the morning, drinking martinis before dinner, and going to bed at 9:00 with a bottle of wine and a plate of boiled potatoes. He had made a number of new friends in the city, and he even took a lover or two, not just one-night call boys but upper middle-class friends for whom he felt a romantic attachment. Sometimes he would dine with the Stravinskys in the Pierre Hotel; sometimes he would see David Protetch, the Weisses, Keith Callaghan. Sometimes he would have drinks and dinner at Chester's father's.

During the sixties his career was going well and he was attracting popular interest. He was then, as always, prolific. In 1960 he had published *Homage to Clio;* in 1962, *The Dyer's Hand,* a compilation of essays as well as his lectures at Oxford; and in 1965, he published *About the House,* a celebration of the individual, as exemplified by his life with Chester in Kirchstetten. His *Collected Shorter Poems, 1927–1957* came out in 1966, and his *Collected Longer Poems* in 1968, along with *Secondary Worlds,* the T. S. Eliot Memorial Lectures given at the University of Kent. In 1969 he published *City Without Walls and Other Poems,* which included the poem in memory of Frau Eiermann, whom he perceived as a victim, as he perceived other personalities in these poems. In 1970 he was to publish *A Certain World: A Commonplace Book.*

During his last decade in New York he continued with his almost secret acts of generosity. He was not only quick to help with money, as he had been in 1956, when he furtively pushed a check for $250 into the hand of the surprised Dorothy Day in order for her to pay a fine levied by the city against her settlement house on Bleecker Street.[1] He was also generous with his talents and his time. Toward

---

[1] Dorothy Day, a Catholic social worker, ran a hotel for derelicts on Bleecker

the middle of the decade, remembering his rewarding experiences at Oxford at the Cadena coffeehouse, where he had met students in an open-house setting, he decided to open his apartment in New York from four to six[1] to American university students with a special interest in English literature. They were invited to visit him and to discuss their work. In fact, it was upon just such an occasion that Auden was to meet the brilliant young Edward Mendelson, a Ph.D. candidate, of whom Wystan said later to Chester: "He knows more about me than I know myself." Mendelson was later to become Wystan's literary executor and the world's foremost authority on Auden.

Wystan was generous not only with the unusually gifted college student but also with the younger student. He believed that students in primary school were being neglected because of the faulty methods of teaching reading. Wystan believed in method, and he believed in only one: intensive phonics. From time to time he helped me study for advanced examinations and became interested in the public high school student.

Due largely to Eddie's ambition for me, my career in New York's public school system changed from what it had been during the early 1940s in the vocational high school. Having passed an advanced examination, I was appointed in the autumn of 1965 to chairman of English, day high schools, of Erasmus Hall in Brooklyn, an event that caused much merriment in the Auden–Kallman circle. The idea of me as head of a department of fifty teachers, as it was then, struck especially Chester as droll, for to him I was still the blonde that danced with him and David Protetch in Yorkville and fell in love with his father. Chester and Wystan were pleased, nevertheless, and Wystan set about giving me advice. He made a number of pronouncements in the hope of changing the way English was taught in at least one New York public high school.

His directions were clear and dramatic. I was to get rid of all books of modern literature immediately and teach only the great books from *Beowulf* through Chaucer and from Chaucer through the Victorians. I was to teach Greek mythology and Homer's *Iliad* at some time in

---

Street across from the San Remo in the Village. Her building had violated New York City fire regulations and she was taken to court and fined $250 in February 1956. Auden met her as she came out of court and handed her the money to pay her fine. He admired her for having the courage to help the "undeserving poor."

[1] Professor Edward Mendelson, recalling his visits to Auden, remembered: "I always took care to arrive *exactly* at four, and was always ushered out at six."

the sophomore or junior years. I was to have formal grammar taught with the diagraming of sentences and a course on the Latin and Greek derivations of English words. I was to require memory work of great lines on every level. I was to permit no adapted or abridged works of any kind except for the mentally retarded. All English literature was to be read in the original; nothing was to be watered down. Outside-reading books were to be assigned specifically from a list. Reports on books of the students' choice, generally called book reports, were a fraud, since students seldom read the books anyway, and to accept such reports encouraged lying. A quiz on all outside reading was to be given instead of book reports. All creative writing classes—also frauds—were to be abolished, as they were even more damaging to students who had talent than to those who had none: "The best way to help a writer is to teach him to write clear expository prose, preferably scientific." Wystan then gave me a book that he had used to teach rhetoric at the Downs School and suggested that its contents be taught in connection with composition.

Although I had always agreed with Wystan's theories about education, I knew that most people of the time did not. However, I managed to apply as many of his ideas as possible, much to the consternation of the progressives in my department but to the delight of the others: "They don't need a paid teacher to learn to read Hemingway," I found myself quoting from time to time Wystan's words. After the first year things went reasonably well, and the students seemed to find the courses significant and valuable. The parents were even more pleased, for now their children could prove that they were learning something when company came to call: Students were quoting Shakespeare on Sunday afternoons. I always believed that Wystan's advice saved my department from the open rebellion experienced by other departments during the widespread student revolts of the late 1960s. Although some of the students complained about the memory work, they never said that the work was not relevant and they were not learning anything. Apparently their teachers had encouraged them to see the eternal relevance in *Beowulf,* Chaucer, and Shakespeare. Wystan's advice to me about education, as his counsel to Anne Weiss about having babies, though it seemed to fly in the face of the conventional wisdom of the day, turned out to be good advice.

Wystan took an active interest in my new position in the world and in the students and teachers of Erasmus Hall, upon whose lives, though they did not know it, he had a considerable impact, having prescribed their course of study. Thus, in the early spring of 1967 he invited to tea at St. Mark's Place some students especially selected by the middle-aged sponsors who accompanied them: Mrs. Mary McNulty, who had majored in Latin, and Mr. Schuyler Bash,[1] who had written his master's thesis on southern writers and adored Eudora Welty.

On the appointed day, Mrs. McNulty and Mr. Bash, together with eight boys and two girls (the only students who could get parents' consent slips), receiving permission from Mrs. Harriet Oxman, the assistant principal, took the BMT subway at Church Avenue, Brooklyn, to Manhattan, and got off at the wrong stop. They had to walk from Union Square to St. Mark's Place, a matter of ten blocks, through pushcarts, crying children, dancing hippies, and tenements, the odors from which, coupled with open garbage cans at entryways, were only slightly modified by the chill spring air. Nevertheless, the twelve persisted, wondering at the ambiance that led them to the home of the Greatest Living English Poet. They finally arrived. Sure that they had reached the wrong building, they sent Ernie Fox,[2] always accurate and willing, ahead to check the street number. There was no mistake.

W. H. Auden was on the landing to greet them, tall and formidable and looking just like his pictures, except that he was more red. Wystan had gone to a great deal of trouble. On the library table was a real English tea service with a real English tea cozy, plates filled with sandwiches and tea buns, even as on Pontiac Trail in Ann Arbor, and a number of thick white mugs. After students and teachers had introduced themselves and set their coats, as directed by Wystan, on chairs in the parlor, Wystan asked Mrs. McNulty to be Mother. Seeing the startled look on her face, he added: "Pour the tea, you know." So Mary McNulty, majestic in her flowered silk, sat at the tea table pouring the tea, her hands still trembling, not only because of the cold walk from Union Square but also because of her nervousness upon meeting the Greatest Living English Poet. Mr. Bash, cold and also nervous, supervised the students at the tea table, got the boys to help the two girls, and sat them properly in a prearranged circle in the music room around W. H. Auden, now drinking from one of the white mugs, but not drinking tea.

While the boys and girls were drinking their tea and gobbling down the sandwiches and buns, Wystan asked the grown-ups whether they would care for something stronger. Mrs. McNulty looked at her watch,

[1] Not their real names.
[2] Ibid.

and, seeing that it was past school time, assured Wystan that she usually did not take alcoholic beverage but that a bit now would prevent her from catching cold and missing school the next day. Mr. Bash readily concurred. Mrs. McNulty and Mr. Bash settled themselves with great dignity on Chester's Folly, a canopied arrangement for seating constructed by one of Pete's friends of the old days, and Wystan served them double martinis in jelly glasses, after which he proceeded to ask each student one of his questions especially prepared for the occasion.

Revived by the tea and going back for more cakes, the students chatted on volubly in answer to Wystan's questions concerning their favorite teacher and why; their favorite books/poems, and why; their favorite course and why; what they intended to do when they finished school and why; were they going on to college, and if so where and why; and so on and why. Wystan made some declarations about not writing free verse until you are forty and about the need for having four years of Latin, but he did not shock them much. They were nice middle-class children, and they had already been shocked to the limit of their capacity by the young hippie teachers in beads and dungarees now being hired in the social studies department, the old guard of which was now retiring.

The two silent teachers who were sitting on Chester's Folly were no longer cold. They were also no longer silent. In fact, they were feeling quite cozy now, and both began to speak at once, Mrs. McNulty about the importance of a Latin curriculum, and Mr. Bash about Eudora Welty and *The Southern Review*. Wystan, the mirror of *politesse,* listened with flattering attention as he sipped from his white mug something other than tea, and the teachers never felt more brilliant in their lives. The students, now nudging each other and winking, were beginning to enjoy the afternoon for the first time. Wystan, noticing that Mrs. McNulty and Mr. Bash had emptied their jelly glasses, offered to refill them, thinking that they would, of course, refuse. Both thought, however, that perhaps just one more would be efficacious in warding off a possible attack of the flu now going round, and they accepted the second with an alacrity worthy of any member of the Auden–Kallman set.

The students were now having more fun than they could remember, and if it had not been for that killjoy Ernie Fox, who insisted that his mother was expecting him home by 6:15, they might have had even more. Wystan, who was beginning to have second thoughts about the entire adventure, took Ernie at his word, rose a mite too quickly, and a mite too quickly started looking for Mrs. McNulty's coat. But when Wystan was helping Mrs. McNulty on with her coat, he noticed that she found it hard to stand up. She said she felt faint and was not sure whether she could find the way to the subway. "Oh, dear, what will the children do?"

Wystan then explained firmly to all how to get to Astor Place: "Just walk west for three blocks." Mr. Bash, full of valor and self-confidence while seated on Chester's Folly, was less assured having risen to his feet. He tipped over a table that stood in his path on the way to the door.

Wystan was expecting a visitor at six o'clock and was now in a panic.

The problem was solved, however, a moment later when, as Wystan stood at the stairwell, he said goodbye to the last of his guests. Mrs. McNulty and Mr. Bash were descending the rickety steps with a student at each elbow. Thus it was that the chaperones found the Astor Place subway stop and got home that night. As the students guided their teachers west on St. Mark's Place, one question remained unanswered: "Why was the Greatest Living English Poet living in the slums?"

Wystan never told me what happened at the tea party, but Chester did. All Wystan ever said was, "I think your teachers were a little tiddly that night."

While Wystan was still living at St. Mark's Place during the winter, he would find time to visit with Chester's father. In the autumn of 1970, when Eddie was seventy-eight, he needed to have an operation. Wystan visited him twice in the French Hospital on West Thirtieth Street, presenting him an autographed copy of *A Certain World,* which had been published the June before. In the course of the conversation, Eddie asked about Chester, never far from his father's mind. "I'm wondering," said Eddie, "whether he's in the right place with those friends in Greece."

"I don't like that whole Greek bunch," Wystan said with disdain. "I am very much concerned about Chester, especially about his health. He is drinking too much."

"Well," said Eddie philosophically, "Chester is now almost fifty years old. I am seventy-eight and growing old. Chester has made his own choices in life and I refuse to suffer for them. He is old enough by this time to take care of himself. I can't be concerned about him if he isn't concerned about himself."

Wystan, who was not pleased with Eddie's answer, said, "Well, I

am concerned." He said it with such emphasis that Eddie was cha-
grined.

Wystan was right to be concerned. After the death of Yannis, the
change in Chester had been dramatic. His drinking became heavier.
His heart, never strong since a siege of rheumatic fever in childhood,
was weaker now. The doctor, whom he saw weekly, said that the swelling on his left side was the result of the spleen affected by a defective
liver. Chester had to stop drinking or he would die. Chester continued drinking. "It's only a psychological pregnancy," he retorted.[1]

In 1971, Chester's younger brother, Malcolm, went to Greece on
another business trip with his wife, Joan, and his daughter, Lisa, now
sixteen. When Chester heard his brother was coming, his spirits improved, and he gathered together all his friends, including Alan Ansen, also a friend of Matt's in the old days, and planned a celebration
at the local café.

They all shared a great many laughs, drinking at the café, and went
to see the old men dancing peasant dances in the square. The brothers,
happy to be together again, discussed days gone by and family problems, particularly those with their father, who, they decided over
ouzo, had been too ambitious for his sons. "Dad doesn't love you for
yourself, but for your accomplishments," said Chester. It never occurred to either of them, of course, that one of the reasons each had
achieved the success he had was because of the value their father had
placed upon it. "Dad has lost interest in me," Chester said. "You're
the successful one now. I went to a party the other day and somebody
said, 'Are you the brother of Matt Kallman?' "

"Well," replied Matt good-naturedly, "I went through it with you
long enough. Now it's your turn."

Both Joan and Matt were worried about Chester because he looked
ill. They knew the cause of the distention in his left side and were
concerned by the fact that Chester was drinking more heavily than
before, but Chester answered them as he had answered the doctor:
"It's only a psychological pregnancy."

"He always drank, but never like that," said Matt. "Alan Ansen
said that he was doing good work, whatever that meant. Maybe he can
write poetry when he's drunk, but he can't do anything else. He can't
even balance a checkbook. Chester lost touch with reality. He invited us for dinner one night for my favorite dish, lamb stew. Ches-

[1] This and subsequent quotes from the author's conversation with Matt Kallman, March 23, 1983.

ter had always been a great cook, but not now. When we arrived at his house that night he was already drunk and puttering around in the kitchen. He didn't know what he was doing and had forgotten to put the lamb into the stew. It was awful."

Chester had for some time toyed with the idea of returning to New York. He had not been feeling well lately, and he knew in his heart that his drinking had become worse. With the wishful thinking of the active alcoholic, he believed he could find solace from his grief in the familiar places of his youth and in close contact with his family, to whom he was still the brilliant, beautiful boy. Eddie had been much on his mind, and he wanted to see his father for what he believed would be the last time. In 1971, Braziller of New York had published his new book, *The Sense of Occasion,* and Chester had dedicated it to his father and me. Perhaps if he came back home he would be able to stop this heavy drinking and be able to drink as he did when he was young. He sent a telegram to his father and one to Wystan, and he took the next plane for New York. Travel always rejuvenated him, and he was able to control his drinking during the trip and for the next few days.

He arrived in New York two days before New Year's. Wystan was waiting for him at St. Mark's Place with coffee and a brandy, and they talked for an hour or so before Chester went to sleep off the jet lag. As he lay on his bed in the alcove next to the music room he knew he had made a mistake. No sooner had he stepped off the plane at La Guardia than he wished he had not come.

On New Year's Eve they arrived at his father's new apartment, an old cooperative near University Place and Tenth Street. The living room was large for New York, filled with chandeliers, mirrors, and old furniture. It was also filled with people who rushed to greet him. Eddie was prepared to treat him like the prodigal returned. There were platters of food, all Chester's favorites, on a large buffet table near the fireplace. Eddie had prepared fillet of white fish, Nova Scotia salmon, lake sturgeon, and even caviar and smoked fish. The liquor was laid out on a desk in the foyer and Wystan and Chester made drinks for themselves.

Bringing their drinks to a coffee table, they sat on a tapestry settee as people came over to talk to them. Mary in a red dress sat across from Chester, and Getel and Frank Nastasi sat close by. Wystan, uncomfortable and glum in crowds, sat next to him on the tapestry and Malcolm sat on his other side. The room was warm. From somewhere a piano was playing Chopin.

The drink had gone to Chester's head. His friends were asking him questions he suddenly could not answer. He found that he was weeping, and he began quietly wiping his tears with his hand, and his hand on the tapestry. Wystan turned to him and whispered something, but Chester was thinking of Yannis. His cousins and his brother looked alarmed. Mary and I, now sitting together across from him, watched him with that old familiar feeling of bewilderment and fear. His father was still mercifully in the kitchen. Those of his friends who noticed pretended they did not. After a while he got control of himself, went to the desk in the foyer, mixed another dry martini, and circulated among his relieved friends.

In a day or so, when Chester made the announcement he was going back to Greece, his father walked over to St. Mark's Place to see him one more time and say goodbye. Chester was sitting in an armchair, his legs crossed, talking, his cigarette poised insolently in his right hand. Chester and Wystan were having an argument. Wystan was pacing the floor, clearly upset about something. They were expecting some friends over for the evening: "Not your kind of people, Dad."

"When am I going to see you again, Ches?" asked Eddie.

"I am going to be very busy arranging to leave."

"Then I'll say goodbye now."

"Wait, I'll walk you a block or so."

Chester walked his father to Astor Place and said goodbye. Then he turned around and walked back. The night was misty, still, and cold. By the light of the streetlamps he could see the snow turning to slush in the gutters. Stray bits of paper drifted feebly along the street. The lights in the empty shops still decked for Christmas gave the street a false festivity. Here and there were noisy groups of young people in beads and long hair. As he approached the familiar entrance he stopped a moment to listen and then walked past the stone lions and up the steps. From an apartment across the street a clarinet was playing "Show Me the Way to Go Home."

The next day Chester returned to Athens.

When Chester left, Wystan was shaken and haggard. He had expected Chester to remain longer in New York, and they had argued bitterly about his leaving. Now it would be spring again before they met, and Wystan still had three more months on St. Mark's Place alone. He was angry because Chester would not permit himself to be helped. He knew that Chester was ill, and he himself no longer had the stamina to argue or exert his will to try to save him. Perhaps Wystan feared as well the loneliness that had begun to assail him more frequently now, a loneliness that had caused him in August 1971 to write the following poem:

LONELINESS

Gate-crashing ghost, aggressive
invisible visitor,
tactless gooseberry, spoiling
my tête-à-tête *with myself,*
blackmailing brute, behaving
as if the house were your own,
so viciously pursuing
your victim from room to room
monotonously nagging,
ungenerous jabberer,
dirty devil, befouling
fair fancies, making the mind
a quagmire of disquiet,
weakening my will to work,
shadow without shape or sex,
excluding consolation,
blotting out Nature's beauties,
gray mist between me and God,
pestilent problem that won't
be put on the back-burner,
hard it is to endure you.

Routine is the one technique
I know of that enables
your host to ignore you now:
while typing business letters,
laying the table for one,
gobbling a thoughtless luncheon,
I briefly forget you're there,
but am safe from your haunting
only when soundly asleep.

History counsels patience:
tyrants come, like plagues, but none
can rule the roost for ever.

Indeed, your totter is near,
your days numbered: to-morrow
Chester, my chum, will return.
Then you'll be through: in no time
he'll throw you out neck-and-crop.
We'll merry-make your cadence
With music, feasting and fun.[1]

Chester could fill a loneliness no one else could, and now Wystan began to perceive he was losing him forever.

Toward the middle of the 1960s Wystan's health, too, had begun to decline, and David Protetch had diagnosed a heart condition. Yet Wystan refused to give up any of his habits. He still took Benzedrine each morning and still drank too much. He once told Eddie, who himself had stopped smoking, "If I have to give up smoking and the other things I like, I'd rather die." He had written a poem, one of his "Shorts," in 1950 about an ideal doctor, and though David Protetch was hardly an endomorph in any sense of the word, he let Wystan have his way quite as the doctor in his poem would have:

Give me a doctor, partridge-plump,
Short in the leg and broad in the rump,
An endomorph with gentle hands,
Who'll never make absurd demands
That I abandon all my vices,
Nor pull a long face in a crisis,
But with a twinkle in his eye
Will tell me that I have to die.[2]

By the late 1960s the world around Wystan had changed. Crime had increased along with the flourishing drug culture in the neighborhood of St. Mark's Place, as it had elsewhere. The world suddenly went mad with its flashing lights, mod culture, wild dances, and rock music. Then, too, New York was lonely; Chester now remained in Europe for years at a time.

All that was familiar had suddenly become grotesque and distorted as reality is distorted in the mirrors of a Coney Island funhouse or the visions of a nightmare. In 1969, David Protetch died. Alone dur-

[1] Auden, "Loneliness," in *Collected Poems*, pp. 649–50.
[2] Auden, "Shorts," ibid., p. 436.

ing the winter on St. Mark's Place, Wystan wondered what would happen if he himself were suddenly to die. "Supposing I had a coronary. It might be weeks before I was found . . ." he said.[1] Yet he made little effort to contact old friends, unaware of his plight, who, believing he wanted to be undisturbed, did not call him regularly and knew little about his illness.

It was at this time that Wystan thought of Oxford, remembering with nostalgia the many happy hours he had spent there in the late fifties when he was professor of poetry. He remembered the regular time schedule, the monastic repose, the nightly ritual of dessert and drinks in the Senior Common Room. He remembered the friends he had made. Not only had Oxford in 1956 elected him professor of poetry, and recently awarded him an honorary doctor of letters. He was, after all, an Englishman. Christ Church, Oxford, had been his own school as a young man, and the college had made him an honorary fellow in 1962. Now he thought of it as his home, and he wanted to go home. He was ill and growing old. He had had enough of travel, of excitement, of living all over the world with surrogate families that would not or could not care for him now when he needed them most. Further, he felt betrayed by New York, which now appeared to him dangerous, threatening, and lonely.

He let it be known that he wanted to return to his old college and spend the remainder of his life there; and Christ Church, almost unanimously, voted him the small sixteenth-century cottage, which had once been a brew house, in the garden of one of the canon-professors, near Christ Church Hall, near the old Senior Common Room and the new one. Wystan agreed to pay a monthly rental fee, live there during the winter, and be free in the spring and summer to go back to Kirchstetten to be with Chester. He said goodbye to his friends in New York on his birthday in a farewell party at the Coffee House on West Forty-fifth Street. He had packed his thousands of books and other belongings on St. Mark's Place and sent them on ahead.

Then he packed his bags. Orlan Fox and Dr. Oliver Sacks, old friends, called for him on April 15 to take him to the airport. All three descended the rickety stairs at 77 St. Mark's Place for the last time. They went out the frosted glass double doors and passed the

---

[1] Auden quoted in the London *Evening Standard*, February 7, 1972, in Carpenter, *Auden: A Biography*, p. 439.

stone lions that had guarded Auden's exits and entrances for almost twenty years. They passed the Ukrainiàn bar downstairs where Chester and Pete had long ago spent happy hours. They listened as the boy across the way now dutifully practiced on his clarinet his only and favorite tune—"Show Me the Way to Go Home."

Wystan went to Kirchstetten for the summer and to England in the fall of 1972. He arrived at Oxford in October, and photographers from the press were there to greet him when he got off the train from London. While the Brew House was being made ready for him, he stayed with a friend at All Souls. When he moved into the house that was to be his for the remainder of his life, the first words he said were "It's not my style."

Reality now confronted him as it had confronted Chester at the airport in New York. Oxford, too, had changed. The life he remembered as professor of poetry was no more; even the Cadena coffee-house had vanished. The baby boom of World War II, now approaching college age, had increased the number of students and teachers. The hall that he loved was crowded and noisy, and the newly appointed fellows had given up the once or twice weekly ritual of dessert, coffee, and drinks after dinner on guest nights. Wystan, stubborn and solitary, often sat alone in the Senior Common Room drinking his glass of red wine. As a substitute for the Cadena coffeehouse Wystan chose St. Aldate's Church Bookshop and Coffee House. For some reason, students did not flock to his table as they had flocked twelve years before when he was the rage. Many regarded him as passé.

Wystan himself had changed. He was drinking more heavily now, even adding brandy to his list of after-dinner drinks, and inclined to be repetitious and cantankerous. He was lonely without Chester, who seldom if ever wrote to him that last year. He was worried about Chester's health and took to writing him one-line letters frequently, letters that Chester often left unopened for days: "Why don't I hear from you?" or "Please let me know how you are."[1]

According to one of his biographers, Charles Osborne:

[1] The letters Auden sent to Chester Kallman during 1972–1973 were among the material returned from Greece, upon Chester's death, to Dr. Edward Kallman. The author had an opportunity to examine these letters, along with photographs and other papers, before they were turned over to the Humanities Research Center at the University of Texas, Austin. The author is indebted to Dr. Kallman and Edward Mendelson for permission to quote from them here.

In general, he tactlessly and ungratefully complained about most aspects of Oxford life. The traffic was worse than in New York. The streets were becoming as dangerous as those of New York. The intellectual atmosphere was, in comparison with that of New York, intolerably provincial. Clearly he was homesick for New York in winter! He became involved in prosecuting a twenty-seven-year-old labourer who he claimed had stolen his wallet containing £50.[1]

"I had to come to Oxford to be robbed," Wystan was heard to say too many times. His companions at table resented not only the complaints but also his conversation, which gave evidence of too many preprandial martinis. Those who wanted to invite him out in the evening were confronted by his insistence upon going to bed at 9:00. His working day had begun hours before at dawn.

What Wystan did not realize when he returned to Oxford was that he was homesick for New York. Over the years, despite his travels, his years in Italy and in Austria, he had become a New Yorker. The city had worked its magic spell on him and refused to relinquish him. Oxford, Ischia, and even Kirchstetten were fine as long as at the end of the summer he could come back to New York. No matter how the city had changed, there was still no substitute, not Oxford, not anywhere.

He attempted, however, to keep up his own work as well as to contribute to the intellectual life of the college. In December 1972, he spent the Christmas holidays with his old friends, the Sterns.[2] It was at their home that he wrote the poem that formed the title of his last book, *Thank You, Fog,* published posthumously. In January 1973, he recorded an interview with an old friend, Richard Crossman,[3] for television. In February he attended in Brussels the première of *Love's Labours Lost,* for which, with Chester, he had done the libretto for Nicolas Nabokov's[4] score. When he returned to Oxford he attended a party for graduate English students and planned to take part in a seminar on Shakespeare. He also attended a performance of his early

[1] Charles Osborne, *W. H. Auden: The Life of a Poet* (New York: Harcourt Brace Jovanovich, 1979), pp. 304–5.

[2] James and Tania Stern, old friends who in the forties shared with Auden the cottage on Fire Island. James Stern is a writer now living in England.

[3] Richard Crossman, one of Auden's friends from Oxford days, was a member of the Labour government under Prime Minister Harold Wilson and later became editor of *The New Statesman.*

[4] Nabokov, the composer, was an old friend of Auden's.

play *The Dog Beneath the Skin*. The performance was successful and well attended, particularly since the character of Auden himself, complete with cigarette, was written into the play. In April he traveled to Yorkshire to read his poems at the Ilkley Literature Festival.

The summer of 1973 he spent at Kirchstetten with Chester, making plans for future work. He was to edit with Edward Mendelson a new edition of his *Oxford Book of Light Verse* and to translate some poems by the Swedish Nobel prize winner, Par Lagerkvist. In June he read at Poetry International Festival in London. This time Chester was with him, and Wystan's mood seemed lighter. He and Chester that summer wrote an antimasque, "The Entertainment of the Senses."

In September they would again part, Chester for Athens and Wystan for Oxford. On Friday evening, September 28, having closed the house in Kirchstetten for the winter, they went to Vienna, Chester to the opera to see *Rigoletto* and Wystan to the Palais Palffy in Josefplatz to give a poetry reading for the Austrian Society for Literature. When he was offered supper, he refused, saying that he was feeling tired. He was driven back to the old hotel where he always stayed when he was in Vienna, and he went to his room. At some time before nine o'clock the next morning he died in his sleep.

CHAPTER 16

Last Days
in Athens

AFTER THE FUNERAL in Kirchstetten, Chester returned to Athens, where, since 1963, he had been spending the autumn and winter. He took up his life again on the first floor of Dr. Basil Proimos's house on 23 Deemocharous Street, down the hill from the apartment of Alan Ansen and near friends in the American colony. Despite the compatriots around him, he was alone in the world now. Without Wystan, he would never again be the same brilliant, beautiful boy. He was fifty-two years old going on fifty-three. He was gaining weight and beginning to lose his blond hair, and he had to pay more now in cold cash for the feigned passions of lovers. His health, too, was beginning to fail. The swelling in his left side had increased. The years of Strega and ouzo and strong wine had not promised to prolong his youth. He began immediately to dissipate his health and his inheritance.

He went nightly to the bars where the ouzo allowed him to forget. The cold morning light brought the same emptiness of the day before, and the same awareness of loss. The boy of the night before with whom he had shared his bed had perhaps already left, to go to a job somewhere or to return to his wife—the richer by a number of drachmas. Chester would try putting off facing the day for yet a while by rolling over in bed and sleeping for another hour, but eventually the strong Greek sun would rouse him. He would get out of bed, take a swallow of wine, make himself some coffee, and put a record on the phonograph.

The days went on more or less the same. Depending upon his health, he would escape into the old habits, listening to music, visiting friends, cooking, giving and going to parties, celebrating as fêtes the most unimportant anniversaries, now and then opening his notebook and jotting down lines for a poem. This was to be his last poem—"The Dome of the Rock"—about his trip in 1970 to Jerusalem with Ansen and Auden. Sometimes he would just sit in the sun with his glass beside him, waiting through the long afternoon for the excitement of the night. He had never learned Wystan's mastery of time.

Toward six o'clock his neighbor and old friend, Alan Ansen, who had already done the shopping for groceries and meat, would come over and Chester would start the dinner. After dinner he and Alan would play music for a while, talk a bit, and then Chester would go off, sometimes with Alan, but more often without him, to the bars and the Greek boys.

Chester had not been well for some time, and he had been consulting a physician, George A. Anastasopoulis. Dr. Anastasopoulis's bills found in Chester's effects show that he had been seeing a doctor regularly through 1972, 1973, and even more frequently during 1974. In the spring of 1974, Chester's health began to fail. His Greek doctor had ordered him to stop drinking. In addition to the heart murmur he had had since childhood as a result of rheumatic fever, he now had a duodenal ulcer and an enlarged liver and spleen as the result of alcohol. He was able to stop drinking for two months or so, and, along with the medication given him by Anastasopoulis, he began to feel better. Then he started drinking again.

In May 1974 he returned to Kirchstetten for the summer. On May 5, 1974, having come to a decision about selling his property there, he wrote a letter to me:

> I am answering (briefly) by return mail because "time is of the essence." Tomorrow I mean to call someone to get an estimate on my "property." Yes, that means that my intention is to sell. You

see, I can't maintain, now that Wystan is dead, both this place and an apartment in Athens. Also (it is fair to warn you), because of bad and dishonest advice, I am in an Income Tax situation here which has, added to my Greek "responsibilities," become very burdensome. Taxes are rather high, for one (even for a non-citizen, if you're in residence and/or own property); and for another (since one pays in advance quarterly), they appear to have decided that I've fallen heir to the authoress of "Gone With the Wind," things are more expensive than before, and the dollar is down; but of course it's nothing like New York.

As for cabbages, the garden about the house is full of them and green beans and peas and corn and strawberries and raspberries and apples and beets and what you will. And there's a housekeeper who has to be prodded a bit, but washes up and drives and tends the garden and does the laundry and talks too much. . . . The house would be almost fully furnished—I should imagine the asking price (with the ground and a garage and pool) will be about $50,000. . . . Please let me know immediately.

I am feeling fine now, though I rather broke up after Wystan's death (and finding the body as well) and came down in February with a bleeding duodenal ulcer. Drink minimally now (since May 1). More news after we get business settled.

Love to you, Dad, and Mary.

In addition to British death taxes and United States estate taxes, Chester had to pay Austrian death taxes for which he could claim no refund of any kind, since no tax treaty existed between the United States and Austria. Then, if he remained in Austria, there were income taxes, both Austrian and United States taxes, which threatened the few royalties he might receive over the years from the Auden estate. His family in New York, not having been apprised of these problems until after his death, could not give him advice, since he did not ask them for it. He thus thrashed about wildly for a tax shelter, but he did not acquaint himself sufficiently with the tax laws of each country to make an intelligent decision, and he would not hire an attorney. At any rate, his first solution was to sell the property in Austria to me and to quit Austria as a resident.

When Chester said that he wanted fifty thousand dollars, I assumed I would either have to get a mortgage or gather the fifty thousand in another way and pay him in a lump sum. I had no idea that property could be sold on an annuity basis, a practice, I learned later, which was not uncommon among Austrians. Further, I was put off by Chester's stories in his next letter about Austrian income taxes, in addition to property taxes, on foreign residents (May 21, 1974): "I'd hate to expose you," he wrote, "to their murderous income tax laws. And when I say murderous, I'm not being over-wrought, but simply remembering what they did to Wystan. . . ." I finally told him that I could not afford to buy the property. Chester now had to find someone else. He allegedly had a number of offers, one from a literary society, but he refused them, probably because he would have to pay exorbitant taxes on a lump-sum payment for the property.

But Chester's tax problems were only a small part of the essential problem after Auden died. There was in Chester Kallman a deep, self-destructive impulse. Chester courted destruction and drove himself obsessively to it. Forces that could have been positive in his life and brought him happiness he turned against himself, either by excesses or by dissipation, despite the fact that few people in this world have been given more than he in opportunity and native intelligence. His excesses in alcohol and sex are well documented. His dissipation of money and cultivation of poverty merely symbolize the dissipation of his spiritual goods.

The will he made before Yannis Boras died is an example. Chester had made Yannis the sole heir of his estate with Wystan's full knowledge and consent. Hence, had Yannis lived after the death of Chester, he would have been the sole heir to the Auden estate. Yannis could neither read nor speak English. He was an auto mechanic who had no education. When Wystan died, Chester made a new will naming Nikos Piraeus,[1] his new Greek lover, the heir to all his household furnishings. However, Piraeus was under the impression that Chester had promised him more, and perhaps he had. The Greek translation of Chester's English will, made by a translator, not an attorney, had worded the original English "my household furnishings" as "the contents of my apartment."[2] On Chester's death, Piraeus made a number of scenes, insisting that the contents of the apartment, including all books, records, and valuable papers, were his.[3]

It is indeed possible that, had Chester continued to live in Greece,

[1] Not his real name.

[2] The author's conversation with Joel B. Miller, attorney for the estate of Chester Kallman, November 30, 1983.

[3] The author's conversation with Barnett B. Ruder, December 2, 1983. Ruder, Dr. Edward Kallman's old friend and patient, a professional appraiser of books, was Dr. Kallman's surrogate in settling Chester's estate in Greece.

he in fact would have made Piraeus his sole heir, if for no other reason than that Piraeus kept nagging him to do so, and Chester wanted
to be left in peace. Piraeus had no more grasp of English poetry than
did Boras.

Chester was in Austria in June 1974, and in July he made a trip
to London with Auden's notebooks, letters, and manuscripts—all the
material that later was known as the Auden Collection. Edward Mendelson, Auden's literary executor, was in London at the time, and
Chester directed him to take the collection to the New York Public
Library. "I urged Chester to do this," said Mendelson, "because I
knew that if he wasn't going to sell them they would quickly disappear."[1] Apparently Chester had told a number of people he intended
to donate the material and that the collection "would never be sold."

In September, Chester returned to London to be present at Westminster Abbey on the anniversary of Wystan's death when John
Betjeman, the poet laureate, would unveil a memorial stone for Auden in Poet's Corner. But Chester's health was poor again. He was
now shaking severely and needed help in walking. He notified the
friends in London with whom he was planning to stay, and they flew
to Kirchstetten to help him pack and fly him to England in time for
the ceremony.[2]

Chester was clearly in no condition to handle with efficiency and
good judgment the inheritance that had come his way. Although
Wystan had left Chester a sufficient income, the estate had not been
settled, and the New York attorneys, at least so Chester said, were not
sending him enough money. Actually they sent him more than enough
to pay his living expenses in Greece. What they did send him each
month in stipends was, for some reason, gone before the month's end.
Sometimes, for example, when he went out to a bar with enough
drachmas in his pocket for a month's board, he would find the next
morning that nothing was left,[3] and he was as penniless as he had been
long ago in New York when he lived on Twenty-seventh Street. He
had to raise money. He borrowed from friends in the American
colony.

As Chester had been dissipating his health, he had begun also to
dissipate his inheritance. If he had set about consciously planning to
get rid of everything as soon as possible, he could not have done so

---

[1] Letter to the author from Edward Mendelson, July 6, 1983.

[2] Letter to Dr. Edward Kallman from Michael Yates, February 6, 1975.

[3] The author's conversation with Stavros Kondylis, February 27, 1975.

with more alacrity than he was to do in the fourteen months that remained to him after Wystan's death. Chester, now viewed as prosperous by the citizens of Athens, was, according to his neighbors, turning over sums of drachmas to young men who wished to start up in business for themselves, and in a short time after Auden's death, a number of glass shops and grocery and fruit stores were opened because of Chester's generosity. Chester, characteristically, received nothing in return. In addition, Chester, plied with ouzo, would be persuaded to make loans in response to sad stories told him in the local bar, loans he did not remember and that the borrowers never repaid.[1]

Two weeks before he died, he literally gave away his house, the house that to Wystan was Cockaigne, over which Wystan wept tears of gratitude and quoted Psalm 16:6, the house that Wystan had intended for Chester's security should Chester outlive him. In early January 1975, Chester made a trip to Kirchstetten. What he actually did there is no more clear than his motives, and his motives were mysterious. The court records at Neulengbach show that on January 2, 1975, he sold the house and lot at 6 Audenstrasse (once Hinterholz) to his caretaker, Frau Strobl, for an annuity of $125 a month for life, plus privileges to stay in the house when he visited Austria. The housekeeper made no down payment. Suspicious of lawyers, having had an unfortunate experience with one in Austria, he managed the sale of the property himself and thus made no provisions as to what was to happen should he predecease Frau Strobl. Whether he collected the first annuity payment is unknown. What is known is that he collected no others, and Frau Josefa Strobl, a stranger, acquired Wystan's beloved Cockaigne without paying anything.

At some point Chester did sell one of the two lots remaining on the three-acre estate to a Josef Dorfinger for eighty thousand Austrian schillings (five thousand dollars). Frau Strobl probably managed the sale while Chester was in Athens, for she had written him an undated letter earlier in the winter of 1974, saying in German "Today we finally had a sale." (*"Heute haben wir endlich einen Kauf gehabt."*) She said that she would pay him thirty thousand Austrian schillings ($1875) when he arrived in Kirchstetten and fifty thousand Austrian schillings ($3125) later.[2] When Chester returned to Athens in January 1975, he had, according to his neighbor, a substantial sum of money in his pocket, "a thousand dollars or even more," and was "spending

---

[1] The author's conversation with Stavros Kondylis, February 27, 1975.
[2] Undated letter to Chester Kallman from Frau Josefa Strobl, 1974.

it like water" in a local pub.[1] When Chester awoke the next morning, he went to his pockets in panic to discover that the money was gone.[2]

By January 1975 Chester had not only squandered the money given to him in stipends by the attorneys in New York; he had not only given away the house in Kirchstetten—he had also disposed of the Auden manuscripts without compensation. To the end the pattern was the same. Had Chester lived on, he would eventually have lived in poverty. He was to his last days the same Chester who had, by mistake, given his last twenty-dollar bill as a tip to a waiter in a ship's bar. But who was to protect him now when Wystan, his only true friend in the world, was gone?

The trip to Kirchstetten had been too much for him, and his health rapidly became worse starting in early January. "He came back in terrible shape," said Alan Ansen, "and though his physician . . . was able through drug therapy to achieve a temporary stay of execution the end seems in retrospect to have been inevitable."[3] On January 15, 1975, Chester attended a poetry reading by one of his friends in the American colony, but he was too ill to attend the reception afterward. On the night of January 16, Alan Ansen found him:

> . . . lying on his side on his bed and very vague when I switched on the lights and insisted on his getting up. He attempted to leave the living room to supervise the cooking, but found himself unable to walk without assistance and eventually returned to bed. The next thing I knew was that the boys who had stayed with him overnight had found him dead about eight the next morning— and according to his doctor, who arrived around eleven, he had died only a short time before they discovered him. The preliminaries of the autopsy indicate an enlarged liver and damage to the heart muscles, both characteristic of too much alcohol.[4]

An official autopsy was performed on January 19, 1975,[5] by the Athens coroner, Dr. A. Loutselinis. The pathological findings were as

[1] The author's conversation with Stavros Kondylis, February 27, 1975.
[2] Ibid.
[3] Letter to Dr. Edward Kallman from Alan Ansen, January 20, 1975.
[4] Letter to Dr. Edward Kallman from Alan Ansen, January 20, 1975.
[5] Embassy of the United States of America, Consular Section, Athens, Greece, Republic of Greece, Athens Coroner's Office, Report No. 922, Coroner's Report of Autopsy and Necrotomy dated January 19, 1975, Kallman, Chester, as a result of written instruction No. 243 dated January 17, 1975, of Police section KD, performed at 10:00. The author has summarized only the pathological findings.

follows: His brain was swollen by a superabundance of fluid and a congestion of blood. The blood vessels at the base were hardened. The pericardiac (heart) fluid was above normal, the weight being 800 grams. The valves and vessels of the heart were hardened and the tissue of the myocardium was impaired (ischemic necrosis of myocardium). His liver was cirrhotic and his spleen swollen. There were sclerotic lesions in his kidneys. The alcohol in his blood was indicated as 69 milligrams.

The brilliant, beautiful boy was dead. He was buried on February 20 in the Jewish Cemetery in Athens, and his friends of the American colony rallied round as Alan Ansen, unused to the requirements of death, made telephone calls to New York and saw to the ceremonies of burial. Malcolm in Pittsburgh made arrangements for money to be sent. Eddie, now eighty-three, was deaf, almost blind, and, at the time, scheduled for a series of operations on his eyes. Unfit to travel, he now needed my constant care, so none of Chester's family could be present in distant Greece.

In his will (which bequeathed all his belongings to Wystan except the furniture in his Greek apartment), Chester had asked that he be cremated, and that his ashes be spread over the grave of Yannis Boras in Livadaki. But the Greek government forbade cremation, so even Chester's last wish was denied. Chester now lies beneath the marble monument that Eddie provided for him in the Jewish Cemetery in Athens. He is alone, without Wystan, without Yannis, without even a friend or a cousin to keep him company through the dark nights and burning days.

When Auden died, Chester was heard to say, "I have lost my criterion." He lost more than that—he had lost his life's mate, his well-wisher, his guardian. The golden wedding bands that Wystan had bought many years ago had symbolized a true marriage. "I have always felt that Chester was enormously good for Wystan," Alan Ansen wrote to Chester's father on January 20, shortly after Chester's burial. Alan was right. Chester gave Wystan someone to love, someone for whom to work, someone with whom to share his life. Chester had the gift of laughter and companionship. In the end, Chester, always light of love, could not live two years without him. Their lives were joined by an indissoluble tie. Let us hope they are together now and have found peace. Let us hope they have finally found the way to go home.

DOROTHY JEANNE FARNAN was born in Winona, Minnesota. She is the wife of Dr. Edward Kallman, Chester Kallman's father.

She met W. H. Auden, and, shortly afterward, Chester Kallman, when she was a student at the University of Michigan in 1941. After receiving her master's degree in English language and literature in 1943, also from the University of Michigan, she moved to New York with her friend Mary Valentine, and both women became intimate members of the Auden–Kallman circle of the forties.

Miss Farnan taught English at De Witt Clinton High School in the Bronx for ten years before being appointed Chairman of English at Erasmus Hall High School in Brooklyn, where she served until her retirement in 1975.

She lives in Manhattan with her husband and a family of cats.